CREDIT QUESTIONNAIRE

How can I get my credit rating—and how can I improve it?

What are the new government regulations—and how do they affect my rights and obligations regarding my credit?

How long will a bad credit rating hurt me—and what can I do to change it?

How can I get free credit cards—and cut the interest rates on the cards I already carry?

How can I cut my expenses and pay off my bills faster?

This is just a tiny sampling of what you will find out in the one guide that tells you all you want and need to know—

THE ULTIMATE
CREDIT HANDBOOK

Gerri Detweiler is the former director of Bankcard Holders of America, a nonprofit consumer credit and advocacy organization that has helped thousands of consumers solve their credit problems, and the former director for the National Council for Individual Investors. She has been featured on the *Today Show, CBS This Morning,* and in *The New York Times, The Wall Street Journal, USA Today, The Washington Post,* the *Los Angeles Times,* and *Money* magazine, among others. She lives in Sarasota, Florida.

THIRD EDITION

THE
ULTIMATE
CREDIT
HANDBOOK

CUT YOUR DEBT
AND HAVE A LIFETIME OF
GREAT CREDIT

GERRI DETWEILER

A PLUME BOOK

PLUME
Published by the Penguin Group
Penguin Putnam Inc., 375 Hudson Street, New York, New York 10014, U.S.A.
Penguin Books Ltd, 80 Strand, London WC2R 0RL, England
Penguin Books Australia Ltd, 250 Camberwell Road,
Camberwell, Victoria 3124, Australia
Penguin Books Canada Ltd, 10 Alcorn Avenue, Toronto, Ontario, Canada M4V 3B2
Penguin Books (N.Z.) Ltd, 182–190 Wairau Road, Auckland 10, New Zealand

Penguin Books Ltd, Registered Offices: Harmondsworth, Middlesex, England

First published by Plume, a member of Penguin Putnam Inc.

First Printing, March 1993
First Printing (revised edition), March 1997
First Printing (third edition), February 2003
10 9 8 7 6 5 4 3 2 1

The following trademarks and service marks appear in the text of this book:

American Express®, Optima True Grace℠, Optima®, Gold Card®, Membership Miles®, and Platinum Card® are trademarks of American Express Co.
Discover®, Cashback Bonus®, and Private Issue® Card are trademarks of Dean Witter, Discover & Co.
Master Money™, MasterCard®, Cirrus®, and Maestro® are trademarks of MasterCard International.
Visa®, InterLink®, and Plus® are trademarks of Visa International.

Ⓟ REGISTERED TRADEMARK—MARCA REGISTRADA

LIBRARY OF CONGRESS CATALOGING-IN-PUBLICATION DATA
Detweiler, Gerri.
    The ultimate credit handbook : how to cut your debt and have a lifetime of great
credit / Gerri Detweiler.—3rd ed.
        p.   cm.
    Includes bibliographical references and index.
    ISBN 0-452-28392-2
    1. Consumer credit—United States—Handbooks, manuals, etc. I. Title.
HG3756.U54 D48 2003
    332.7'43—dc21   2002028256

Printed in the United States of America
Set in Melior

PUBLISHER'S NOTE
This publication is designed to provide accurate and authoritative information in regard to the subject matter covered. It is sold with the understanding that the publisher is not engaged in rendering legal, accounting, or other professional services. If you require legal advice or other expert assistance, you should seek the services of a competent professional.

While the publisher and author have made every effort to provide accurate telephone numbers and Internet addresses at the time of publication, neither assumes any responsibility for errors, or for changes that occur after publication.

*To my father, Gene Detweiler, who showed his children
how to live happily with less,
and to my mother, Gerda, who generously made sure
we never really had to!*

CONTENTS

Contents

PART TWO: CUT YOUR DEBT

PART THREE: A LIFETIME OF GREAT CREDIT

THE
ULTIMATE
CREDIT
HANDBOOK

INTRODUCTION

Credit fuels the American economy and finances the American Dream. For many of us, credit means homes, cars, boats, shopping sprees, and the Good Life. For millions of others, though, credit means bills they can't pay, phone calls from collection agencies, and rejection letters from credit card companies.

This book is designed to help you take control of credit. It will show you how to:

- Save $200 or more each year by choosing the right credit cards and loans.
- Pay off your debts a lot faster (and save lots of money while you do).
- Solve your credit problems—even if you've been through bankruptcy, divorce, or other credit nightmares.
- Get credit when you need it—even if you've been turned down before.

The Ultimate Credit Handbook is for the millions of people who are buried under a pile of plastic, struggling to get out of debt. If you feel as though you can't get ahead, if you're on the edge of the "debt cliff," just hoping some financial problem won't push you over the edge, you're not alone. Every year, hundreds of thousands of people file for bankruptcy. Many others flock to Consumer Credit Counseling Services for help in paying off their debts.

Even if you don't have serious credit problems, you can probably still use some advice on how to cut your credit costs, pay off your bills a lot sooner, and really start getting ahead. That's what this book is about.

I wrote *The Ultimate Credit Handbook* as a result of both my personal and professional experiences with credit. In 1987, I took a job at Bankcard Holders of America, a nonprofit organization dedicated to credit education and advocacy.

In the late 1980s, it really was a seller's market for credit cards. Almost all of the major credit card issuers charged 19.8 percent interest, and people accepted those rates without question. In fact, issuers often would market credit cards without mentioning the price (interest rates, annual fees, etc.) at all. There were very few issuers offering secured cards for people who had had previous credit problems, and few of those that did were legitimate. Consequently, there was a lot of work to be done for a nonprofit group that wanted to educate people about credit.

I had a lot to learn myself. When I started working at BHA, I was headed for serious credit problems and didn't even realize it.

When I graduated from college in the mid-1980s, I moved from the Midwest to Washington, D.C., found a job and an apartment, and figured I was on my way. I didn't have much furniture and really couldn't afford any, so I went to one of the big department stores. There, they approved me for a credit card with a $1,000 limit. The couch I wanted to buy was only about $800, so I threw in a lamp and an answering machine as well. I didn't even look at the interest rate—all that I cared about was the low monthly payment of about $35. That was the beginning.

Within a few years I had a walletful of credit cards and debt totaling more than $10,000. Every month, I would sit down to a stack of bills on which I could afford little more than the minimum payment. After years of payments, the balance on that first department-store card was still more than $800. I still remember getting sick to my stomach every time I had to "do the bills."

During that time, I was getting into my job at BHA. As I was researching and writing credit education materials, I started to realize that it was going to take me until I retired to pay off these bills if I didn't make some changes. It looked pretty difficult, because I wasn't making a very large salary, and my bills were eating up most of it. I did have a part-time job in a retail store, but I used my paycheck there to buy expensive clothes and makeup on my company discount.

It took a while before I really committed myself to getting out of debt, and when I did, it wasn't easy. I refinanced credit cards, stopped charging, borrowed money from a friend to pay off some debts, took some outside work and used the money I earned toward my credit cards, started keeping track of every penny I spent, and sold my expensive Mustang convertible and bought a used Toyota Tercel from my parents. Basically, I used every strategy I could think of to pay off my bills. It took a couple of years, but I made it out of the hole.

I wrote this book to share what I learned along the way. I've researched *many* different credit questions and problems people have come to me with over the years, and I hope what I found out will be helpful to you. My goal is to provide you with specific answers to your credit questions and proven strategies for solving your personal credit problems.

If you've picked up this book, it's probably for you. Get started: Hopefully it won't be as hard as you think to get your credit in great shape.

Good luck!

PART ONE

DOUBLE YOUR CREDIT

CHAPTER ONE

How Do You Rate?
The Secrets of Good Credit

I'm going to start this book talking about credit reports because that's what it all boils down to. If your credit report "looks good," you'll get the loan you want. If it doesn't, you won't.

Now your next question is probably, "What makes a good credit report?" Good question. That's what I'll tell you in this chapter.

First, I'll explain what credit reports are and how to check yours. Then I'll explain how lenders decide who gets credit—and how to get them to say "yes" to your applications!

Credit Bureaus: Our Business Is Their Business

A good credit report usually makes the difference between a "yes" or "no" on your loan application. Most information in credit reports is positive, and millions of people get approved for loans without a hitch. But it doesn't always work that way. The problem is, you may think you have a good credit rating, but if you haven't checked it, you can't be sure you do.

Credit reports aren't perfect. Some contain mistakes or old information. Those discrepancies are often pretty harmless—an address or employment information that's out of date, for example—but sometimes they are serious enough to cause people to be turned down for mortgages or even jobs.

Even people who are sure they have "good credit" are rejected for loans because they don't really understand what lenders are looking for when they review credit reports. There are a lot of misconceptions about how credit really works. I logged on to one of the popular on-line services recently and started reading some of the members' back-and-forth messages about credit reports. I was shocked by how much wrong advice people were giving one another. Let me try to help set things straight.

Credit bureaus, also called credit reporting agencies, are companies in the business of collecting, packaging, and selling information about our financial lives to lenders, employers, insurance agencies, and other customers. Those customers then use that information to make decisions about whether to offer loans or other services. There are hundreds of credit bureaus across the country, but in most cases you'll deal with one that is affiliated with one of the three major national credit systems: Experian (formerly TRW Information Systems, Inc.), based in Orange, California; Trans Union, headquartered in Chicago, Illinois; and Equifax (formerly known as CBI/Equifax), based in Atlanta, Georgia.

You will sometimes hear references to five major credit bureaus. In addition to the three credit reporting agencies just mentioned, there used to be two other large credit systems: CSC Credit Services and Chilton. In the late 1980s, CSC Credit Services agreed to use the Equifax system as an affiliate, and Chilton was bought out by TRW, which in turn was later sold and its name changed to Experian.

In addition to the three major national credit reporting agencies, there are hundreds of other credit bureaus called *affiliates*. These affiliates generally have collected credit information in specific regions of the country. Instead of being bought out or put out of business by one of the Big Three agencies, they work as affiliates of one of them.

These affiliates collect financial information for customers in their area and then store the information with one of the major credit agencies. They'll pay that agency to store the information in their database, and the agency will pay the affiliate to sell that data to customers outside their market.

So, for example, one of Experian's affiliates is Credit Data of New England. Credit Data stores its information about consumers on Experian's database, and Credit Data and Experian pay each other to sell data about consumers in each other's markets. If there's a problem with information in your credit file and you live in Credit Data's area, you'll probably get referred directly to them (not Experian) to correct it. If Credit Data makes a correction, the correction will automatically be made in Experian's files as well.

There are also *mortgage reporters*. Many of these smaller bureaus use credit report information provided by two or three of the major credit agencies to create detailed or specialized credit reports for real estate lenders. Since they are using information from two or more credit agencies, mortgage reports are usually more complete and detailed than those of a single credit bureau.

There are also *resellers* or *brokers*, which are companies that purchase credit reports for infrequent users of reports. By acting on behalf of several smaller creditors, they are able to buy reports for a smaller fee than the individual granter could do on their own. Generally, resellers purchase reports for medical offices, landlords, and insurance companies.

Although any type of credit bureau can be called a bureau or a reporting agency, I'm going to use the term *credit reporting agency* when I'm specifically talking about the three major bureaus (Equifax, Trans Union, and Experian). Otherwise, I'll just use the word *bureau* to refer to any type of credit bureau that may collect or sell information about you.

What's in Your Personal Credit File?

Credit reports are also referred to as *credit files*, *credit histories*, *bureau files*, or sometimes, *credit ratings*. David Mooney at Equifax says that technically consumers don't have credit ratings.

He's right. But sometimes when I'm referring to how your credit report may look to lenders, the words "credit report" just don't quite work. So I'll use "credit rating" from time to time, but keep in mind that you really don't have a credit rating—you have a credit report that each lender will view differently.

There are two types of personal credit files: standard and investigative. A standard credit file contains a more or less complete outline of a consumer's financial history. Chances are you won't ever have to deal with anything besides a standard credit report.

Investigative reports are much more detailed and may contain information about a person's lifestyle. Investigative reports are usually prepared for companies that want a really thorough investigation of a person's background. For example, an investigative report may be prepared on someone trying to take out a million-dollar insurance policy, or an executive being considered for a high-level job, or someone applying for a job requiring a security clearance.

There are four parts to a standard credit report:

Personal Information

Your name, address, previous addresses for the past five to ten years, your date of birth, your Social Security number, your spouse's name and Social Security number, the names and addresses of your previous and present employers, and your phone number can appear in the personal information section of a credit report.

Tradelines

A *tradeline* is industry lingo for a credit account. In this section, you will find a list of most of your credit accounts, the date each account was opened, whether you have paid each account on time, how much you still owe, whether you share your accounts with someone else, and any negative information about the account (for example, if it was included in a bankruptcy filing).

Public Record Information

Monetary judgments (if you were sued in court and lost, a judgment would order you to pay the person who won), state and federal tax liens, and bankruptcies appear on credit reports. Past-due child support may also be listed. Public record information is usually collected by companies that go to courthouses and gather financial public record information, and resell it to credit bureaus and other interested parties.

By the way, information in credit reports is reported in a factual and straightforward manner. For instance, if you filed bankruptcy, your file would list the date and court particulars of your bankruptcy filing, but it wouldn't say you're a "deadbeat."

Inquiries

A listing of everyone who has seen your credit report recently will appear on your credit report. Each listing is called an *inquiry*. There are three kinds of inquiries:

One kind is usually generated when you apply for some type of credit, insurance, or a job. I'll talk more about that in a minute because the fact is that a company that has a legally acceptable reason for getting your credit report doesn't always have to get your permission to look at your file.

Another kind of inquiry is a *promotional* (sometimes listed as a "PRM") inquiry. These are usually created when lenders ask the credit bureau for lists of people who fit a certain profile so they can mail them preapproved credit card offers. These companies don't actually receive your report, only your name and address if you match their guidelines. (And they don't actually get that either, since the names and addresses go to a mailing house that sends the solicitations.)

While *you* would receive the names of the companies that were involved in a promotional offer under the inquiry section, those types of inquiries are *not* included on the reports that are sent to credit granters and other companies that get a copy of your report.

An account review inquiry is created when lenders want to review the credit of some of their customers. Say, for example, your department-store card issuer wants to increase customers' credit lines before the holidays. They may go to a credit bureau and ask them to run criteria through a certain group of customers' credit reports to find out who meets their qualifications. Those who do will get credit-line increases. Again, this type of inquiry is not reported to lenders.

If you've ordered your own credit report recently, you may also see *consumer* inquiries. Those just indicate that you reviewed your own file. They aren't sent to lenders, either.

The previous three types of inquiries—promotional, account review, and consumer—are called "soft" inquiries because they will appear only when you order your own report, not when a lender orders it for review.

In addition to these soft inquiries, there are several distinct types of "hard" inquiries that will appear on your credit report whether you order it or a lender does. Mortgage-related inquiries, auto-loan-related inquiries, credit inquiries, insurance company inquiries, and employer inquiries are examples of hard inquiries. Later in this chapter I'll explain how these different types of inquiries may affect your credit.

Under the credit reporting law, employment inquiries are reported for two years, all others for one year.

How Do They Get My Information?

If you have never applied for credit, your first application for credit will probably get things started. The creditor processing your application will give identifying information about you (name, address, and Social Security number) to the credit bureau and ask for your credit file. If you don't have any credit, the credit bureau will tell the lender that it cannot find a file on you and will use the information the creditor supplied to start your first credit file.

A lot of people have the impression that there's actually a credit report sitting in some credit bureau with all your information in it. In fact, however, your credit report doesn't actually exist until someone asks for it. When someone requests your credit report, the computer searches and finds all the information in its databases about you and puts together the report. Experian describes the process of putting together a credit report as similar to making beef Stroganoff: You may have all the ingredients in your kitchen, but the dish doesn't exist until you put them together.

Credit bureaus get information about your credit accounts from lenders. Some lenders will send information about their accounts to the credit bureaus on a monthly basis, others on a quarterly basis. They may also report information infrequently; for instance, many gasoline card issuers only report information about accounts that are ninety days or more behind on payments. Lenders often provide information about accounts to the credit bureaus on magnetic tape, which makes it easier to transfer information from the lender's files to the credit bureaus. It's also supposed to help cut down on mistakes.

Credit bureaus add the information they get from lenders to their credit reports, then turn around and sell credit reports back to lenders for anywhere from less than $1 in high volume to more than $10 per report for less frequent customers.

As I pointed out earlier, credit files may contain outdated or wrong information. Part of the problem is the sheer volume of information that is exchanged. Creditors report billions of pieces of information to credit bureaus each year. With that much data going back and forth, mistakes are bound to happen.

The only way to be sure that credit file information is correct is to look at your report and see if there are any mistakes. Unless you have been turned down for credit recently, however, you'll probably have to buy a copy of your report. Most credit bureaus charge an individual $9 per copy.

When I wrote the first edition of this book, I said that people who wanted to see copies of their reports often found it difficult to locate the credit bureaus that held their files, since the major credit bureaus generally don't advertise their services to consumers. A lot has changed since then, and one of the changes is that all three major agencies have national offices that process credit reports. In the Resources section of this book, I'll tell you how to get a copy of your credit report from all three bureaus.

Another problem with credit files is that wrong information can show up on files at different bureaus. Many lenders supply information to all three of the major credit agencies. That means that if a creditor reports erroneous information about your payment history, it will probably show up in the files of different credit bureaus across the country.

The major credit reporting agencies are businesses in competition with each other. They do not share information about consumers' credit files. However, under the revised credit reporting law that went into effect in 1997, lenders are supposed to share corrections they make with all credit reporting agencies to whom they report. It doesn't always happen, but that's the direction things are moving. In the next chapter, I'll explain exactly how it works and how to correct errors on your credit file.

Who Sees Your Credit File?

It's no secret that a "good" credit report can get you the credit card or mortgage you want. But did you also know that it can save you money on car insurance? Or help you get a job?

While there are legal limits on who can get a copy of your credit file (I'll spell those out in the next chapter), the information in credit reports is very valuable to a lot of different companies. In fact, credit bureaus are continually trying to come up with new ways to sell credit report information. Some of these include:

1. Services that predict whether consumers are likely to have credit problems or file bankruptcy in the future.
2. Notification services that warn creditors if their customers are falling behind on other bills. For instance, if you fail to make two payments on your Visa card, the credit bureau may report that delinquency to your other card issuers, to warn them that you may be having trouble paying your bills.
3. Location services that help creditors, landlords, and collection agencies track down consumers. One credit bureau service, for example, sells the names and addresses of a consumer's current or previous neighbors, so debt collectors can contact them to find those who haven't paid. Another service will provide a listing of

the names and addresses of all the people who have applied for credit using a certain Social Security number. The idea here is to catch anyone who has tried to change his or her identity when applying for credit. Some of these lists are sold not only to debt collectors but also to alumni associations and membership groups that want to locate lost members.

This means it's more important than ever for you to make sure that your credit report is complete, error-free, and up-to-date. More importantly, your credit report should make you look as financially attractive as possible. With that in mind, here's how lenders look at credit reports.

How Do You Rate? The Three C's of Credit

When I was in elementary school, I remember a teacher giving us a weeklong project that was designed to get us to eat a balanced diet from the five food groups. Each day, we were told to eat a certain number of servings from each group and report our diet back to the teacher at the end of the project. I loved that project! I remember eating ice-cream bars for my dairy servings and fat-laden bacon and hot dogs for the meat groups. The project was supposed to teach us how to eat a healthy diet, but the *specific* information about what really made a good diet wasn't too helpful.

Well, there's a similar set of guidelines about credit that have been given out for years. It's called the "Three C's" of good credit. The Three C's of credit evaluation are: *character*, *capacity*, and *collateral*. They are frequently used as the guidelines creditors use to decide when to grant credit.

CHARACTER (or "creditworthiness") refers to how responsible you are about paying your bills. If a lender doesn't know you, he or she might review your credit report to see how well you have handled credit in the past.

CAPACITY is your ability to pay a loan based on your money-management skills, income, and financial position.

COLLATERAL is security for the lender if you don't pay back the loan. Collateral can be the car for which you are taking out a loan, stock certificates, a savings account, your house, or other assets.

The problem with the Three C's method of credit evaluation is that it's just too vague. Many loans today are impersonal—the loan officer signing off on the loan may never even talk to the borrower. How can a lender judge your character if you are simply a name on a piece of paper? Just because you have paid your bills in the past doesn't mean you will be able or willing to pay them in the future. And what about capacity? You may have enough income to pay the bills today, but what happens if you get sick and face huge medical bills, or what if you get ten credit cards and run them up to the limit tomorrow?

Most people have an idea about how much credit they can handle and what type of credit habits they have. What they really need to know are the *specific* factors bankers think are important in deciding when to issue loans. Let's get into the nitty-gritty of credit evaluation and try to figure out why one person can get a walletful of cards while another can't get a single loan.

Your Credit Score

There are two ways lenders decide whether an application gets approved: judgmental evaluation and credit scoring. In a judgmental system, the lender looks at each application individually. She will have guidelines to follow and will take into account factors such as your income and credit history but may also consider your individual circumstances when reviewing your application. In other words, the lender may use her own judgment (within guidelines) when deciding whether to approve the loan.

The other way to evaluate loan applications—*credit scoring*—is a way for lenders to predict statistically how risky it is to lend money to someone. Credit scores are created by taking a set of credit data—information in a particular lender's customer base, or a group of credit reports, for example—and analyzing what factors statistically predict credit behavior. In other words, lenders try to figure out what factors people who pay their bills on time (or don't file bankruptcy, or whatever they are trying to analyze) have in common. The data crunching that goes into creating one of these credit scores can be mind-numbing, but it all boils down to what the numbers indicate are risk factors. These credit scores are so accurate in predicting behavior that many times your credit applications are analyzed entirely by computer, and your application is given a thumbs-up or thumbs-down, depending on your score.

You may have heard of the "FICO" score, created by the big player in this business: Fair, Isaac Company. While FICO is the main developer of scores, they are not the only company to create scoring systems. In addition, it is not unusual for lenders to customize their scores based on their own experiences with customers, or they can use different scores for different purposes. Still, using the general guidelines of FICO can be helpful in understanding how scores work and how to improve yours.

What's in a Score?

Information in your credit report will typically most heavily influence your credit score, though information from your application may also be included in some scoring models. Here are the main components of a credit score, as FICO breaks them down:

Payment History: This usually makes up about one-third of your credit score. Here, lenders look at whether you have paid your bills on time. It includes whether you have past late payments, judgments, bankruptcies, or other negative remarks. Lenders look at both how often you were late as well as how late you were—in other words, were you ninety days late or just thirty days late? They also look at how recent your delinquencies were. Recent late payments can be a particular red flag to lenders: a thirty-day late payment just last month can be more detrimental than a ninety-day late payment several years ago, for example.

Amounts Owed: This makes up another third or so of your score. Having debt isn't a score killer, lenders just want to make sure you don't have *too much* debt. They'll look at how much debt you have, what types of accounts carry balances, and how many accounts have balances. They'll also likely look at how much debt you have on credit cards and installment accounts (like car loans) and whether you've paid those installment balances down or are just at the beginning of the loan.

Because of the way your credit report is compiled, lenders generally won't know if you pay your bills in full each month. So, for example, if you charge your daughter's tuition this month to take advantage of frequent-flier miles and end up with a $5,000 bill that you pay off, that $5,000 balance may be treated as debt you currently owe.

Other Factors: Other factors will play a less important role in your score, but still contribute to it. These include:

Inquiries: As I mentioned before, every time you apply for credit (and sometimes for insurance or a job), your credit report may be accessed. Inquiries don't indicate whether you were approved, just that your report was reviewed. Generally it's a good idea to keep inquiries below four to six in a six-month period.

When you check your own credit report, or when your report is screened for a preapproved credit offer (listed as "promotional" on your report), those inquiries are *not* shown to anyone but you, and won't count against you. Also, if you are home or car shopping, FICO uses special rules to try to ensure that multiple car loan or mortgage inquiries don't count against you.

Under FICO's rules, all mortgage-related inquiries and, separately, all auto-related inquiries within the past thirty days are ignored. Going back prior to that thirty-day period, all mortgage-related inquiries and, separately, all auto-related inquiries within a fourteen-day stretch are treated as a single inquiry. The primary reason for this special treatment is to avoid penalizing consumers for shopping for the best mortgage or auto loan (and likely has to do with the rise in Internet loan-shopping sites). The warning that I would give to consumers about this policy is that it only applies to FICO-developed credit scores and only if the inquiry can be specifically identified as a mortgage- or auto-related inquiry.

Length of Your Credit History: A long, stable credit history is good, so scoring systems usually look at how old your oldest account is, as well as how old your accounts are on average. Sometimes this factor includes only open accounts, but may include both open and closed accounts.

Another related factor is the types of credit you are using. Having a mix of several different types of credit (a major credit card, retail car, and auto loan, for example) is helpful because it gives the lender more information from which to evaluate your credit.

New Credit: Most scoring systems do look at how many new accounts you have and how many have balances. Running up balances on a few new credit cards can negatively affect your score.

Age can be considered in a scoring system, but with the caveat that lenders cannot discriminate against anyone who is age sixty-two or older. Anyone who is between the ages of eighteen (the age at which one can legally enter into a contract) and sixty-one, however, may find that age is a factor that is considered.

What's Your Score?

When I bought a home in 2000, my insurance agent told me that my credit score would be used to determine the discount I would get on my homeowner's insurance. No problem, I thought. My payment record is impeccable, I avoid debt, and I have a good mix of credit. Imagine my shock, then, when I was told my score was fourteen points shy of the number needed to qualify for the best rate. That meant I did *not* get the $100 savings a better score would have earned. (Technically, an insurance score, not a credit score, was used. I'll explain the difference shortly.)

As someone who has been writing about credit issues for more than a decade, I think I know more than the average person does about credit reports and scores. Yet I can't say for sure why I didn't hit the mark on my own score. I suspect it was due to all the inquiries placed on my credit file at the time of the home purchase, as well as larger-than-usual amounts I charged for home-improvement supplies. The two new credit card accounts I opened in order to take advantage of interest-free financing on kitchen appliances and cabinets probably had the biggest effect. But I don't—and can't—know for sure.

And there's the problem. While credit scores have been a boon for the lending industry *and* consumers, allowing fast and easy loan decisions and a much greater variety of loan products, my experience with credit scores illustrates how confusing they can be. It also underscores how frustrating they can be when you don't get the score you need. Lenders are required to give you the top three reasons you were denied credit if a score was used, but those reasons typically don't tell you exactly what you can do to boost yours.

Credit scores were tightly under wraps for years. That changed in 2001 when some companies starting showing credit scores. (See the Resources section for information on how to get yours.) The truth, however, is that seeing your score can leave you more confused than before.

When scores are created, the factors involved interact with each other. It's not as if you automatically get ten points for having three credit cards and five points for having six. Instead, the factors are interdependent, making it much more difficult to single out what influenced your score. The same ratio of debt to available credit limits, for example, could have more of an effect on someone with a "thin file" (shorter credit history) than someone with a "thick file"—or vice versa, depending on what the data show. If you hear someone saying that an inquiry automatically means ten points off your score, realize that it's simply not possible to make those kinds of blanket statements.

Checking your credit report once a year or before a major transaction is always a good idea. You'll want to make sure that all information on the report is accurate and up-to-date. Checking your credit score is also a good idea. Keep in mind, however, that your score may vary from source to source. In mortgage transactions, for example, it's not uncommon for a lender to get scores from all three major repositories and use the middle or lowest of the three.

Suggestions for Improving Your Score

I'll say it again: Every lender uses its own criteria, so what makes for a better score with one may not affect your score with another. While getting an inaccurate judgment removed from your report can boost your score dramatically, most changes will not happen overnight. And you never know which direction your score can take if you make changes, so tread cautiously.

In Chapter Four, I'll explain how to rebuild a damaged credit rating. But if you are looking for some simple steps, these may generally help improve your score over time.

Reduce Debt: Paying down debt not only saves you money in interest charges, but it can improve your score if you appear overextended. Ironically, you may score better if you have small balances than if you have none at all. So one strategy is to use your credit cards from time to time, then pay the bill in full to avoid debt while keeping them active.

Get a Good Mix of Credit: Ideally, you'll probably want at least a couple of major credit cards, a department-store card or two, and maybe an installment loan like a student loan or auto loan. Just don't rush out an open a bunch of new accounts at once. You'll end up with too many inquiries and too many new accounts. Also, don't feel you have to run up debt—just use the cards for things you'd normally buy, then pay your balances in full. Still, if you shun credit, you might want to add a couple more over time.

Up Your Credit Limits: Add up all your credit limits and your total debt on your revolving accounts, as shown on your credit report. Are you "utilizing" more than 50 percent of your total credit limits? Then look at each individual revolving account to determine the same thing. If you are using a lot of your available credit, you may want to pay down your debt—or if that's not possible, increase your credit limits—to bring that ratio down. (Note that scoring systems may ignore revolving accounts with very high balances—$25,000, for example—to weed out home equity lines in this calculation.)

Establish Positive References: If your credit is damaged due to past problems, understand that time does heal the wounds. Resolve to make all your payments on time from here on out, and establish new, positive references. Get a secured card if you don't have a major credit card already. (See the Resources section for more information.)

Get a Checking and Savings Account: Most lenders want to see that you have both, and they don't care how much money you have in them unless you are applying for a mortgage.

What Won't Help

Closing All Your Old Accounts: Traditional wisdom has said you should close out accounts you don't use anymore. But I've been told by credit scoring experts that this may actually have a negative effect on your credit by shortening the average length of your credit history (if you close out your older accounts), and by reducing a positive mix of credit, if the system is only evaluating open accounts. If you want to close accounts, do so slowly (maybe one every couple of months) and tell the issuers to report the accounts to the bureaus as "closed by consumer." By law, they must do so upon request.

Closing Negative Accounts: Contrary to popular belief, paying off and closing an account does *not* remove it from your credit report. In fact, there's not much you can do to remove accurate but negative accounts from your report. Still, paying off a collection account or other negative listing *can* help your credit if the scoring system looks at whether these items have been satisfied. Negative information generally can remain on your credit report for up to seven years—ten in the case of bankruptcy. See Chapter Two for more details.

Paying Late: Of course, you know you're not supposed to pay late, but it's not uncommon for consumers to pay their student loans, auto loans, or mortgages after the due date but *before* the late payment kicks in. Sometimes those late payments are not reported to the credit bureaus, sometimes they are. If you apply for a new mortgage or a refinance, however, and you've been paying your current mortgage after the due date, you may not get the loan you want.

In addition, if you do fall behind, it doesn't really help to make a large payment later to "make up for it." The fact that you were late will still be reported to the credit reporting agency and affect your credit score.

Cosigning: Of all the credit problems I hear about, cosigning is one of the most common. Loans you've cosigned for someone else will appear on your credit report and be treated as if they are your own. (You *did* agree to be responsible for them when you cosigned.) If the car you cosigned for is repossessed, the student loan goes into default, or the credit card is maxed out, that will be your problem, too. And until the debt is satisfied or the legal time period for reporting that information elapses, don't count on a whole lot of sympathy from the lender—or other lenders for that matter.

Falling Behind on Child Support: This is a big red flag to lenders. Not only do lenders consider failure to pay child support a sign of financial irresponsibility, but they also stay away from these applicants because child-support payments take precedence over other consumer loans in bankruptcy court.

Finance Company Loans: In the past, I warned people about taking out loans with finance companies because they can often count against you, even if you made every single payment on time. The theory behind it was that finance companies have traditionally been considered the lender of last resort, and if you had to get a loan there you must not be a very good risk.

Now, of course, credit-scoring systems evaluate which factors are risky, and finance company loans aren't always the lender of last resort anymore. Large, legitimate companies like The Associates and Household Finance are making loans to lots of different types of customers. Auto finance companies like GMAC or Ford Motor Credit sell the convenience of on-the-spot financing. That means that it's getting harder for lenders to determine that a category like finance company loans is negative.

Still, some scoring systems will count against a finance company loan, and in a judgmental system, a lender may or may not take it into consideration, depending on where you got the loan. My feeling is that you want to steer clear of the sleazy-type finance companies anyway because of what their loans will end up costing you. As long as you do that, a loan from a legitimate finance company shouldn't be a problem.

Filing Bankruptcy is usually considered the most negative mark on a credit file. A bankruptcy remains on your credit file for ten years from the date you filed for Chapter 7 (straight bankruptcy) or seven years from the date you filed a Chapter 13 (where some debts are partially repaid). In general, both kinds of bankruptcy harm the file equally—in other words, most lenders will not give you a higher rating for having repaid your debts through Chapter 13. Your credit report may also list each separate account that was discharged through bankruptcy for up to seven years. If you filed for bankruptcy but then did not go through with it, the fact that you filed will also be reported, and your credit record will still be damaged.

Earning More: Whether you are applying for a mortgage, car loan, or credit cards, your income might be a factor in determining how much credit you'll get, but that won't always offset a negative credit history. Each card issuer will have a minimum income requirement that can be as low as $10,000, or in the case of most gold-card issuers, as high as $35,000. Some card issuers will reveal their minimum income requirement; others won't.

Issuers don't always confirm employment. If you are self-employed, you may be required to provide tax returns or other proof of income. Some issuers, instead of simply looking at your income, look at your income per dependent. If so, the application will ask for information about your dependents.

A high income usually won't make up for a poor credit record. I've heard from people who say (indignantly), "I had some credit troubles in the past and was behind on several bills. I am all caught up now and make a zillion dollars—why can't I get a major credit card?" In credit card lending, income is usually closely related to your other debts and your credit history. If you have a good credit record, a high income will likely enable you to get a higher credit line. Having a very high income, on the other hand, often will not compensate for bad credit or no credit record.

Are You Who You Say You Are?

Lenders are also constantly on the lookout for credit fraud. Crooks make off with millions of dollars every year by pretending to be someone or something they aren't. When it comes to application fraud, there are a few flags that alert lenders to the possibility that an application isn't on the up and up. They include:

- Post office box addresses (especially if you don't live in a rural area). Some credit bureaus have systems that also catch addresses of prisons, mail drops, or commercial addresses. In addition, a credit granter may be suspicious if the same address appears several times on an application—your home address is the same as your work address, for example; or if the zip code you list doesn't match the address.
- Social Security number discrepancy between the Social Security number you provide on the application and the one listed on your credit report. Credit bureaus also frequently search other files to make sure you aren't using someone else's Social Security number, to check if the number belongs to someone who is dead, and to make sure the number given is a valid number.
- A conflict in the address or employment you listed on your application can raise suspicions, although in general, credit granters do not give a great deal of weight to employment information or addresses on credit reports, since they are so often out of date or incorrect. I've been told that some 30 to 40 percent of credit card issuers verify employment directly with employers—the rest do so on a case-by-case basis.

- Inaccurate bank account numbers. Fraudulent applications frequently do not have accurate checking and savings account numbers listed. In some cases, the accounts are opened shortly before applying for loans, to make the lender believe that the thief is financially stable. Account numbers on credit account references may also be double-checked for validity.

Some fraud-detection systems are quite sophisticated. For instance, listing on your application that you were hired on a date that turns out to be a Saturday or Sunday could raise an eyebrow with a creditor. So could an application or credit file that lists your home address in New York for ten years, but your work address five years ago in Virginia. Zip codes for employers and previous addresses may also be checked and verified to make sure they are correct.

To prevent creditors from rejecting your applications based on potential credit fraud, make sure you fill out the application completely and accurately. It is also a good idea to keep copies of your completed applications to help you fill out new applications consistently and completely.

If you're really interested in this topic of credit scoring, I'll give you some more details here on how it can affect your financial future. If you've read enough already, just skip ahead to the next chapter.

Your Credit Scoring Rights

Credit scoring is legal, but lenders are required to follow some guidelines when using scoring. For instance, the Equal Credit Opportunity Act prevents lenders from discriminating against women and the elderly. It does not allow creditors to discriminate against consumers simply on the basis of race, color, religion, or national origin, or because their income comes from public assistance, part-time work, alimony, or child support.

By law, credit scoring must be based on a lender's actual experience with consumers. For that reason, as well as economic reasons, scoring systems are usually reevaluated every three years or so. The Office of the Comptroller of the Currency, a government agency, also reviews scoring systems when they examine lenders.

Creditors' Crystal Balls

You may be a good customer now, but will you still be one a few years down the line? Creditors can use sophisticated "predictive" scoring systems to calculate how likely customers are to pay their bills on time in the future and even how profitable an account might be.

There are several types of predictive scores: behavior scoring, credit bureau scoring, bankruptcy scoring, and profitability scoring, for example. Here's a brief description of each:

Behavior Scoring: Behavior scores use characteristics from the lender's current customer files to determine which cardholders are likely to pay their bills on time. Behavior scoring systems look at factors such as how close to the limit you are on your accounts, how many times you have been late and for how much, how much you purchase each month, and how much of your credit line is used to obtain cash advances. In other words, it looks at your current behavior on your account, and compares that with other customers' behavior to determine what kind of risk you are. Behavior scoring is commonplace; over half of all bankcard accounts are evaluated using behavior scoring.

How do lenders use behavior scores? One common way behavior scoring is used is to decide when to raise credit limits. Many lenders will automatically review accounts each year, or at some other interval, and decide whether or not to increase credit limits.

These scores are also used more frequently now for authorization purposes. Suppose, for example, you present your card to a merchant to pay for a charge. The merchant calls in for authorization for the charge, and the call is routed to your card issuer, who notices that the charge will put you over the limit. The card issuer can quickly run a behavior score on your account to decide whether to authorize the charge.

Credit Bureau Scoring is similar to behavior scoring but broader. (This is not to be confused with scores sold by credit bureaus. Although a credit bureau may sell a credit bureau score, it may also sell a bankruptcy score, or other types of scores.) While creditors use characteristics from their own customers' accounts to develop behavior or application scoring systems, credit bureau scoring is based upon consumers' records of payments on *all* the credit accounts listed on their credit reports.

Bankruptcy Scoring is usually provided by credit bureaus to lenders who want to know if new applicants or current customers are likely to wind up in bankruptcy court. Bankruptcy scores are based on a very large number of credit characteristics, including many factors found in credit reports. Not all of the factors that contribute to a bankruptcy score are directly related to whether you pay on time. Factors such as the type of job you hold and how long you've held it, how frequently you have moved in the recent past, how many accounts you have, and how close you are to your credit limits can all contribute to a bankruptcy score. In other words, just because you make your minimum payments on time doesn't mean that you won't be pegged as a candidate for bankruptcy.

Profitability Scoring is used by creditors to predict which accounts will generate the most revenue for the issuer. This type of scoring can be used by creditors to target the best customers for special offers or incentives. But it may also be used by creditors who want to weed out accounts that don't make much money for them: those people who don't charge often, or those who always pay their balances in full and don't pay interest, for example.

Pros and Cons: The pros of credit scoring are that it can eliminate discrimination since the decision is made going by the numbers, instead of by what you look like or what neighborhood you live in. It also makes credit cheaper and easier to get since lenders can evaluate stacks of applications quickly by computer.

The problem with scoring is that some lenders use it to reduce consumers to a set of numbers. If, for instance, you always paid on time but then were in a serious accident that cost you thousands of dollars and set you back on your finances, your application would be treated just like that of anyone else who didn't pay his or her bills on time. Or maybe you just moved here from Canada. You had credit cards and paid the bills on time there, but when the lender pulls your report here, it comes up blank and the computer turns you down for "no credit history."

The other problem is that it's hard to get any helpful guidelines from lenders about what makes for a good credit score. It's true that it's extremely complicated to explain how the systems really work—the math is mind-boggling. But it's also frustrating for people to see college students getting cards with no income and no credit history yet have their applications turned down for cryptic reasons such as "level of utilization on revolving lines of credit."

Insurance Bureau Scores

Most auto insurance companies, and an increasing number of homeowner's insurance companies, use insurance bureau scores to help predict how likely a customer is to file claims. The information used to calculate an insurance score is the same type of information used in a credit score, and it comes from the credit report. However, the score is calculated separately from a credit score. Therefore, you can't tell from your credit score how "good" an insurance risk you may be. (If you have a poor credit score, though, don't expect a strong insurance score.)

Insurance scoring has been under scrutiny by a number of state regulators and has been criticized for unfairly making consumers who have great driving records, but poor credit histories, pay more for insurance. Insurance bureau scores are generally used for evaluating new applicants for insurance, as well as customers who are up for renewal. The insurance score is often used to help determine whether you will be eligible for discounts, but in some cases it may actually be used to deny coverage. Some states prohibit insurers from turning down consumers for insurance based solely on an insurance score, but most do not.

If you are turned down for insurance based on a score, by law you should be supplied with the name and address of the credit reporting agency that supplied your information so you can order a free copy of your credit report. As of this writing, however, there is no source that supplies insurance scores—either for free or for a fee. In several states, you can get the main factors in your credit report that contributed to your score, but this is not mandatory nationwide.

You can get more information about state laws regarding the use of insurance scores at insure.com or you can contact your state's insurance commissioner (for information or to file a complaint) at www.naic.org.

CHAPTER TWO

Improving Your Credit Reputation: Your Credit Report

Most people go through life getting credit cards, car loans, and mortgages with no problem. In fact, some 95 percent of the information found in people's credit reports is positive. But mistakes happen. And when they do, they can be a hassle—sometimes even a nightmare—to straighten out.

In 1989, when I was working at the advocacy group Bankcard Holders of America, I became involved in an effort by consumer groups and some members of Congress to update the Fair Credit Reporting Act, a law passed in the early 1970s, which governs how credit bureaus operate. Changes were long overdue. For years, people had fought inaccuracies and poor customer service from credit bureaus that in many cases couldn't care less if the reports they sold were ruining people's financial lives.

In 1996, eight years after reform efforts began, Congress finally passed a bill updating the Fair Credit Reporting Act. Most provisions in the new law became effective on October 1, 1997. Even before that new legislation passed, however, the credit reporting agencies themselves made a number of voluntary changes. The Big Three credit reporting agencies each consolidated their customer-relations offices in national centers and installed toll-free numbers, speeded up the time it takes to get a credit report and dispute mistakes, and generally became more responsive to consumers. Experian started offering free credit reports once a year to anyone who asked (which they have since stopped doing). All three agencies made their reports easier to read.

The system still isn't perfect. I still hear horror stories from consumers who have had a terrible time trying to straighten out report mistakes. But there are fewer complaints than there used to be. It's better than it was a few years ago, and some of the agencies are trying to make sure the improvements continue.

Looking Good

What can you do to make sure that your credit report accurately and fairly reflects your creditworthiness? In this chapter, you will learn

- Your legal rights when it comes to credit reports.
- How to fix mistakes on your file.
- How to exercise your legal rights when things go wrong.

The Fair Credit Reporting Act (FCRA) was enacted in 1971 to give Americans the opportunity to find out what information is contained in their credit files, and to help ensure that the information being exchanged with others is correct and complete. When Congress passed that law, however, the credit-reporting industry was much different than it is today.

In the early 1970s, if you wanted to see your credit report, you probably would have gone down to the local credit bureau office and asked to see your file. The clerk would disappear into a room lined with folders and bring out your report—a page or more of notes describing your payment history. Today, if you want to order your credit file, chances are you'll order it from a large national credit reporting agency in another state.

The original FCRA was important legislation when it was passed but became outdated in the electronic age. Using that law to regulate the modern credit reporting system was something like applying horse-and-buggy traffic laws to automobiles.

The following are your rights, including those under the newer credit reporting law passed in 1996.

Your Credit Report: Legal Right #1
You Have the Right to Find Out What Your Credit Report Says

If you have never seen your credit report, get it. If you haven't seen it in the past year, it may be time for a "check-up."

Here's a good example of why it's important to check it: My friend's car died on her one weekend. She had been hoping to nurse it along, but it just couldn't hang on any longer. Suddenly, she had to buy a car right away. She went shopping, found one, and applied for the loan. She knew her credit wasn't perfect, but she was also confident that she knew everything that would show up on it. Apparently, it contained some surprises.

The finance manager told her she had to order a copy of her credit report (which she could only get by mail, since the local credit bureau office no longer handles consumer requests), wait for it to arrive, then explain and dispute the mistakes. That took about a week. In the meantime, she had to scramble for transportation.

Don't wait until there's a problem to get your credit report. If you are thinking about getting a car loan or mortgage, get a copy ahead of time.

If you have been turned down for credit recently because of information in your credit report, it is fairly easy to get a copy of the report. The rejection letter (called an "adverse action" letter) you received from the bank or credit card company must list the name of the credit bureau from which it obtained your credit report. Save your rejection letter! Call the credit bureau listed on that letter, tell them you have been turned down for credit based on information in their report on you, and ask how to get a copy of your credit report.

If you have *not* been turned down for credit recently and you want to see a copy of your report, it will cost you about $9 (plus tax in some states). In the Resources section of this book you'll find complete information for ordering a copy of your report.

One thing you have to decide is which bureau to get it from. In some areas of the country, there may still be one credit bureau that is more dominant than others. For example, when I lived outside Washington, D.C., most lenders would get a copy of my credit report from Equifax. You might want to try calling your local bank or credit union and ask someone in the consumer lending department which is the major bureau for your area and get your report from that bureau.

As far as paying for your report is concerned, some state laws require lower prices than the $9 the major agencies charge. Those limits are: Colorado, Maryland, Massachusetts, New Jersey, and Vermont: one free report each year (from each major agency); Georgia: two free copies per year; Maine and Minnesota: $3; Connecticut: $5; California: $8. Elsewhere you'll pay $9 (a figure that may be adjusted for inflation), and double that if you order a report for two spouses.

The fastest way to get your credit report these days is to order and receive it directly on-line. If you go this route, be prepared: You'll likely be asked some detailed questions about open accounts on your credit report (including the names of lenders and payment amounts) to make sure you're ordering your own report and not someone else's. You may not always be able to order your report on-line if you are requesting a free copy.

If you order your report by mail, jot down on your calendar when you ordered your credit report. It usually takes about two weeks to get a copy, faster if you've ordered it because you've just been turned down for credit. Always pay by check, credit card, or by money order so you have a record of receipt. Follow up in about thirty days if you haven't heard from the credit bureau.

When you order your credit report, always be sure to provide very complete information. They want your name (including maiden name, and whether you're a senior or junior or I, II, or III), spouse's name, Social Security number, current address and addresses for the past five years, including zip codes, and your year of birth. Providing all the details helps the credit bureaus dig up all the information on you, instead of someone else.

One common frustration under the old credit reporting law was that lenders in many cases wouldn't show consumers their own credit reports. You could be sitting in front of a banker who was holding your credit report, explaining that it contained negative information, but if you wanted to find out what it actually said, you had to order a copy from the credit bureau and wait until it arrived. This policy originated with the credit bureaus, which strongly discouraged their subscribers from showing people their reports because they often look different from the ones consumers get (full of codes, or formatted in a special way).

The new credit reporting law specifically says that credit bureaus cannot prohibit lenders of credit reports from showing them to consumers if adverse action has been taken by the lender because of information in the report.

The new law includes some additional disclosure rights. You can also get a free credit report if you are unemployed and intend to apply for employment within sixty days, you are a welfare recipient, you believe you are a victim of credit fraud, or you have been notified by a collection agency affiliated with a credit bureau that it has already, or may, report negative information to that credit bureau.

Your Credit Report: Your Legal Right #2
You Have the Right to a (Reasonably) Accurate and Complete File

One of my friends was turned down for a car loan because of a bankruptcy on her credit report. She got a copy of her file and found out it listed an account that was supposedly charged off in a bankruptcy when she was five years old! Because she has a common name, her file was mixed up with someone else's.

The Fair Credit Reporting Act says consumers have the right to reasonably accurate and complete credit files. But mistakes happen. Creditors can make mistakes when they enter information you scribble on your application, or occasionally errors occur in transmitting or translating data.

Here are some examples of the types of errors that I've seen on credit reports:

- *Your file contains information about someone with a similar name.* Called "comingling," this problem can plague people with common names, or juniors or seniors in a family. You can help cut down on the chance that your file will get mixed up by always filling out your complete name on a credit application (including if you're a junior or senior, for example), and by being consistent in the name you use when you apply for credit.

The credit bureaus are developing systems to reduce the number of comingled files, and they say they've already been successful in stopping a lot of it. If your file has already been mixed up with someone else's, make sure you notify the credit bureau of the problem. Experian, for instance, offers a "blocker" to keep files separate. And check your report periodically to make sure it doesn't happen again.

- *Your ex-spouse's information appears on your report.* If the information on your report is about joint accounts you both shared, that information can and will remain on both your reports for seven years or more. But if information about accounts you *never* held together appears on the report, dispute the entries with the credit bureau. Be sure to mention that you never held those accounts.

- *The most recent information reported about one of your accounts is months—or years—old.* Subscribers (lenders) are *not* required to report their information regularly to the credit bureau. They can report information only once, or as often as once a month. It's their choice. Most do report information monthly. Bureaus are required to report accurate information, though, so if an account lists outdated information, you can ask the credit bureau to update it.

- *Your report lists accounts you do not recognize.* If you have a relative with a similar name, first check with them to make sure it is not their account. If it does belong to them, notify the credit bureau—and the creditor that reported the information—of the error. If you can't figure out who the extra information belongs to, dispute it with the credit bureau—they may be able to trace it to someone with a similar name and remove it.

If there are several accounts you don't recognize, you

must find out why they are on your file. Application fraud, where a thief applies for credit in someone else's name, is a serious crime. If your report lists a bunch of accounts that do not belong to you, especially recent ones with balances, it could be because of this type of fraud. For more information on how to handle application fraud, see Chapter Eleven.

- *Your credit report does not list all your accounts.* Credit bureaus are required to keep their files as complete as possible. But that doesn't mean they have to include accounts from all your creditors. It is totally up to a lender or credit card company as to whether or not they report information, and how often they report it. Accounts that may not show up on your report include utilities, small local retailers, finance accounts, some credit union accounts, some student loans, gasoline cards, debit cards, checking accounts, medical and attorneys' bills, and some mortgages.

  If you have an account with a lender that doesn't report to credit bureaus, you probably won't have any luck getting it added to your report. Credit bureaus won't add information from someone that's not a subscriber. To help make sure that the information they get is accurate, they'll only accept information from customers they've been able to check out. If they aren't getting information on a regular basis from a customer, they won't take a one-time report.

  Sometimes, "mistakes" on credit reports don't turn out to be mistakes at all. Here are two common complaints that I hear that are perfectly legal.

- *Your credit report lists accounts that you have paid off.* I worked on a credit hotline for a couple of months, answering people's credit questions. This complaint came up a *lot*. I clearly remember the first call like this. A woman told me her rejection letter said she had been turned down because "Your credit report shows ninety days or more late on other accounts." She told me, "I've never been ninety days late on anything." I assumed there must be a mistake on her credit report and explained to her how to get a copy. Then I told her that if she found anything wrong on it—say a student loan that was reported paid late but wasn't—she could write to the credit bureau and dispute it.

"Oh," she said, "I did have a student loan that was late but I paid that account off a couple of years ago. I didn't think it could stay on my credit report once I paid it."

Under law, negative information stays on your report for seven years. A credit bureau *can* legally keep accounts on your file after you have paid them off. If there is any negative information (a late payment, or an account that was sent to collections, etc.) it can stay on your report for seven years. If the information is *not* derogatory, it can stay on your report indefinitely. The credit bureau must, however, report complete information about the account. So, for example, if one of your accounts has been paid off and closed, your report should say that it has been closed, but it will still show that you were late. If it is a collection account that has since been paid, your report should list that fact as well.

- *Your report lists negative information, such as delinquency or collection activity, about an account, but fails to list the years of on-time payments you made on that same account.* Subscribers are free to report only negative information, or both positive and negative information. A few issuers, such as gasoline card issuers, may report your account to the credit bureau only if you fall behind more than three months on payments. While these creditors are not required to report a positive payment history on a regular basis, they are required to update the listing if payment status on the account changes. So if you get caught up, the report should say that, even though it can and will still show the late payment.

Your Credit Report: Your Legal Right #3
You Have the Right to Ask the Credit Bureau to Fix Mistakes

If you find wrong or incomplete information on your report, the credit bureau is required by law to investigate the error and correct it if it's wrong. If the bureau can't verify the information with the lender that reported it, they must delete it from your file.

Most credit bureaus include a form you should fill out if you want to dispute information. If you don't have one of the forms, you can simply write a letter. Be as specific as possible. For instance, don't simply list: "Bloomingdale's, Discover." Instead, describe your dispute something like this:

Bloomingdale's	I paid this account off a year ago and closed it. Please update the file to show a zero balance and account closed by me.
Discover	Acct #1010. I have never had a Discover Card. Please investigate.

You don't have to be nasty in your original dispute. Remember, the people who are handling your complaint get hundreds of letters from irate consumers every week. Politely enlisting their aid may even score you a few points. (There's plenty of time to get mad later if your report is not corrected.)

Be sure to list your name, address, Social Security number, and phone numbers (day and evening) in your dispute. Type or print if possible to make sure it is readable. Do not simply send in a marked-up copy of your credit report unless the credit bureau asks you to do so.

Return your form or letter by certified mail, return receipt requested, and keep a copy. Sending your letter by certified mail is usually worth the small expense and the inconvenience of going to the post office. If there is a problem later, you may want proof that the credit bureau received your letter.

You may also be able to file your dispute on-line, though my experience to date with this has been that the on-line forms don't leave room for a lot of flexibility in describing the problem. That will probably change as the agencies gain more experience with on-line disputes.

Credit bureaus now have thirty days to investigate and correct information. If they cannot verify the information in that time period, they must delete it. If, in the meantime, you supply additional relevant information about your dispute, the bureau can have fifteen more days to investigate.

If you do not hear back from the credit bureau within thirty days, write again, enclosing a copy of your original letter of dispute. If the credit bureau again fails to respond, you may want to enlist the help of an attorney, or one of the federal agencies listed in the Resources section.

How Do Investigations Work? When you dispute wrong or outdated information with a credit bureau, the bureau must verify the information with the source that reported it or else delete it. In addition, the credit bureau must supply the lender with all relevant information you have provided about the dispute. If you have proof that the information is wrong, send a copy to the bureau. If you don't have anything to show that the information is wrong and the lender continues to report it as wrong, you could have a tough time getting it removed from your file. After all, in the credit bureau's view, you could be one of the thousands of people who are just trying to get some accurate but negative information taken off their files.

Sometimes a credit bureau will contact a lender to confirm if information is correct, and the creditor just never responds. Under the FCRA, if a credit bureau cannot verify disputed information, the agency has to drop it from your file. That doesn't mean, however, that the agency can't put the information back on at a later time if the creditor shows it's correct.

Before reinserting disputed information that has already been deleted, however, the person supplying the data must certify that it is complete and accurate. Then the credit bureau must send the consumer a notice within five business days, stating that the information has been placed back in the file. The bureau must also include the name, address, and phone number of the company that supplied the information (as long as those details are "reasonably available") and explain the consumer's right to add a statement of dispute to the file.

In the past, if you found wrong information on your credit report with one of the three major agencies, you had to make sure you disputed it with the other two to make certain it didn't show up somewhere else. That is supposed to be changing.

In 1995, the Associated Credit Bureaus (now called The Consumer Data Industry Association) developed the Automated Consumer Dispute Verification (ACDV) system, which automatically reports corrections to all major bureaus. For example, suppose you get your Trans Union report, and it shows that one of your gasoline card issuers is reporting you as being ninety days late on your payments last year, but you know you weren't late at all. You write to Trans Union, tell them about the error and ask them to correct it. Instead of filling out a written consumer dispute form and mailing it to the card issuer as they used to, Trans Union sends a Consumer Dispute Verification Request via an automated system that works in a way similar to e-mail. The card issuer checks its files and finds out you're right, you never were ninety days late on that account. So they respond via the same system to Trans Union and *also* to Equifax and Experian. That means the correction should be made at all three bureaus, not just the one you wrote to.

The advantages of the ACDV system are that it eliminates the mail time in the dispute process, so information can be verified in days, not weeks, and if the creditor makes a correction via the ACDV system, it's automatically corrected with all three credit agencies, so you don't have to dispute the same information again.

The drawback to the ACDV system is that it is voluntary. However, more and more creditors are participating. Still, if you find mistakes on your report, it's vital you check your report with all three agencies to make sure they are corrected everywhere.

If wrong information was deleted from your report as a result of an investigation, you can ask the credit bureau to report the correction to any companies that saw your report in the past two years for employment purposes, or the past six months for any other purpose. They'll do this only if you ask, and under the new law they can charge you for them, but no more than they would normally charge the recipient. (Since many credit grantors pay less than consumers do, it may well be less than the usual $9.)

Another major improvement in the credit reporting law is the section that holds those who supply information to credit bureaus responsible for correcting mistakes. Under the old FCRA, credit grantors were off the hook completely—even if they repeatedly reported wrong information. No more. The new law makes it illegal for anyone to report information to a credit bureau that it "knows or consciously avoids knowing" is inaccurate.

If a creditor is notified of a possible mistake, either through a credit bureau or directly by the consumer, it must investigate and, if necessary, correct the error within the same thirty-day time frame as credit bureaus (with an extra fifteen days for additional information supplied by the consumer). Furthermore, it must report the correction to all bureaus to which it originally supplied the information, as described above.

The fact that lenders, too, must investigate disputes raises the question, Should you contact the credit bureau or the creditor when you find a mistake? There is no correct answer. In many cases, you will find more than one error on your report when you review it. In that case, it makes sense to notify the bureau that supplied your report of all the mistakes and ask them to investigate each. If one (or more) is not resolved, you can request contact information for the creditor and go directly to them with your dispute.

If you are applying for a time-sensitive loan and you know the mistake is seriously impacting your credit, it probably makes sense to go directly to the creditor and try to get it straightened out as quickly as possible. And if you know that the creditor has mistaken information in its files and will simply confirm with the credit bureau that your information is correct if you dispute it that way, then go directly to the source.

When I found an erroneous late payment on my credit report in 2000, it took three months and finally a call to the public-relations department of the lender to get it corrected. It should not be that difficult, but it certainly can be.

Your Credit Report: Legal Right #4
You Have a Right to Tell Your Side of the Story

What happens if you dispute information as wrong, but the credit bureau and the creditor refuse to change it because the creditor says it's correct? What else can you do? The FCRA gives you the right to tell your side of the story. You can add a statement to your file explaining your version of the dispute. This statement will become a permanent part of your credit file and must be given to all creditors who receive the disputed information.

Unfortunately, statements aren't always helpful. If your application for credit is being evaluated by computer, which many are these days, the creditor may not even see your statement. If you're applying for a loan in person, or a live human being is reviewing your credit report, then it's more likely to at least be read. If your statement seems plausible and it seems accurate and consistent with other information in your file, then it can be helpful.

The credit bureau may limit your statement to one hundred words or less, but if it does, it has to help you summarize it. Some consumers have complained that credit bureaus automatically summarize statements without getting their input. If you see your file after you have added a statement, and don't like the summary of the statement, ask that your own words be used. Steve Rhode, president of the financial crisis organization Myvesta.org, generally does not recommend people add statements to their credit files because they can remain on the report long after the problem is resolved.

When writing your statement, be factual, brief, and clear. Ranting and raving about how unfairly a creditor treated you is unlikely to impress other creditors. If you have documentation supporting your version of the dispute, be sure to mention that it's available.

The FCRA right to add a statement to your file applies only to cases where you are disputing the *accuracy* of information in your file. It doesn't include situations where you are trying to explain the *circumstances* that led to credit problems. If, for instance, your ex-spouse illegally opened an account in both your names after your divorce and the creditor refuses to take it off your report, you can add a statement to your file because that information is not accurate and should not be on your report. If, however, your divorce caused financial problems and you fell behind on some bills, you do not have a legal basis for adding a statement explaining why your report contains late payments.

Some credit bureaus, like Experian, will allow consumers to add statements that explain circumstances but they don't encourage it. Others, like Equifax, encourage it. For example, during the 1994 floods that caused so much damage in the Southeast, Equifax notified local and regional media that consumers could call a special toll-free number (set up for that purpose) to add statements to their credit files explaining that they were victims of the flood. `

Your Credit Report: Legal Right #5
You Have the Right to a Fresh Start

Millions of people go through financial setbacks that hurt their credit histories—divorce, a period of unemployment, or a temporary interruption in income (moving, changing jobs, having a child) can cause even the most careful person to fall behind.

Fortunately, a bad credit rating can't haunt you forever. Congress gave consumers a chance to start over again. Under the FCRA, damaging or negative information can usually stay on your file for only seven years. There are a few exceptions—bankruptcy can stay on the file for ten years, for example—but the general rule is seven years.

If you are trying to get out from under a bad credit rating, read Chapter Four carefully for details on how long specific information can remain on your report.

Your Credit Report: Legal Right #6
You Have the Right to Understand What Your File Says

In the past, credit reports have been extremely difficult to read. Filled with confusing codes, they were often very hard to decipher. But they're getting better. Experian has gone to a "plain English" format, which makes their reports much easier to read.

Equifax and Trans Union have also gone to a written-out format, without codes.

If there is anything on your report that you don't understand, the credit bureau is *required by law* to explain it to you. If there is a creditor that you don't recognize listed on your report, ask the credit bureau to supply you with the name and location of the creditor so you can find out if you really do have an account with them.

Most of the credit bureaus used to have "consumer-relations" offices in local bureaus across the country. Now they've consolidated them into their national offices. You'll have to either write to the credit bureau or call a toll-free number to try to speak with someone about your question. Some credit bureaus have been easier to reach than others. Under the new law, credit bureaus must maintain staffed toll-free numbers to assist consumers who have been denied credit based on information in their reports. If you have a really hard time finding someone knowledgeable to help you, you may want to let the Federal Trade Commission, or FTC, know about it. (See the Resources section for information on contacting the FTC.)

Your Credit Report: Legal Right #7
You Have the Right to Find Out Who Has Seen Your Credit File

Credit bureaus are required to tell you who has seen your report in the past two years for employment purposes and during the past year for all other purposes. As I mentioned in Chapter One, the names of the firms that have accessed your file will be listed in the "inquiries" section of your report.

In the past, it has often been difficult to tell exactly which companies accessed your credit report, because their names were often abbreviated on the reports. Experian was the only reporting agency that gave complete names and addresses for inquiries. Now, however, credit bureaus must list the full name or business name of anyone who reviewed your report during the time frames listed above. In addition, the bureau must also supply the address and telephone number of the company if you ask for it. Creditor contact information may be listed on your report.

If you find inquiries from companies you don't recognize on your report, and they aren't promotional inquiries, dig a little deeper to make sure your file wasn't illegally accessed. The following section explains who can legally access your credit report.

Your Credit Report: Legal Right #8
You Have the Right to Confidentiality

If you provide someone with written permission to obtain your credit file, the credit bureau may supply it to them. But your written permission is not always needed to get a copy of your report. The Fair Credit Reporting Act allows another person or business to access your credit file *without* your permission for:

1. *Credit purposes:* The user is considering extending credit to you, reviewing your credit account, or attempting to collect a debt. The credit being considered or reviewed must be for personal, family, or household purposes only.

   For purposes of collecting a debt, the FTC's interpretation of the law outlines a number of circumstances under which a person or business may obtain a credit report. Those include: a private detective attempting to collect a debt owed by the consumer, an attorney deciding whether to sue a consumer to collect a debt, a judgment creditor attempting to collect a judgment debt, a district attorney's office or child-support enforcement agency trying to collect a delinquent child-support obligation, a tax collection agency that has a tax lien or judgment against the consumer, and someone attempting to collect on a bad check.

2. *Employment purposes:* The user is an employer or potential employer considering you for employment, promotion, reassignment, or retention. The law requires that employers must have your written permission to obtain your report. Before denying you a job, promotion, etc., because of your credit report, the employer

must give you a copy of it with a statement describing your right to dispute wrong information.

3. *Insurance purposes:* The user is obtaining the report in connection with the underwriting of an insurance policy. Again, the insurance policy must be for personal, family, or household purposes. While a credit report may be obtained to decide whether or not to issue a policy, the amount and terms of coverage, the duration of the policy, the rates and fees charged, and whether or not to renew or cancel the policy, the credit report *cannot* be obtained to evaluate a claim—unless you give your permission for the creditor to get one to evaluate claims. According to one of the major credit reporting agencies, insurance companies will frequently make consumers sign "blanket consents" on their applications for insurance, so that the company can run a credit check if a claim is filed.

4. *Business purposes:* The user has a legitimate need for the information in connection with a business transaction that is initiated by the consumer.

5. *Other purposes:* The new law also specifies that a user can obtain a credit report if the intent is to "use the information, as a potential investor or servicer, or current investor, in connection with a valuation of, or an assessment of the credit or prepayment risks associated with, an existing credit obligation." This would apply, for example, to an investor buying pools of mortgage obligations. When your mortgage is sold, you may continue to make the mortgage payment to the same servicer you have been using, but someone else is actually taking the "risk" if you don't pay.

It also specifies that a credit report can be obtained by someone with a legitimate business purpose to review an account to "determine whether the consumer continues to meet the terms of an account."

In addition, the FCRA lists several circumstances under which someone can obtain your credit report other than for insurance, employment, or credit purposes:

"In response to a court order"; or

"In connection with a determination of the consumer's eligibility for a license or other benefit granted by a governmental instrumentality required by law to consider an applicant's financial responsibility or status." For example, this provision allows government agencies to access reports in cases where consumers have applied for welfare benefits, a government security clearance, or even a license to practice law.

"In response to the written instructions of the consumer to whom it relates." If you agree in writing to allow someone to access your credit report, they *may* do so. It is important to note, however, that the credit bureau is *not* obligated to sell someone a report, even if you have asked them to do so. If, for instance, you are trying to rent a home from someone, or trying to buy their home on an owner-financed basis, the credit bureau may require you to order your own credit report and give it to them, rather than supply it directly to someone else.

Child Support: In the case of child support, a credit report can be obtained by an enforcement agency to determine whether the person who will be obligated to pay it can make the payments, or to set the level of the payments. However, that person must be given ten days' prior notice via certified mail that the report will be reviewed, and the report must be kept confidential. A report can also be used by an enforcement agency to set an initial or modified child support award.

A friend of mine was at a party and met a car salesman. She didn't give him any information about where she worked or her unlisted home phone number. She was very surprised, then, when he called her a couple of days later at work. "How did you get my number here?" she demanded. "Oh, I just used your name to pull up your credit report here at work, and it gave me the name of your employer," he responded. He didn't seem to think there was anything wrong with accessing her information like that, but in fact what he was doing was illegal. Just because someone can get credit reports doesn't mean he or she is allowed to.

No Peeking: Based on interpretations of the Fair Credit Reporting Act, there are a number of reasons for which credit reports may *not* be obtained:

Credit reports *cannot* be used in most cases by attorneys for litigation purposes. They can, however, be used by attorneys trying to collect debts.

Ex-spouses' credit reports *may not* be used by creditors or other third parties. If you are divorced, in the process of divorce, or legally separated, your spouse or ex-spouse may not obtain a report on you.

Credit reports *may not* be used to evaluate insurance claims (unless, of course, you've given your permission).

Credit reports *cannot* be used for general marketing purposes, or for marketing research. Prescreening is the exception.

Preapproved Cards: In prescreening, a card issuer or other lender supplies the credit bureau with a list of names of prospective customers. The list of names may be purchased from a list broker, or the issuer specifies a geographic area and relies on the credit reporting agency to develop the list of names. In either case, the card issuer will chose various criteria they want their customers to meet. The card issuer, for example, may ask the credit bureau for all the people on the list who have three to five credit cards, at least one bankcard, and no late payments or public record information. The credit bureau will then run through the credit files of the people on the list or in the chosen geographic area to determine which ones meet those criteria. The computer spits out a list of all the people who "pass" and they are all sent preapproved offers for credit cards.

The updated FCRA changed the rules regarding prescreening. First, the bureaus now have a toll-free number you can call to block your file from prescreening for credit or insurance purposes 1-888-5OPT-OUT. If you decide to "opt out," they must block your file within five business days and keep it blocked for two years. (You can sign a form supplied by the bureau to leave the block in effect until you say otherwise.)

If you don't opt out, your file can be reviewed for preapproved offers. Don't assume, however, that if you do accept one of these preapproved offers you will automatically be approved. While the new law says that a prescreened offer must be a "firm offer" of credit or insurance, it also has a sneaky provision that appears to make the definition of "firm" rather loose.

The new law says that a lender (or insurer) can set additional requirements ahead of time and may turn you down if you don't meet those requirements. The problem is, of course, you won't know exactly what those requirements are. In addition, if any of the criteria on which you were prescreened have changed by the time you accept the offer, you can be turned down (if, for example, you've defaulted on a credit card between the time your file was prescreened and when you responded). Finally, if collateral is required for the offer, you can be turned down if you don't have it.

The credit grantor is required to keep its criteria on file for three years, presumably so you can challenge any deceptive offers. If you do respond to a preapproved offer and are turned down, talk to the credit grantor. If the answer is not satisfactory, I strongly suggest you write to the Federal Trade Commission's Credit Practices Division and complain.

Remember, inquiries for prescreened offers are "soft" inquiries and are not shown to anyone except the consumer, so they can't hurt your credit. But if you respond to a preapproved offer, the creditor will likely pull a complete copy of your credit report, creating a "hard" inquiry, which can affect your credit. So if you do decide to respond to these offers, do so cautiously and try to avoid more than four or five hard inquiries in a six-month stretch.

Snooping in Your File: What happens if someone accesses your report illegally? The FCRA states that anyone who "knowingly and willfully obtains information on a consumer from a consumer-reporting agency under false pretenses shall be fined under Title 18 U.S.C., or imprisoned not more than two years, or both." The penalty for an officer or employee of a credit bureau who "knowingly and willfully" provides information to someone who is not authorized to obtain it is similar.

The names of firms that have accessed your credit report will be found under the "inquiries" section of a credit report. While credit bureaus are clamping down on illegal access to credit reports, it does happen. Smaller credit bureaus and resellers have been known to sell credit reports without making sure the users had legal reasons for getting them.

New provisions in the FCRA require credit reporting agencies to make sure that all credit reports are supplied only for legal purposes. In particular, resellers cannot obtain credit reports unless they identify the end user of the report, as well as each permissible purpose for the report. Before reselling reports, the identification and certification of the end user must be reasonably established. Still, if you suspect that someone has gained illegal access to your file, report your suspicions to the credit bureau and the FTC.

Your Credit Report: Your Legal Right #9
You Have the Right to Know When Your Credit Report Has Been Used for Adverse Action

Anytime you are turned down for credit or insurance for personal, family, or household purposes, and the creditor bases that decision either partially or completely on information in your credit report, they have to tell you the name and address of the credit bureau that supplied your report. You'll then be able to order a free copy. This is also true if the cost of your credit or insurance was raised in whole or in part because of information they got from your credit record.

As I mentioned earlier, employers may see your credit report if they are evaluating you for "employment, promotion, reassignment or retention" as an employee. Before you are denied a job, you lose your current job, or you are denied a promotion or new job because of information in your credit report, the employer must give you a copy of your credit report.

Your Credit Report: Your Legal Right #10
You May Have the Right to Sue the Credit Bureau

The Fair Credit Reporting Act allows consumers to sue credit bureaus if they willfully violate the Act. If you are planning on suing a credit bureau, be forewarned: It may be expensive and difficult to win.

Suits can be brought in either state or federal court; an attorney can help you decide which is most appropriate for your case. Although class-action suits against credit bureaus are not common, they are not prohibited by the FCRA. Nor are jury trials, which are sometimes used successfully in these types of cases.

The FCRA allows consumers to bring civil action against credit bureaus for willful noncompliance or negligent noncompliance. In cases of "willful noncompliance," a consumer sues a credit bureau or user because it willfully fails to comply with any requirements of the Act. The consumer can sue for an amount equal to the sum of actual damages (not less than $100 or more than $1,000), attorney's fees, plus punitive damages.

Negligent noncompliance suits allege that a credit bureau showed negligence in failing to comply with the requirements of the Act. Often, it can mean that the credit bureau does not have reasonable procedures in place to ensure that it is in compliance with the Act or, if it does have appropriate procedures, an employee fails to follow them in a particular case. In the case of negligent noncompliance, a consumer can sue for actual damages plus attorney's fees.

These two types of noncompliance are very closely related. If you are considering suing a credit bureau, seek the assistance of an attorney familiar with consumer credit protection laws to help you determine how to proceed. If you are interested in researching remedies yourself, the National Consumer Law Center's *Fair Credit Reporting Act Manual* can help. See the Resources section for more information.

Going One Step Further: ACB Voluntary Guidelines

The Consumer Data Industry Association (formerly ACB) is an international trade association representing the consumer credit, mortgage reporting, and collection service industries. Their members include more than five hundred credit reporting, mortgage-reporting, collection-services, and employment reporting companies.

Before the new credit reporting law was passed, they developed a set of guidelines their members agreed to follow to improve credit reporting accuracy, privacy, and responsiveness to consumers. In most cases, the guidelines went above and beyond what was required by the FCRA at the time. Virtually every one of those guidelines will be redundant under the new law, but one in particular was not addressed in the legislation: the reporting period for Chapter 13 bankruptcies.

All three major credit reporting systems have agreed to their recommendation that successfully completed Chapter 13 bankruptcies be kept in the credit file no longer than seven years from filing, rather than the ten-year period allowed by federal law.

Summary of 1996 Credit Reporting Law

In late 1996, Congress passed amendments to the Fair Credit Reporting Act. The effort to reform the law was due to years of hard work by Congressmen Joe Kennedy, Esteban Torres, and Senators Charles Schumer and Richard Bryan, and several consumer groups including Consumers Union, U.S. Public Interest Research Group, and Bankcard Holders of America.

The bill that was enacted is called the Consumer Credit Reporting Reform Act of 1996. Following is a summary of the major provisions of that act. Most became effective October 1, 1997, except as noted.

Investigations of Disputed Information: Credit bureaus must promptly investigate consumer disputes at no charge, in most cases within thirty days. They must take into account any relevant documentation or proof provided by the consumer and must supply that documentation to the person who originally reported the information. Within five business days of completing their investigation, the bureau must send the consumer the results, a revised copy of the credit report, and information about the consumer's rights.

Credit bureaus must share corrections with other bureaus through an automated system, so consumers do not have to contact several bureaus to correct the same information.

Reinserting Disputed Information: Credit bureaus must maintain reasonable procedures to prevent deleted information from being reinserted into credit files. A credit bureau cannot put previously disputed and deleted information back on a credit report unless the furnisher supplying the information certifies it is correct, and the credit bureau notifies the consumer with the name, address, and phone number of the furnisher and a description of the consumer's right to add an explanatory statement to the file.

Responsibilities of Creditors and Other Furnishers: Anyone who supplies information to credit bureaus cannot provide information they "know or consciously avoid knowing" is inaccurate. Furnishers also must promptly investigate and correct, if necessary, any mistakes brought to their attention by a credit bureau or consumer. Corrections must be sent to all major credit bureaus to which they reported the information.

If a consumer notifies a creditor or other furnisher that information is not correct, the furnisher cannot report that information to a credit bureau without noting that it is disputed by the consumer.

Costs of Credit Reports: Credit reports will be available to consumers for $9, adjusted annually for inflation. Free reports are provided to: anyone who has been turned down for credit or insurance in the past sixty days based on information in their credit report; the unemployed; those on public assistance; and fraud victims.

Closed Accounts: When a consumer closes an account, the creditor must notify the bureaus, which must report the account as closed at the consumer's request.

Employer's Responsibilities: An employer who wants to review an employee or prospective employee's credit report must first get that person's written permission to do so. Before taking any adverse action against the consumer based on information in the report, the employer must provide a copy of the report and a description of the consumer's credit rights.

Inquiries: Consumers who request their credit reports must be shown the name or full trade name of anyone who has requested their credit report in the past year (two years for inquiries by employers). Upon request, the credit bureau must also supply the addresses and telephone numbers of these companies. Inquiries from prescreening cannot be shown to anyone except the consumer.

Prescreening: Credit reporting agencies must offer a toll-free number consumers can call to block their files from prescreening. The bureaus then must block the files of consumers who "opt out" from prescreening for two years, or at the consumer's written request, indefinitely.

Preapproved Offers: Credit or insurance companies that use prescreening to qualify customers must make a "firm" offer of credit to anyone who meets the initial prescreening criteria. If the consumer responds to the preapproved offer, the lender may still review the customer's credit report and application to make sure nothing screened for in the initial prescreening has changed and that additional predetermined criteria in the application are met.

Obsolete Information: The law clarified that the seven-year reporting period for collection, profit-and-loss, or similar accounts begins 180 days after the payment leading to the delinquency should have been made. This provision applies only to information added to the report on or after December 29, 1997. It also raised the limits for circumstances under which information can be reported longer than seven years to: credit or life insurance transactions involving $150,000 or more, or jobs at an anticipated salary of $75,000 or more.

Other Provisions: Credit bureaus do not have to reveal risk or credit scores. Users, or lenders, may show consumers their credit reports if they are taking adverse action based on information in the report. Resellers of credit reports must verify the end users of the reports and that the purpose for which the report will ultimately be used is legal. Credit reporting agencies must offer staffed, toll-free numbers consumers can call for questions when they are denied credit based on information in their credit reports.

CHAPTER THREE

Credit Cards:
Money-Saving Choices

It all seems so easy. You open your mail and find that one of the biggest banks in the country wants to give you a credit card. A letter from the bank's executive vice president tells you that your superior credit qualifications entitle you to the best, most prestigious piece of plastic in the world. You don't even have to fill out an application. Just sign on the dotted line and two weeks later, it arrives: your major credit card.

You whiz on over to the shopping mall, pick up a few things you don't really need, plop down the plastic on the counter, and it's all yours. No pain, lots of gain.

Until the bill arrives, that is.

You can't believe your eyes. You really charged $1,500 worth of stuff that day? And the credit card company is really going to charge you twenty-three bucks in finance charges—*in one month*—if you can't pay the bill off? Soon, your major credit card is giving you a major headache.

This scene has probably been repeated countless times across the country. With more than six thousand financial institutions pushing Visas and MasterCards, plus countless others hawking department-store cards, charge cards, and gasoline cards, competition for customers is stiff. Lenders are scrambling to attract new customers, each claiming it offers the best credit card. Millions of offers for easy credit flood Americans' mailboxes each year.

How do you figure out which credit card is best for you? How many cards should you carry? How much money can you really save by using the right credit cards? In this chapter, I'll give you the information you need to choose the best credit cards, based on your credit profile. I'll also show you how to save money on credit cards—without sacrificing quality.

Choosing the Best Credit Cards

Visa and MasterCard

Many people think a Visa is a Visa and a MasterCard is a MasterCard, not knowing that there is a wide variety of prices and perks available on these brand-name cards.

Visa cards and MasterCards are *bankcards*, which means they are issued by banks or other financial institutions (credit unions or savings banks, for example). Visa and MasterCard are two large associations of financial institutions. Visa and MasterCard *do not* themselves issue cards but instead provide the systems and support to thousands of individual banks across the country that do. You can think of each issuer operating as sort of a "franchise" of the Visa and MasterCard systems. Lenders must abide by the basic rules of those two companies in order to keep the whole operation running smoothly. Each issuer, however, is free to set its own credit standards, prices, credit limits, and many of the perks offered to cardholders.

MasterCard and Visa are quite similar in terms of buying power and convenience. It's not unusual for someone to have a Visa and a MasterCard or two or more of each. (Why not?) In addition, most merchants accept both types of cards.

Since each Visa and MasterCard issuer decides what type of customers to give cards to, you could find your application for a Visa (or MasterCard) turned down by one bank but accepted with no problem by another.

Discover

The Discover Card is a bankcard offered by Discover Financial Services, a business unit of Morgan Stanley Dean Witter and Co. Designed to be a competitor to Visa and MasterCard, Discover was introduced in the mid-1980s. Millions of cardholders quickly signed up for it. The Discover card is accepted by fewer merchants than Visa or MasterCard and is not an international bankcard. (You can only use it in the United States.) Its claim to fame has been its 1 percent cash-back rebate program, which promises to reward cardholders who spend, spend, spend. For the word on rebates, see Chapter Twelve.

There are Classic, Gold, and Platinum Discover cards as well as affinity cards.

American Express

American Express used to be in a different category. For many years, all they offered were *charge cards* (also called a "travel and entertainment card") because they required that you pay off your balance in full each month. Charge cards—the American Express personal (a.k.a. "Green cards") and Gold cards—are still the majority of the cards they issue.

But American Express has also added *credit cards* to their menu. Their cards include Blue, Optima, and Optima Platinum. All allow a consumer to pay in full or pay over time. The Blue card has a built-in Smart Chip to give consumers "an added level of security when shopping on-line." (In Chapter Ten I point out that your level of liability for fraud when shopping on-line with a credit card is always $0, regardless of which card you use.)

One of the advertised benefits of AmEx charge cards is the fact that there is "no preset spending limit." This doesn't mean that American Express is going to allow you to spend as much as you possibly can on the card. It just means you don't know how much they will allow you to spend. (They are flexible about this.) Their computers keep track of your spending and, if it looks like you are going overboard, someone might call you to find out what's going on, freeze your card if it looks like you aren't going to be able to pay the bills, or even decline some of your purchases.

American Express' greatest pride, however, is their customer-service staff, which they say goes above and beyond that of other card companies. That, along with lots of perks, is primarily what they seem to be banking on for success.

The first benefit that comes to many people's minds when they think of an AmEx card may not be service, however, but prestige. Millions of Americans now hold American Express cards, and even college students can get them, but the perceived exclusivity of the card still attracts new customers.

Department-Store Cards

Department-store cards are easy to get, but they are often very expensive. Although these cards are almost always "free" in terms of annual fees, if you don't pay off the balance in full, the finance charges are often astronomical—sometimes as high as 26 percent and almost never under 18 percent.

Perhaps the only good reason to get department-store cards is the opportunity for special sales and discounts. Department stores often send their charge customers advance notice of sales, hold private sales for them, and offer periodic discounts on merchandise. If you rarely pay off your cards in full each month, however, don't use high-rate department-store cards; pull out a low-interest-rate bankcard instead.

Gasoline Cards

Gasoline cards (also called "oil cards") are T&E cards—you will usually be required to pay your balance in full every month. (I'm *not* talking here about cobranded gas cards, where the gas company offers a Visa or MasterCard with their name on it—I'm talking about the gasoline cards that have been around for a long time.) Most gasoline cards offer revolving credit for certain higher-ticket purchases like car repairs, tires, and travel. The interest rates for these revolving purchases are usually high, like department-store cards. Each card may also offer perks like credit card registration, travel clubs, and emergency road assistance. Best of all, gasoline cards are by far the easiest cards to get.

Credit Card Costs

Credit cards can be one of the most expensive types of consumer loans available today—or the cheapest. Fairly priced cards are available, but they're sometimes harder to find (and get), and if you don't read the fine print, you could pay more than you thought you would.

It used to be that credit card companies wouldn't even tell you how much a credit card cost until you actually got the card in your hands. Congress put a halt to that, however, by passing the Fair Credit and Charge Card Disclosure Act of 1989. Card issuers now, by law, have to give you details up front about how much a credit card costs. Under this law, which is part of the Truth-in-Lending Act, the costs of credit cards must be displayed in an easy-to-read box format on most applications and solicitations. The box that lists the costs of the card is dubbed the "Schumer Box," after Senator Charles Schumer (D-NY), who led this consumer-protection legislation through Congress.

Here's an example of a credit card disclosure table:

Annual Percentage Rate for Purchases	Grace Period for Purchases	Minimum Finance Charges	Balance Calculation Method for Purchases	Annual Fees	Transaction Fees for Cash Advances	Late Payment Fee
19.8%	Not less than 25 days	$.50 when a finance charge at a periodic rate is charged	Average daily balance method (including new purchases)	Annual fee: $25 per year	2% with a minimum fee of $2	$10

There are five basic elements to look at when you're selecting a credit card: finance charges, annual fees, grace periods, penalty fees, and balance calculation methods. First, I'll explain what each of these terms means and how they affect the cost of the credit you use. Then I'll show you how to save money by choosing the cards that best fit your personal financial needs.

Finance Charges

A finance charge (also called "interest") is the "commission" you pay the bank for lending you money. Most people don't pay their credit card bills off each month—in fact, somewhere between one-third and one-half do. If you *do* pay in full, you'll usually, but not always, be charged no interest at all. Those who fail to pay off all their credit cards in full at the end of every month pay interest (or finance charges).

You will see finance charges listed on your credit card statement in two ways: as a "monthly periodic rate" and as an "APR." APR stands for "annual percentage rate," and it simply means the stated amount of interest you will pay on a yearly basis. An APR of 19.8 percent means you will pay 19.8 percent interest over the course of a year on your balances. Divide that 19.8 percent APR by 12 (months), and you have a monthly periodic rate of 1.65 percent.

An interest rate of 1.65 percent a month seems harmless enough, but that depends on your balance. A monthly periodic rate of 1.65 percent on a balance of $1,000, for example, would mean about $16 of interest per month, and over $165 per year.

Even worse, the stated finance charge the card issuer charges is often lower than the *actual* amount of interest you will pay on the card, because of the way interest is calculated on credit cards. Later, I'll explain how that works.

Annual Fees

Free Credit Cards: An article in the December 18, 1980, issue of the *New York Times* announced that Citibank was going to begin charging cardholders a $15 annual fee. In those days, many bankcards did not charge annual fees. American Express, Diner's Club, and Carte Blanche cost $35 back then.

Annual fees (or "membership fees," as they are sometimes called) now range anywhere from $0 to $100 or more, while the average is about $20. These fees can add up. Suppose you have three bankcards, each charging $25 apiece—that's $75 a year. There are, however, cards that carry no annual fees. A free credit card isn't a giveaway for the issuer. Most cardholders pay interest, and that's where issuers really make money. In addition, every time you use your card, the merchant pays a percentage of the purchase (called a "merchant discount fee") to the card companies for the privilege of accepting the card. A small portion of the merchant discount fee, which typically ranges from 1.5 to 4 percent of the purchase amount, is passed on to the card issuer.

If your credit card carries an annual fee, your card issuer must warn you thirty days before the card will be renewed, so you will have the opportunity to cancel the card before you pay the fee. This notice will appear on your billing statement; it must disclose how much the annual fee will cost and tell you how and when to close your account if you don't want to pay the annual fee.

Grace Periods

A Free Ride? A grace period, or "free-ride" period, is the time between the closing date of the billing cycle and the due date that you have to pay the balance in full and be charged no finance charge. If it sounds really confusing, that's because it is.

If your card has a grace period, the bill will usually read "Pay this amount to avoid further finance charges . . ." next to the total balance. If your card does *not* have a grace period, you can pay off your bill in full at the end of the month, and you will find next month that you were charged interest anyway.

People are usually confused about how grace periods really work, and I don't blame them. The way interest is calculated on credit cards is very complicated. Just remember this: *You usually get the benefit of a grace period* only *if you pay the entire bill in full by the due date.*

Later, in the section on balance calculation methods, you will learn more about how this works. For now, however, you should understand that unless you pay off every last penny at the end of the month, the grace period is useless.

Some credit cards do not offer a grace period. That doesn't necessarily make the card a bad deal. Some people can actually save more money with a card that offers no grace period than one that does. I'll tell you why in a minute.

Penalty Fees

Late fees, over-the-limit fees, transaction fees, and bounced-check fees on credit cards were uncommon, if not unknown, in the mid-1980s when I started watching this industry. But as soon as a few large banks wised up to the fact that they could charge additional fees to cardholders who didn't pay their accounts as agreed, penalty fees became almost commonplace. These days, most issuers charge penalty fees, although you may find a few issuers that don't.

Penalty fees can be very expensive, and in few cases do they actually reflect the bank's cost of processing the transaction. Besides, that is what interest is for: to cover the bank's costs and make a reasonable profit. Even worse, some banks will add the fee to your current balance and charge you interest on the fee as well as the balance!

Wells Fargo Bank, one of the largest card issuers in the country, in 1991 settled a class-action suit over its over-the-limit fees. The verdict? It could not charge over-the-limit fees for the next four years, a loss of probably $1 million in fees it could have collected. Wells Fargo was also sued because of late fees. In a separate story reported in the February 16, 1989, issue of *The Wall Street Journal*, a California state court jury determined that Wells Fargo had illegally overcharged its credit card holders with its late fees of $10 and over-limit fees of $3 to $5. The total overcharge: $5.2 million.

Here's what to look out for in penalty fees:

Cash Advance Fees: Card issuers already can make a tidy sum off cash advances, since they usually charge interest from the day you take out the cash advance (regardless of whether you pay the balance in full at the end of the month). Often they make even more by charging higher interest rates on cash advances than on purchases. On top of that, most issuers add on a cash advance fee—as much as 2 to 4 percent of the amount of the cash advance (sometimes capped at $25 to $50)—simply for the privilege of borrowing cash instead of making a purchase. Be sure to check with your bank before you take out a cash advance to find out what kinds of fees they charge.

A few issuers have advertised in the past that they charge a fee instead of interest right away, but don't assume that makes them a better deal. The banks that pulled that trick in the past charged more for the fee than it would have cost for one month's interest at their already high interest rates! And even those banks that do offer a "grace period" on cash advances will start charging interest if you can't pay the advance off in full by the due date.

Late Fees: Some banks charge a fee of $10 to $35 if you fail to pay your bill on time. Most issuers used to wait until you were a full month behind before charging a late fee. Then some started charging if you fell behind by fifteen days. Now most will impose a late fee if you are just one day late with a payment. In addition, many cardholder agreements specify a time (say 11 A.M.) by which payments must be received on the due date in order to be considered on time. Your interest rate may also skyrocket if you are late with your payments.

Over-the-Limit Fees: Card issuers shouldn't get away with charging an over-limit fee of $10 to $35, but they do. After all, if you are over your limit, you are either carrying a high balance (which likely means you are a profitable account for the bank, since you pay a lot of interest), or you charged a lot during the month (which also makes you a profitable account, since you generated income in merchant discount fees).

If you go over the limit, your card issuer is likely to send you a notice asking you to pay the over-limit amount in full immediately. Regardless, you'll pay interest on the over-limit amount and may pay a penalty fee as well. Sometimes they'll charge an over-limit fee every single month until you are able to bring the balance down under the limit.

Transaction Fees: These are particularly onerous because most consumers don't know about them until it is too late. A transaction fee is a fee that is charged each time you use the card. A typical transaction fee from a card issuer that charges one would be fifty cents per charge. Fortunately, most issuers don't charge transaction fees, but if you find one that does, you're probably smart to just say "no" to the offer.

If you see this language on a credit card disclosure statement: "A minimum finance charge of fifty cents will be charged in any month during which a periodic finance charge is payable," don't confuse it with a transaction charge. This simply means that if your finance charge for the month is between one cent and forty-nine cents, it will be rounded off to fifty cents on your bill.

Balance Calculation Methods

How much your credit cards will cost you depends on the costs mentioned above. It will also depend on the method the card issuer uses to calculate the finance charge. Think about this for a second. A credit card isn't like a car loan or mortgage where you have a set amount you borrow and then fixed payments you make each month. With a credit card, you're constantly borrowing different amounts and paying back some or all of the balance. The question is, then, how do they figure out which balance to charge you interest on? That's where the balance calculation method comes in.

Balance calculation methods first came to my attention a few years back when a woman wrote to me because she had a question about her credit card. She had made a fairly expensive purchase of jewelry, and decided to pay it off over a couple of months. Normally, she didn't carry a balance on her credit card. She was smart enough to figure out in advance what the finance charges would be, but absolutely flipped when she got her first statement—the finance charge was *double* what she had expected! She called the credit card company for an explanation and they said that was how the "two-cycle billing method" worked. She wrote to me asking if this was legal. I didn't think it could be, but I researched it and found it was perfectly legal.

There are several main ways that credit card balances can be calculated, some more expensive than others. Almost all credit card issuers use the "Average Daily Balance, including New Purchases" method, but you'll see some other methods from time to time. Balance calculation methods are quite complicated, but I've listed a brief, and hopefully understandable, description of each. I have listed these in the order of "best" to "worst" for many but never all—consumers.

1. Adjusted balance. This balance is figured by deducting payments and credits made during the billing cycle from the outstanding balance at the beginning of the billing cycle. *If your beginning balance was $1,000 and you paid $900 of that, you would only be charged interest on the remaining $100.*

2. Average Daily Balance *Excluding* New Purchases. This balance is figured by adding the outstanding balance (excluding new purchases and deducting payments and credits) for each day in the billing cycle, and then dividing by the number of days in the cycle. *New purchases made during the billing cycle do not raise your balance or increase your finance charge.*

3. Previous balance. This balance is the outstanding balance at the beginning of the billing cycle. *Payments or charges made during the month won't affect your finance charge this billing cycle.*

4. Average Daily Balance *Including* New Purchases. This balance is figured by adding the outstanding balance, including new purchases, and deducting payments and credits, for each day in the billing cycle, and then dividing by the number of days in the billing cycle. *Purchases made during the billing cycle raise your balance and increase your finance charge.*

5. Two-Cycle Average Daily Balance, *Excluding* New Purchases. This balance is the sum of the average daily balances for two billing cycles. The first balance is for the current billing cycle, and is figured by adding the outstanding balance (excluding new purchases and deducting payments and credits) for each date in the billing cycle, and then dividing by the number of days in the billing cycle. The second balance is for the preceding billing cycle and is figured in the same way as the first balance. *Adds interest on the current month's balance (not including new purchases) together with interest on last month's balance (not including new purchases).*

6. Two-Cycle Average Daily Balance, *Including* New Purchases. This balance is the sum of the average daily balances for two billing cycles. The first balance is for the

current billing cycle, and is figured by adding the outstanding balance (including new purchases and deducting payments and credits) for each date in the billing cycle, and then dividing by the number of days in the billing cycle. The second balance is for the preceding cycle and is figured in the same way as the first balance. *Adds interest on two months' balances together, as above, but includes any new purchases in the current month's balance.*

This last method can result in the highest finance charges of any common calculation method, but the two-cycle method (either type) usually *only* applies in cases where you start the billing cycle with a zero balance, charge something, and then fail to pay the bill off in full by the due date. If you're consistently carrying a balance from month to month, the two-cycle method won't usually raise your credit costs—except in the first month where you went from carrying no balance to carrying a balance.

Does the balance calculation method really make a difference in costs? Absolutely. Here's an example from the Maine Bureau of Consumer Protection: Suppose we are comparing two credit cards. One uses the average daily balance method excluding new purchases. The other uses the two-cycle average daily balance method including new purchases.

Now suppose that each company mails out bills on the first of the month. You make two purchases of $200 each, one on November 2 (which first appears on your December statement) and the next on December 2 (which appears on your January statement). You don't pay your December bill, but you pay your January bill in full within the grace period.

Your January billing statement will carry a $3 finance charge from the card issuer that uses the average daily balance method excluding new purchases. On the other statement, however, the finance charge is more than double that at $8.79. There is a big difference—especially when it adds up over the years.

What Kind of Card User Are You?

Fortunately, you don't have to find a card that has everything: a low fee, cheap rate, no extra fees, and a full grace period. Instead, the card you choose will depend on your personal credit habits. Which type of credit card user are you?

Credit User: You frequently carry a balance from month to month. You often pay only the minimum payment each month, or you pay part—but not all—of the total bill at the end of the month.

Convenience User: You pay off your balance in full every month.

Combination User: You do some of each. You pay off your balance in full most—or at least half—of the time. You may carry a balance from time to time, but it's usually paid off in several months at the most.

Choosing the Card for You

Credit Users should choose a card with the lowest interest rate they can find. If you are a credit user, the annual fee is *not* as important as the interest rate, since you will likely benefit more from a low rate than a cheap fee. You don't need a grace period on your card, since you do *not* take advantage of it.

Convenience Users should look for cards with low or free annual fees. If you are a convenience user, the interest rate is not of much importance to you, since you don't revolve a balance. Make sure your cards carry interest-free grace periods. If there is no grace period, you are likely to wind up paying a bundle in monthly interest charges.

Combination Users must do a little math to make their decision. If you are a combination user, pull out your credit card statements from last year. If you don't have them, look in your tax records for the year-end billing statements that listed how much interest you paid during the year. For each card, compare how much interest you paid, and how much you paid for the annual fee. If there is not much difference between the two, you can likely cut your costs in half by choosing a card with a similar interest rate and no annual fee. You will save even more if you choose a card with no annual fee and a low interest rate.

If, however, you find there is a large difference between the amount you paid in interest and the annual fee, then you should try to reduce the most expensive one first. If, for instance, your card carries a $25 annual fee, but you paid $85 in interest during the year, you should try to reduce the amount of interest you pay. Compare the interest rate on your card to other offers.

Credit Card Shopping List:

Credit Users should look for: low interest rate	Don't worry as much about: grace period, annual fee
Convenience Users should look for: grace period, no annual fee	Don't worry as much about: interest rate
Combination Users should look for: grace period, low interest rate, low or no annual fee	

How Do You Save Money?

There are two ways to save money on your credit cards. One is to save with your existing cards; the other is to switch to new cards.

If you want to keep one of your major credit cards, but it carries a high rate or fee, try what my colleague Marc Eisenson calls "dialing for dollars." Call your issuer and explain you want to close your account to get a cheaper card elsewhere. Some banks will actually waive or reduce the fee, or offer you a better rate, to keep you as a customer.

Don't be intimidated or embarrassed to ask for a better deal. If the first person you talk with isn't helpful, ask to speak to a supervisor. If they aren't helpful, consider switching to another card. A warning: Issuers usually will bargain with good customers, but if your payment history is spotty, you may have a hard time negotiating a better deal.

I remember a radio show where I gave out this advice early on in the show. A woman called in halfway through the show and said she had just called her issuer and they waived her annual fee for a year. In another case, a woman I know quickly reduced the interest rate on five out of the eight cards on which she held balances. One of my relatives used this method to play two of her card issuers against each other and ended up with a rock-bottom rate.

If it doesn't work because you have too much debt, too low a credit score, or your issuers just won't play ball, you can always shop for a better deal somewhere else. If you want to switch to new, cheaper credit cards, here are some tips:

First, you can switch to cheaper cards even if you still owe money on your current ones. Don't cut up your cards and send them back right away, however. Many cardholder agreements contain "acceleration clauses," which allow the card issuer to demand payment in full for any reason, at any time. If you close out your account, your card issuer may ask you to pay off your balance immediately. It doesn't usually happen, but it can.

Before you close those expensive accounts, go shopping. Find a card or two that you consider good deals. Apply for one, wait until you receive an answer, and then apply for the other, if necessary. Don't apply for several cards at one time, as that may cause the other card issuers to think you are on a credit binge, and it will result in a rejection. Once you have the new cards in hand, you have several options.

Option #1. Let your card issuer do the work for you: Some card issuers will pay off your other accounts for you. All you do is sign a form specifying the accounts you want paid off, and they will take care of it for you. The balances on those accounts will then be transferred to your new, cheaper card. These days, you may even get a form with your application that authorizes your new card issuer to pay off other cards if your application is approved. Or the new issuer may even take care of it over the phone.

Option #2. Write a check: If your card issuer won't pay off the balance for you, you can request convenience checks. Convenience checks look similar to regular checking account checks, but instead of accessing your bank account, they draw against your credit card's line of credit. Purchases made with convenience checks are usually billed to your account at the cash advance interest rate, so make sure that rate is not expensive. There may also be transfer fees charged for these checks—be sure to ask.

Option #3. Hit the bank: If your card issuer doesn't offer convenience checks or a balance-transfer feature (very unusual now) you can always use the old-fashioned method: a regular cash advance. Simply go to any bank sporting the Visa or MasterCard logo in the window and request a cash advance. Immediately purchase a cashier's check or money order for the amount of the balance you are paying off, and make it out to your other card issuer.

Of course, it can't be *that* easy (is anything?). There are a couple of pitfalls you'll want to watch out for:

How low can they go? More and more issuers are promoting balance transfers at very low introductory rates. If you really want to use one of these super-low-rate offers, mark your calendar. In a few months, when the rates go up, you're going to have to switch again—or pay a lot more.

Nickel and diming us . . . Some issuers charge fees for balance transfers or purchases made with convenience checks. If that's the case, call your card issuer, explain that you are using the checks to pay off other credit cards, and ask them to waive the fee. Many will be willing to oblige—especially since they will be getting an instant outstanding balance!

Another tip: Don't let the location or the size of the credit card company deter you from switching. People have told me they are afraid to take out a card with a bank across the country because they are worried that the card may not be accepted by local merchants. Credit cards are not like personal checks. Every merchant that accepts Visa or MasterCard must accept every Visa or MasterCard, regardless of the issuer.

Or maybe you want to stick with a local bank because you like the comfort of knowing your bank is right around the corner in case of a billing problem. Just keep in mind that federal law *requires* you put your billing disputes in writing to the card issuer whether they're five miles away or five hundred.

Finally, the solvency, or "safety," of the card-issuing bank shouldn't be a major concern. After all, you have their money, and not vice versa. If the bank that issues your card does go under or get bought out, the new bank that takes over will probably continue the card program (since credit cards are usually the most profitable area of banking), or at worst, the card portfolio will be sold to another bank.

How much can you really save by switching to a cheaper credit card?

Suppose you have a balance of $1,000 on a credit card that carries a 19.8 percent interest rate, a full grace period, and a $20 annual fee. If you make only the minimum monthly payment of 3 percent per month, you will pay a little over $165 in interest over the course of one year. If you continue making only minimum monthly payments for the rest of the loan, it will take you eight years and three months to pay it off, and you will have paid $843 in interest over that period of time! Plus, you will pay eight annual fees that total $180.

Now suppose you carry a credit card with an interest rate of 14 percent and a $12 annual fee. If you make only the minimum monthly payment of 3 percent per month, it will take you six years and six months to pay off the balance, and you will pay $455 in interest over that period of time. Your annual fees will total $84.

Your net savings by switching from the high-rate card to the lower-rate one would be $483.96!

Interest Savings

The following chart shows how much interest you'd pay and how many months it would take to pay off several balances by just making the minimum payment each month. Notice the big savings to be had by using a low-rate card.

Balance/Rate	14%	17%	19.8%
$500	$136.91 (43)	$181.49 (45)	$231.90 (49)
$1,000	$455.04 (80)	$628.80 (89)	$843.05 (100)
$3,000	$1,727.89 (140)	$2,418.29 (158)	$3,287.43 (181)

Source: The Banker's Secret Credit Card Software (see the Resources section).

Hidden Credit Card Costs

When Does the Interest Clock Start Ticking? Issuers can charge interest on purchases from the date of posting—the date the charge slip reaches your card issuer and is placed on your account. The current trend, however, is for issuers to charge from the date of purchase, adding anywhere from one day to several days' interest to their coffers.

Minimum Payments: Credit card minimum payments have been shrinking to the point that it's not unusual to see a minimum payment of 2 percent of the balance due (and that *was* unusual not that long ago!). At that rate, it will take a long, long time to pay off a balance. While low minimums can be a bonus when cash is tight, they also make it possible to run up very large balances that may, in reality, be unaffordable. In Chapter Seven we'll talk about digging out from under. In the meantime, though, remember that you can always pay more than the minimum due, and often save a lot of money in the process.

The Fixed-Rate Credit Card That Isn't: When you take out a fixed-rate mortgage, you know what the rate will be for the entire life of the loan. When you take out a fixed-rate car loan, you know that the interest rate will be the same on the first payment as the last. When you take out a fixed-rate credit card, it's an entirely different story.

A fixed interest rate means nothing in the credit card business. Under federal law, card issuers need only give consumers fifteen days' prior written notice in order to change the rate on credit cards. They can then apply the new rate to any outstanding balance as well as new purchases.

Variable-Rate Cards: Just like with mortgages, a variable rate means the interest rate is tied to another interest rate in the economy, and will change if that interest rate changes.

Every card issuer that offers a variable-rate card is free to decide how it's going to compute the rate. One, for instance, may determine the rate by adding 5 percent to the prime rate as listed in the *Wall Street Journal*. Another may choose to tie the rate to the federal discount rate.

Most variable-rate cards change rates quarterly but some do semiannually—it is up to the card issuer to decide. Information about how the variable rate is determined, and when it changes, has to be disclosed up front in applications and solicitations. According to CardTrak.com, most variable-rate cards have interest rate "floors" below which the interest rate cannot go, even if the index rate goes lower. If rates dip very low, as they did in 2001, consumers may be better off getting a lower-rate card elsewhere than sticking with a bottomed-out variable rate.

Tiered-Rate Cards: A few credit card programs offer tiered rates: The interest rate depends on the balance on the card. For example, a tiered card may charge 17 percent on balances up to and including $1,000, and 13 percent on balances above $1,000. This rate structure is designed to reward higher balances and make more money off lower balances. Tiered-rate cards are usually not good deals because they "reward" customers for going deeper into debt.

Different Rates for Different Balances: Many cards now charge different rates for different balances. There may be a lower rate for the balances you transferred from another card during a promotion, for example, or another rate for cash advances. If you have balances subject to different interest rates, your issuer will print an "effective" rate on the statement, which is basically an average of the different rates you are paying.

A caution: All issuers, as far as I know, allocate payments to the lowest-rate balance first. That means you'll be wiping out the cheapest balance first. This is directly contradictory to the most common advice for paying off debt, which recommends you pay off your highest-rate balance first. Consider yourself forewarned.

Teaser Rates: 5.9 percent or even 0 percent interest sounds great. And it can be. But remember: Card issuers would not continue to offer teaser rates if they weren't profitable. Many teaser rates just don't last that long. Six months sounds like a long time, but by the time you've completed the transfer (which can take a few weeks), you may not benefit from the new rate that long. And if you don't find a new card or negotiate a better deal, you may be stuck with a higher rate than you need. We'll discuss "card surfing" to lower rates in Chapter Seven.

So which do you choose: a fixed-rate, variable-rate, or tiered-rate card? It really doesn't make a difference whether you choose a fixed-rate or variable-rate card, since neither is completely stable. So far, there have been no studies that tell whether fixed or variable-rate cards change rates more dramatically. I personally think it's a matter of finding a bank that has a general reputation for charging low rates (fixed or variable) and hoping they don't decide to suddenly change their marketing strategy. Whatever you choose, you are taking something of a chance. The exception are cards from Arkansas banks, where state law keeps rates very low. If you can get one of these cards, you know the rate will be good as long as that law's in place!

When Your Account Changes Hands

It's true that the big banks keep getting bigger—at least in the case of credit card issuers. Credit cards are so profitable for banks that "do it right" that many of the larger banks want to get more and more customers. Sometimes, they'll just buy them from other issuers.

As I mentioned earlier, card issuers have to give you fifteen days' advance written notice before changing the terms of the credit card. This is also true if a bank buys another bank's cards and raises any of the costs. In addition, individual states may have laws that cover banks located in that state.

If, for instance, your new credit card issuer is located in Delaware or New York, you will have extra protection against a sudden rate hike. Delaware and New York laws require issuers to give customers thirty days' advance written notice before raising the rate, *and* also require banks to give customers the opportunity to pay off the card at the old terms and surrender the card.

Marquette v. First Omaha Services

Have you ever wondered why so many major credit cards are issued by banks located in Delaware and South Dakota? (Okay maybe you haven't, but I have been asked that question more often than you might think.) Some states have laws to protect consumers from sky-high interest rates, although they are few. But even if you live in a state that caps interest rates on credit cards at a reasonable level, you may find yourself paying an expensive rate on your card because of a Supreme Court decision made in a case called *Marquette v. First Omaha Services*, 1978.

In this decision, the Court ruled that it was legal for nationally charted banks to export the terms of their cards to states where the laws regarding interest rates are stricter. The card issuer need only follow the law of the state in which its credit card operations are located. South Dakota and Delaware are particularly kind to card issuers, and that's one of the main reasons they have become hubs for some very large credit card businesses.

It is also getting easier for department stores to sidestep state interest-rate caps. If you have ever looked at the fine print on the back of one of your department-store card statements, you may have noticed a listing of states and the interest rates charged in each. Department stores weren't covered by the Marquette decision, so they were forced to stagger interest rates according to the laws of the state where each cardholder lived. No more. A 1987 federal law permits retail cards to create special-purpose "credit card" banks, which can export credit card rates under the Marquette decision. A number of large card-issuing chains have opened up these special banks and are sending their high-priced cards into states where the ceilings are lower.

Special Credit Cards: Gold Cards, Affinity Cards, and Debit Cards

Gold cards and affinity cards are variations on the basic Visa and MasterCard theme. The question is, do you really need—or want—one?

Gold and Platinum

Gold cards are a favorite of cardholders and card issuers alike. These cards are usually touted as prestigious plastic, offered only to exceptional customers. Banks like gold cards because they are often more profitable than standard cards. Since you often have to make at least $35,000 or more a year, and have a good credit record, chances are you'll pay your bills on time.

If you really want a gold card for the perks or prestige, here's what you should know:

Higher Credit Limits: Gold card credit lines often start at $5,000 and go as high as tens of thousands of dollars. By contrast, opening credit lines on standard cards are often $2,000 to $3,000. What's important to realize is that many standard cards can offer credit lines competitive with those on gold cards. If you're a big spender, or anticipate needing a higher credit line, call your card issuer and ask for an increase in your limit. If you pay on time and have sufficient credit qualifications, you'll probably get it.

Prestige: It's true that several years ago, gold cards probably did confer some degree of exclusivity upon the owner. For a while, American Express was the only issuer to offer gold cards, and at that time, most Visas and MasterCards looked alike. The American Express Gold Card probably did, then, identify its holder as someone with superior financial credentials. Today, however, there are millions of gold cards in circulation. In addition, Visa and MasterCard issuers have freed up the fronts of their cards so that issuers can design colorful cards. All that means is that gold cards simply don't make as much of an impression as they used to do.

Perks: Gold cards do offer one thing that many standard cards don't—a menu of perks. These extras include emergency medical and legal services for cardholders when they travel, collision damage waiver coverage when a car rental is paid for with the card, extended warranties, and purchase protection plans.

On standard bankcards, most enhancements are chosen and offered by the individual banks that issue the cards. On gold cards, however, Visa and MasterCard have developed packages of "core" enhancements that are generally offered on *all* gold cards. Since the competition among gold card issuers is intense, these core enhancement packages carry a lot of perks.

This also means, however, that if you want a particular perk, you can shop among lots of gold card issuers to find one that also offers the low rate and/or no annual fee you're looking for.

Keep in mind that most people never take advantage of many of the perks offered on credit cards. There's more detail on enhancements in Chapter Twelve, but my basic advice is: Shop for a credit card on the basis of price, not perks.

Affinity Cards

Sponsored by groups as diverse as the Sierra Club and the National Rifle Association, affinity cards hit their peak in the saturated credit card market of the late 1980s. These special Visa and MasterCard programs were a dream for bankers and a boon for charities and associations but, more often than not, a mediocre deal for consumers.

Affinity cards traditionally are linked with a charity or association, and the card often bears the name or logo of the sponsoring group. Most promise that part of the annual fee or a portion of each purchase will be donated to the sponsoring organization.

Credit card companies love affinity cards because they help

conquer two major marketing problems: getting prospective customers to open and read *another* credit card offer, and getting
cardholders to use their card over the other ones they already
hold. People like the idea of donating to their favorite charity
through one of these cards, or they like to show the world that
they're members, for example, of their alumni association or the
American Bar Association.

In general, these cards have not been great deals for the people
who are going to use them, for the same reason that many credit
cards are not good deals: They often cost too much! The interest
rates on affinity cards may be higher than what you could get
elsewhere, and many charge a standard fee of $20 or so (although
it may be waived for the first six months or the first year).

Some people don't care how much an affinity card costs,
they'll take the card anyway for the chance to make a "painless"
charitable donation. But how much of the profits actually go to
charity? Most programs won't reveal how much is being donated
to the sponsoring organization. "It's proprietary," the banks argue, but I would argue it is not particularly ethical to advertise to
customers that they'll be making a donation, but not tell them
how much will actually end up in the sponsor's pockets.

Let's take a hypothetical case: Good Causes Affinity Card
charges 17.5 percent with a $20 annual fee. Half the annual fee
plus one-half of 1 percent of purchase amounts are donated to the
charity that sponsors the card. Let's suppose you charge $1,500
over the course of the year, and carry a balance of about $1,000 of
that balance. Your donation will be $17.50 for the year ($10 from
the annual fee + $7.50 from purchases). By contrast, you will pay
more than $150 in interest, plus the $20 annual fee, over the
course of the year. It is easy to see that if you simply took a card
with no annual fee, you could save $20 and donate that to the
sponsoring organization. If you switched to a card with a cheaper
interest rate, you would save even more.

In addition, your donation through an affinity program is *not*
tax-deductible, but your direct contribution to a charitable organization may be.

Once bankers found out how lucrative affinity cards were,
they started coming up with ingenious twists on that theme.
Affinity card offers aren't always affiliated with a charity. Some

banks, in an effort to get on the bandwagon quickly and avoid having to really pay a royalty to an outside organization, have actually *invented* sponsoring groups. There are cards for golfers and for mystery book lovers, for example. There's no real sponsor behind them, just the bank.

There are some good deals out there, however. The AFL-CIO, for example, used the clout of its millions of members to negotiate a low-rate, no-fee card for members with special perks like suspended payments during a strike or lock-out. The difference between cards like the AFL-CIO's deal and many others is that the good programs are usually developed first as an attractive benefit for members, and *then* as a fund-raiser for the sponsor.

The bottom line? If your university or a charity group offers a good deal on an affinity card, go ahead and take advantage of it. Otherwise, get a cheap credit card and write your charity a check.

Debit Cards

Debit cards can sometimes look like Visa and MasterCard credit cards, but they're not credit cards at all. Debit cards basically access money in your checking, savings, or brokerage account, instead of a line of credit. ATM cards are a type of debit card, and some gasoline cards offer a debit feature where the amount you pump will be drawn directly from your checking account.

Debit cards may work in two different ways—off-line and on-line. Many do both. It may seem confusing at first, but once you've used them a few times it should be clear.

On-line Transactions: These transactions require you to enter a Personal Identification Number (PIN) and the money is taken right out of your account. Taking money out of an ATM is an on-line transaction, but making a purchase at a store using a debit card and PIN is also an on-line transaction.

On-line transactions are often routed through one of several networks that process the transaction. This won't be apparent to you as a consumer; in fact, you won't even know which network handled your transaction. It only matters in a few cases where there may be a problem with a MasterCard or Visa debit transaction. I'll explain that in a moment.

Off-line Transactions: These transactions work more like a cross between a credit card and check. You can swipe your debit card through the terminal at the cash register—but choose "credit" instead of "debit." Alternatively you might present it to the clerk, who rings it up like a credit transaction. The money is then taken out of your account in a period similar to what it might take a local check to clear—anywhere from one to three days.

Merchants often prefer on-line transactions because they're cheaper than off-line transactions. Issuers of debit cards, however, may prefer off-line transactions because they earn a portion of the merchant fee that is paid.

Read your debit card agreement carefully to see what fees may be associated with their use. Your bank *as well as* the merchant may charge fees for the use of debit cards. My credit union, for example, allows free off-line use of my MasterCard debit card. But if I use my PIN, I am allowed only four free transactions per month. I'll be charged $1.50 for any PIN-based transactions above my four monthly free ones.

Debit Card Pros and Cons

Spending Limits: Your debit card may allow you to access only a certain amount of money each day. Holds on your account (from a car rental agency or hotel, for example) may block you from getting access to your cash from an ATM.

Convenience: A debit card carrying the MasterCard or Visa logo must be accepted by any merchant that accepts MasterCard or Visa. This is true when it comes to paying for a purchase. In the case of car rental agencies, however, some do not accept debit cards to *reserve* a car—a lesson I learned the hard way when I got to the car rental counter in Washington, D.C., and realized I had forgotten to bring a credit card. Check with each rental agency if you want to use a debit card exclusively instead of a credit card.

Many merchants also accept regional debit cards (typically issued as ATM cards).

No Float: When you pay by debit card, your purchase will be deducted from your account quickly. You won't have free use of the bank's money the way you will with a credit card that you pay in full each month.

Issuance: If you have a bank account, you should have no trouble getting a debit card. You may have trouble getting one with off-line purchasing capabilities, however, if your credit or check-writing history is spotty.

Benefits: Though debit card perks are not nearly as common as credit card ones, some issuers offer benefits such as frequent-flier miles and rebates with debit cards. Visit Cardweb.com or Bankrate.com for the latest deals.

Dispute Assistance: Debit cards are not included in the Fair Credit Billing Act, which allows you to withhold payment in the case of certain disputes (see Chapter Ten). Your debit card transaction is typically treated the same as a cash or credit purchase, and you have to deal with the merchant directly if there's a problem with your purchase. That, of course, can become a *big* problem when the merchant isn't legit.

Credit History: Debit cards are typically not reported to credit reporting agencies and therefore do not help build a credit rating.

When Your Debit Card Is Lost or Stolen

The biggest problem with debit cards, as compared to credit cards, is exposure in the case of fraud. Debit cards are covered by the federal Electronic Funds Transfer Act. Under that law, if your card is lost or stolen and a thief uses it to go on a spending spree, your liability is $50 (the same as credit cards), but only if you notify the bank within two business days of a problem. If you wait too long, your liability could become unlimited. The good news is that MasterCard and Visa both have policies that protect you from unlimited loss if your debit card carrying one of their logos is used fraudulently. See Chapter Ten for details.

Internet Shopping

The first edition of *The Ultimate Credit Handbook* was published before the Internet came widely into use, and at that time if you wanted a comprehensive list of low-rate credit cards you had to write to Bankcard Holders of America (which is now defunct). We used to receive thousands of requests for that list every week.

Now, of course, you can log on to your computer and find out about thousands of different card programs. There are a couple of different types of shopping sites. Information sites, like bankrate.com, cardtrak.com, and creditcardmenu.com, provide information about different offers. You have to apply for those in which you are interested.

Other sites offer to take your information and shop it to different lenders to find the best deal for you. The main thing to watch out for is whether you will be creating potentially negative multiple hard inquiries from different lenders who want to check out your full credit report before they will quote an offer. Also investigate the privacy policies of these sites—will you be inundated with unwanted calls, e-mails, or faxes?

Finally, one of the concerns I have about online offers is that they tend to quote a "range" of rates and tell you you'll find out which rate you qualify for after you apply. This, to me, goes against the spirit of the Truth-in-Lending Act disclosures and could set you up for unnecessary hard inquiries on your credit report if you don't receive offers you like.

While you're shopping, you may also want to check out consumer ratings of various card issuers at www.gomez.com.

CHAPTER FOUR

Starting Over: How to Rebuild a Bad Credit Rating

If you have "bad credit" you are not alone. Literally millions of Americans have less-than-perfect credit ratings—but not all because they are deadbeats who just aren't responsible enough to pay their bills on time. Many people with bad credit ran into tough financial situations that set them back for a while. Some have bad credit because they went through a messy divorce or a temporary period of unemployment. Others may have faced credit difficulties because of a serious illness, a new child in the family, or a small business that didn't make it. The trouble is, bad credit ratings usually hang around long after financial problems are over.

Living with a bad credit rating can be a hassle. Often, you can't get a major credit card, which means you have trouble reserving hotel rooms, renting cars, or even writing a check at a retail store. Utility companies may require deposits from people with no major credit cards, and landlords hesitate to rent apartments to people who don't have good credit. Some employers will even turn down job applicants if their credit reports don't look good.

It's no surprise then that a whole industry has sprung up to help these people. Credit repair companies, issuers of special credit cards for people who can't get credit, and publishers of credit repair books (selling for as much as $100 or more) are examples of some of the businesses that say they can help people hungry for a way back into the financial mainstream.

Credit repair companies often make a lot of money, but rarely say anything new. There are no surefire ways to a great credit rating, just as there are no guaranteed ways to become a millionaire. There are, however, proven ways to improve a credit rating, and those are contained in this chapter. I have reviewed many credit repair manuals and books, and attended credit repair seminars. I can assure you the information in this chapter and the following chapter is complete and should contain all the legitimate advice you will find from another source.

There is really no such thing as a "bad" credit rating. The standards for who gets credit and who doesn't vary from lender to lender. Here are some examples, though, of the types of marks on credit reports that many creditors consider negative:

Late Payments: Some creditors don't mind lending money to people with histories of late payments, as long as they haven't been behind frequently or in the past year or so. Other lenders will reject applicants with one or two payments only thirty days late.

The important thing to remember is that creditors may not be as concerned with how much you were late, but *how late you were*. In other words, a small $10 payment that was ninety days late can hurt your credit rating more than a $1,000 payment that was thirty days late.

Having said that, there are some cases where the amount does matter. A scoring system may be set up to ignore all collection accounts for less than $250, for example. In that case, a small late amount may not matter as much. But to be safe, you'll want to avoid any late payments of any amounts.

Collection Accounts, Profit-and-Loss or Charged-Off Accounts, Judgments, Tax Liens, or Lawsuits: These marks are considered very negative by most lenders. Some creditors will automatically reject applications when they see these marks—

especially if they have not been paid off, or if they occurred in the last two years.

Bankruptcy is often considered the most negative mark on a credit report, and again many creditors will reject outright those applicants who have been through bankruptcy (especially if it's recent).

Delinquent Child-Support Debts: Though traditionally not a factor in credit evaluation, more and more lenders are unwilling to lend money to someone who's behind on child-support payments.

There are ways to repair and rebuild your credit, however, and put the past behind you. Here's how:

Face the Music

Get a copy of your credit report, preferably from all three of the major credit reporting agencies. You'll need all three to find out what each is reporting and to learn where you need to make corrections or improvements.

Know the Ground Rules

You'll no doubt find information on your report that you think is inaccurate or incomplete. Here are some common areas of concern:

Collection Accounts: In most cases, lenders must charge off delinquent accounts after 180 days of nonpayment, but some do so sooner. After it is charged off (written off the lender's books as bad debt), it may be placed for collection. When that happens, you'll find two marks on your credit report: the listing from the original lender showing that the account has been charged off, and the other remark showing a collection account. But if you don't pay one collection agency and they pass it on to another agency, you should *not* see duplicate listings from different collection agencies for the same account. Only the most recent one should be listed, so feel free to dispute duplicates.

Ex-spouse's Debts: If you're divorced, you may think you're off the hook for any debts of your ex-spouse, but don't be so sure. Any joint accounts you held together will be reported to the credit bureaus in both your names—*even if they've been assigned to your ex in the divorce decree.* The divorce decree does not erase the original agreement with the lender. Any accounts you never held with your ex, however, should not be reported on your credit file.

Paid Accounts: Many people erroneously think that once an account is paid it is removed from your credit report. Not true. Negative accounts can generally be reported for seven years.

Missing Accounts: There's no law requiring lenders to report information to credit bureaus, so you may find that not all your accounts—gasoline credit cards or personal loans with local lenders, for example—appear on your report. While you can ask the credit bureaus to add those accounts, they don't usually accommodate those types of requests. They want to have a business agreement with a company before they will accept sensitive consumer credit information.

Medical Bills: Just because you think your insurance company should have paid a medical bill doesn't mean you are immune from collection activity. The provider of the medical services can collect from you if the insurance company doesn't pay, and may send it to collections. The collection company isn't required to get the insurance company to pay either; that's your job. In the meantime, if you don't pay the bill yourself, the collection account on your credit report may hurt you for seven years. Some creditors will ignore medical collection accounts if they can correctly be identified as such.

Don't Let the Past Linger

If negative information that is out of date, and can no longer legally be reported, appears on your report, write to the credit bureau to dispute it. The general rule of thumb is that negative information can remain on your credit report for up to seven years—ten in the case of bankruptcy. (Positive or neutral information can remain forever.) The tricky part is determining exactly when that seven-year period starts.

Late Payments can stay on credit reports for seven years from the *last schedule payment*. If your report lists that a payment was three months late because a payment that was due January 1, 1990, wasn't made until May 1990, that late payment can remain on your report until January 1, 1997—seven years from the date the payment was supposed to have been made.

Unpaid Lawsuits and Judgments by law can be reported for seven years from the date they were entered (by the court) or the governing statute of limitations—*whichever is longer.* The governing statute of limitations is the time under state or federal law that the courts allow for collecting the judgment. In many states, that period of time can be as long as twenty years or more. Once the judgment is paid or the suit is settled, however, the seven-year limitation for paid lawsuits or judgments takes effect. If you want to find out the governing statute of limitations, check with your attorney or your state attorney general's office, or Robin Leonard's book *Money Troubles* (see the Resources section).

In practice, all the major credit agencies remove all judgments after seven years—whether they are paid or not. The problem is the plaintiff who is owed the money may be able to get a new judgment filed with the court if you haven't paid within seven years, and that new judgment could go on your credit record.

Paid Lawsuits and Judgments can be reported for seven years from the date they were entered by the court, *not* the date you paid them.

Unpaid Tax Liens may remain on your credit report until they are paid, although again, all the major credit agencies say they will remove them after seven years.

Paid Tax Liens may remain on your credit report for seven years after they were paid. Again, the credit agencies will remove this type of negative information if it is more than seven years old.

Nontax Liens can be reported for as long as they remain filed against the consumer's property, or until the applicable statute of limitations expires. (Equifax does not report property tax liens.) Again, credit bureaus will usually remove information after seven years, but there may be ways to get it back on your report.

Collection or Profit-and-Loss Accounts added to your credit report after December 29, 1997, can be reported for seven and a half years from the original date of delinquency—*not* from the date they were charged off or placed for collection. For example, suppose you missed a payment that was due in January 1999. You didn't make any payments for five months and your account was charged off in May 1999. The charge-off listing could then remain on your report until the end of June 2006—seven and a half years after you missed that first January payment that led to the charge-off.

Now let's say your account was turned over to a collection agency in December 1999. That collection account (and *all* subsequent collection accounts for that same debt) can be reported until the same date as the charge-off (seven and a half years from that first missed payment): June 2006.

Collection agencies sometimes tell consumers they have ways to report an account forever till they pay. They may have their tactics, but that statement—and falsifying information to carry it out—is *not* true and is also illegal. The Fair Credit Reporting Act requires collection agencies to provide credit reporting agencies with the *original* date of delinquency for tracking purposes.

Having said that, those requirements only apply to accounts added to your report *after* December 29, 1997. For any accounts added before that time, it is a little more complicated. Under the old law, collection accounts were often reported for seven years from the date they were placed for collection. Each time a collection account was passed on to a new agency, a new seven-year period was started. The law was revised to end that problem but many people still have older charge-off and collection accounts on their reports.

The good news is that if you can prove that original date of delinquency, the credit reporting agencies will honor the newer seven-and-a-half-year rule. But the challenge is to find something to prove it! An old credit report showing the original information, an old collection notice, or even copies of your statements from that time period can work. Even if you don't have that documentation, try disputing it and state that the information is outdated. It might work.

Foreclosures

Those added to your report before December 29, 1997, can be reported for seven years from the date of foreclosure. Those reported after that date can be reported for seven and a half years from the missed payment that led to the foreclosure.

Repossessions

Both voluntary (where you turn in the car or property) and involuntary (repo man) repossessions added to your report before December 29, 1997, can be reported for seven years from the date of repossession. Those reported after that date can be reported for seven and a half years from the missed payment that led to the repossession. Again, it's up to the lender to report that original delinquency date along with the repossession listing to the credit bureau.

Student Loans

The Department of Education would like delinquent student loans to be reported forever, and although the Higher Education Act has been amended to allow for them to be reported longer, all of the credit reporting agencies with which I have spoken say the FCRA requires them to remove negative student loan information in seven years, just as with other delinquent debts. If you have a student loan that is behind but you catch up and make twelve on-time payments, the lender in many cases is required under the Higher Education Act to remove the delinquency from your report.

Some unpaid delinquent student loans are reported for longer than seven years. That's because it can be difficult to prove the original date of delinquency that starts the clock ticking. If student loans are sold, consolidated, or turned over to collections, the original date of delinquency can get "lost" in the process. And often there's no easy solution for straightening these messes out. See Chapter Eight for suggestions for dealing with delinquent student loans.

Records of Arrest, Indictment, or Conviction of a Crime may remain on a credit report for seven years from the date of disposition, release, or parole. Records of this type usually do *not* appear in standard credit reports but may appear in more extensive investigative reports used by insurance companies or prospective employers.

Bankruptcy: Both Chapter 13 and Chapter 7 bankruptcies can legally be reported for ten years from the date the bankruptcy was filed. All three major agencies and all CDIA members, however, have agreed to remove successfully completed Chapter 13 bankruptcies (where you pay back a portion of your debts) seven years from the date you filed. If your Chapter 13 bankruptcy is not successfully completed (discharged), it will be reported for ten years.

In addition, each debt that was discharged under the bankruptcy petition may remain on the report for its applicable seven-year period. (For example, if you held a department-store card that was charged off and later discharged in bankruptcy, the bankruptcy may be listed under the department store's tradeline for seven years.)

None of These Limitations Apply if a credit report is being supplied for a transaction involving a loan of $150,000 or more, or if the consumer is applying for a job at a salary of $75,000 or more, or applying for a life insurance policy of $150,000 or more. In those cases, negative information may be reported forever, although as a practical matter it usually is not. It might be collected for a more investigative report, but not for a consumer credit report.

Six Steps to a Better Credit Profile

While you may not be able to wipe the slate clean, there are ways you can improve your credit record. Here are steps I suggest:

Dispute Information

If you find mistakes on your report, you absolutely should dispute them. Some might not result in a change in your credit score (closing old accounts, for example), but others may result in a dramatic improvement (getting an inaccurate judgment or old collection account off your file, for example).

If you dispute information with the credit reporting agency, and it comes back to you saying that it has verified the information with the lender, your next step is to go directly to the lender reporting the mistake. The revised federal Fair Credit Reporting Act says that lenders may not report information they "know or consciously avoid knowing" is wrong. That means they have to take your dispute seriously, investigate it, and confirm that it is correct before continuing to report it.

Establish New Credit

Establishing positive new credit references can really help your credit if you need them. The best? A couple of major credit cards paid on time. If you already have one (or more), use it to charge only what you can afford to pay at the end of the month, and make sure you mail the payment well in advance of the due date. If you don't have one, get a secured card, which requires a security deposit. (Secured cards are discussed later in this chapter.)

Negotiate a Better Rating

Though this tactic is frowned upon by credit reporting agencies and lenders, it is sometimes possible to negotiate an improvement in a particular tradeline in exchange for payment, or just because you are a good customer. You'll probably have the most success with this technique if you are working with a collection agency early on in the debt collection process. For example, as soon as you are contacted, you may offer to make a lump-sum payment to settle the debt as long as they agree not to report it to the credit reporting agencies. Caution! You must get that agreement in writing. If you do not, you may find they report you anyway. Some balk at doing so, but if they agree to your proposal, they should be willing to back that agreement up in writing.

In other cases, a company may be willing to remove or stop reporting a negative remark if you can show that your late payments were temporary or due to unusual circumstances *and* if you otherwise have a good credit history with them.

If a company has gone out of business or sold your loan, you may be able to simply dispute the account through the credit reporting agency. If the agency cannot confirm it with the lender, the account will be deleted.

No company is obligated to remove negative but accurate information, but neither are they obligated under federal law to report an account in the first place. Some lenders or collectors may, however, have agreements with credit reporting agencies stating that they will not change or delete accurate consumer information.

Watch Out for Preapproved Offers

Despite your difficulties, you may receive many "preapproved" credit card offers in the mail. Don't get too excited. Lenders are allowed to "prescreen" names through a credit bureau, then offer a preapproved card to those who pass the prescreening. But once you accept, they can run a second screening and decline you based on any other factors they choose— including your poor credit history. Alternatively, they may still give you a card but at a sky-high interest rate. If you really need a major card to help rebuild your credit, you can take a shot at one of these offers, but understand that you may not get the card you wanted at first.

Go to the Source

Believe it or not, lenders want to make loans. But they also want to make sure you'll pay them back. As I discussed in Chapter One, most lenders use some form of credit scoring system to evaluate applications. If you have unusual circumstances, such as divorce or medical bills that ruined your credit, make it a point to apply for loans *only* when you can talk to a loan officer to whom you can explain your circumstances. Otherwise, you're likely to be judged only by the numbers. Even then, a scoring system may prevail—but it's still worth a shot.

Remember, Time Heals

While you can't remove truthful, negative information, the older it becomes the less important it will be. A thirty-day late payment last month will probably hurt your credit rating more than a ninety-day late payment five years ago. People buy homes, get credit cards, and buy new cars, even after bankruptcy. So hang in there, and keep building good credit references by paying your bills on time all the time. It may take a little while to get your credit where you want it to be, but it will happen over time.

What Pitfalls Should You Avoid When Rebuilding Credit?

Passbook Loans

It's common advice that a good way for people to rebuild a credit rating is to deposit a couple of hundred dollars in the bank, then ask for a loan against that deposit; pay it back promptly, then ask for a larger amount, etc. I'm not a big fan of that route, because a small passbook loan may not be reported to the credit bureaus and, if it is, may not be as strong a credit reference as a secured card. If you have several hundred dollars you can afford to put into a savings account, then you're probably better off using it as collateral for a secured credit card.

If you decide to go this route, however, just make sure that the loan will be reported to all three credit bureaus each month, and make sure you make the payments on time. Some lenders will automatically take the payments out of your checking account— that's a good way to handle it.

Finance Company Accounts

In the past, finance companies were considered lenders of last resort. Therefore, in many cases creditors have actually held it against people if they had loans from finance companies—*even if the bills were paid on time.* That's changing as more and more large, legitimate finance companies are aggressively selling loans. Still, some lenders don't look favorably upon references from finance companies. Steer clear of the ones that claim they can give loans to anyone. At a minimum, you'll save money—and perhaps you'll also help your credit rating.

One-Time References

Some smaller companies will tell you they can make a "one-time" report about your account to the credit bureau or say that they will provide a credit reference if a lender contacts you directly. It's probably not worth the bother. Creditors want to see a record of good payments over a period of time. A one-shot report to a credit bureau will not be helpful in that regard. Most credit bureaus won't add one-time references from companies that aren't regular subscribers, since it would take too much time and money to check out the company to make sure it's legitimate. In addition, many card issuers and lenders won't contact those kinds of firms for credit references. If it isn't on the credit report, they don't want it.

Catalog Cards

These "credit cards" (they are often paper cards, not plastic) are good only for purchasing merchandise from a catalog provided by the company. They often charge high up-front fees, and the merchandise in many cases will be low quality and high priced; used electronic equipment and cheap jewelry are typical. One-shot credit cards are often marketed under names that make them sound as if they are major credit cards. They may be called "gold cards" or "national credit cards," for example. Some promise that if you use the card for a period of time and pay your bills promptly, you will be eligible for a Visa or MasterCard. Ask the catalog issuer the name of the bank they work with to issue Visas or MasterCards, and call the bank directly to confirm that they work with them. If they won't reveal the names of any banks, then they're probably just passing on applications from secured card issuers that they have no relationship with. I have yet to see one of these cards that I would recommend to people.

Rent-to-Owns

Not only are rent-to-own accounts rarely reported to credit bureaus; they are frequently one of the biggest consumer rip-offs. Since rent-to-owns are not usually covered by state usury laws, and since they often target low-income consumers, they may charge as much as 200 percent interest. They won't really help your credit, either. Find a better alternative.

Credit Repair Clinics

You've seen the advertisements in your e-mail inbox, the backs of magazines, or the classified sections of newspapers: "Clean up bad credit. Credit guaranteed. Bad credit/bankruptcy no problem." These advertisements are often placed by credit repair clinics. These companies prey upon the millions of consumers with damaged credit ratings by making it sound as if it is possible, with the proper know-how and enough money, to erase bad credit ratings forever.

Like many consumer advocates, I have often recommended against all credit repair clinics. And most of them are not worth the money you'll pay. On the other hand, I have spoken with experienced mortgage brokers and others in that industry who have had "success" with these firms. (Success usually means getting a negative entry off long enough to get a loan application through, or boosting a credit score for the same reason.) *Washington Post* writer Kenneth Harney wrote a two-part series in July 2001 about "rapid rescoring" companies that have boosted consumers' credit scores, saving them money on mortgages.

Because credit repair is so fraught with bogus claims and firms, I recommend you read the warnings I list here, then carefully check out any company that promises to improve your credit rating. I'd also take a careful look at your goals in using one of these firms. Is it a temporary fix or do you want long-term change? Will their work leave you in an ethical and legal dilemma (lying on loan applications about previous bankruptcies or collection accounts, for example)? What kinds of recommendations can you get for them? Using one that is recommended by a mortgage broker who has been working with them for the past five years is a lot better than relying on dubious testimonials in a junk e-mail. Above all, go with your gut. If it doesn't feel right, save your money and work your way through these problems yourself.

How They Work

The last thing I want to see is for you to be ripped off by an unscrupulous credit repair firm. So here I'll tell you more about how they work and what you want to watch out for.

Frivolous Disputes: One of the first things credit repair clinics do is try to make you believe that the system is against you but with the right knowledge you can beat it. They claim knowledge of little-known provisions in the law that give you the right to remove negative but accurate information from their credit files. One of their common advertising themes is: "Based on little-known loopholes in federal law, we can show you how to clean up your credit report!"

They base that claim on an interpretation of the Fair Credit Reporting Act (FCRA), the federal law that governs credit reports and credit bureaus. In the FCRA is a section entitled "Procedure in Case of Disputed Accuracy." Under that section, consumers have the right to require credit bureaus to reinvestigate any information in their credit reports that they believe is incorrect or incomplete. If a consumer challenges information on his credit report, the credit bureau must check with the source reporting the information to determine if it is correct. If it cannot be confirmed with the source, or if the creditor fails to respond to the reinvestigation request, the data must be dropped from the file.

How can this help you remove accurate but negative information? Credit clinics generally advise people to dispute negative information in their files *repeatedly*. They will instruct their clients, for example, to send in letters or forms disputing the same negative information every day for several weeks. Their goal is to jam up the system so that some requests will not be verified and the information will be dropped. While there was probably some success with this tactic in the past, it almost always fails now for several reasons:

1. Credit bureaus and credit granters respond to disputes much more quickly now than in the past. The ACDV system makes investigations even faster.
2. If you dispute information in your credit file and the creditor who reported the information does not verify it, the credit bureau must take it off your report. There is nothing in the law, however, to keep the *creditor* from reporting the same information again at a later date if the creditor verifies it is correct.
3. Credit bureaus have their own "legal loophole" in the FCRA that allows them to refuse to reinvestigate "frivolous" disputes. That means that if the bureau notices repeated disputes of the same information, without any proof, it may assume you are working with a credit clinic and refuse to reinvestigate information you've already disputed.
4. In 1996, Congress passed the Credit Repair Organizations Act, which, among other provisions, made it illegal to advise a consumer to make an untrue or misleading statement to a credit bureau. In other words, they aren't supposed to help you dispute accurate information.

Credit clinics often offer to "do it for you" by sending the dispute forms to the credit bureaus on behalf of clients. This is really ineffective, because credit bureaus will quickly refuse to acknowledge disputes that look as though they originated from a credit repair clinic. It's extremely difficult to get a credit bureau to continue to investigate information if it looks as if you're working with a credit clinic.

Starting Over Again: Credit clinics may also suggest that you dispute *everything* in your file, including identifying information such as your name, address, and Social Security number. They hope to distort the file so that when a lender goes to pull your file, it won't find anything. You can then start creating a brand-new credit file. Again, these are exactly the types of disputes that credit bureaus flag as being "frivolous" or "fraudulent."

You've no doubt seen the ads saying that you can get a "new credit identity" for just $99, and figure that anything—including a clean credit report—is available for a price. Don't buy it. These credit repair companies are often operating on the edge of legality. Here's what they'll tell you to do: apply for an Employer Identification Number (EIN), which is the same number of digits as a Social Security number (and used by employers for tax reporting purposes). Then, they will tell you to get a new address (a P.O. Box, for example) and apply for credit using your new EIN and address. Voilà! You've got a new credit history—or rather no credit history at all, which allows you to start from scratch.

Follow that advice, however, and guess what? You're committing fraud against the lender and the IRS. If you want to take that risk, that's your mistake. But at least don't fork over your hard-earned money to learn this system.

Create a New File: Rather than create an entirely new identity, some repair clinics instruct clients to create a new credit file with information similar to the old one but different enough to avoid mingling with the old file. For instance, they will suggest you change your name slightly or use another version of your name, get a post office box, and use it as a new address, and transpose a number or two in your Social Security number. Then try applying for credit—say at a car dealer—with this information. If the car dealer cannot locate your credit file using the new name and identifying information, then you know you have a "hit." You can now use this "new identity" to apply for credit.

Not only is this strategy illegal, but it often backfires because the large credit agencies' computer systems are quite sophisticated. Credit bureaus cross-reference names and addresses, weed out incorrect Social Security numbers, and search for similar names when accessing files and gathering data. Experian, for example, is using advanced technology to make sure they can match up the right information about each consumer.

Negotiating Payment: Credit clinics often teach consumers to "negotiate" their way out of a bad credit record. If you have an account that's currently delinquent, they'll instruct you to contact the creditor or collection agency and offer payment in exchange for removal of the negative credit information. Or they'll advise you to write a disclaimer on your payment check stating that, by cashing the check, the creditor or collection agency agrees to remove any negative information from the credit file.

Some creditors won't accept these types of checks, and in some states the creditor can cash the check without being legally bound to the disclaimer. Some lenders flatly refuse to negotiate payment in exchange for taking information off the report, while others—collection agencies in particular—are more than willing to strike a bargain (although under the new credit repair law they may not be able to remove accurate information). If you want to repair your credit this way, do it yourself as I described earlier. It's much cheaper than paying someone else hundreds of dollars to try it for you.

Delay-the-Payment Trick: Although not directly related to credit repair, this tactic is offered by credit clinics as a stopgap measure when bills pile up. You may notice that many credit card and utility bills today carry numbers on the bottom that appear to be computer generated. These numbers are often scanned by machines to speed the processing of payments. Credit repair clinics may advise you to scratch out or mutilate these numbers. If they are magnetized, they advise running a strong electric magnet over them. The idea is that the bill will be kicked out of the system for manual processing, which will delay it for several days.

Others teach that you can buy weeks or a month of extra time by leaving the signature off your check. Some creditors—if they catch it—will return the check for your signature, which adds a couple of weeks to processing time. If you are having so much trouble paying your bills that you have to resort to these tactics, see a counselor, or at least contact your creditors to set up modified payment schedules.

Credit Doctors: Credit doctors really can patch up a credit problem—but their price is steep and their methods extremely risky. Credit doctors work in one of two ways: cleaning up files, or finding new files. Working with a credit doctor requires an "in" with someone at a credit bureau or at one of the locations that has access to credit files. The most common type of credit doctoring involves stealing credit files from good credit risks and selling them to bad risks. The "victims" whose files were stolen probably won't know about the scam until they start receiving dunning notices for bills they know nothing about.

To clean up a file, a credit doctor will actually change the credit file of the consumer. To be really effective, of course, the credit doctor needs access to all three major credit bureaus' files, and an employee of one credit bureau probably could not provide that access. An employee of a credit bureau *user* that processes disputes, however, *may* be able to correct all three files.

An employee of a used car dealer in Florida searched credit files while at work and found other people who had the same name as his (the spelling was slightly different on some). He then applied for credit in those people's names and ran up more than $100,000 in bills before he was detected!

Not only do you risk criminal penalties against obtaining credit files under false pretenses, but do you really want credit bad enough to destroy someone else's good credit as well?

Make a Thousand Dollars Your First Week: If you don't have credit problems or need the services of a credit repair firm, perhaps you know someone who does. Credit repair or "counseling" is advertised as a lucrative and rewarding profession that can be handled right out of your own home. I am not referring to nonprofit consumer counseling firms here. I am referring to firms that give customers the types of advice I've just discussed.

If you are considering a career in credit repair, proceed with caution. Some thirty-five states have laws governing credit repair clinics. While some states actually make credit repair services illegal, most state laws require that credit clinics be licensed and bonded, offer cancellation periods, and tell consumers up front their rights and what services will be performed. In addition, Congress passed a tough law in 1996 regulating the activities of credit repair companies. See below for a summary.

Many of the credit clinic techniques outlined just won't work anymore, so you may find yourself in the frustrating position of being unable to help your clients. As with any other business opportunity, check with your state attorney general's office, your local consumer-protection agency, and the Better Business Bureau before putting your money down.

Credit Repair Organizations Act

These are the main protections offered by the credit repair law enacted in 1996. All became effective April 1, 1997:

1. It is illegal for a credit repair company to make any statement that is untrue or misleading, or advise anyone to make a statement that is untrue or misleading, to a credit reporting agency or a credit grantor. (They can't tell you to lie about accurate but negative information!)
2. It is also illegal to advise a consumer to alter his or her identification or alter the identification of his or her credit report in order to remove or hide negative, accurate information in that credit report.
3. Credit repair organizations cannot accept payment for services until they have been performed. (This provision alone should put many out of business.)
4. Before you sign a contract with a credit repair organization, it must give you a statement that explains your credit reporting rights under state and federal laws. The company must get your signature on that document and keep it on file for two years.
5. You must be given a dated, written contract to sign that

explains the services that will be performed, any guarantees about services, how much it will cost you, and the date by which the services will be performed.

6. You have the right to cancel the contract, without penalty, within three business days of when you sign it. Your contract must explain how to cancel.

Keep in mind that additional state laws may also require credit repair firms to be licensed or bonded. If you are still considering doing business with one, check with your state attorney general or consumer-affairs office for more information.

"Get a Major Credit Card— Regardless of Past Credit!"

Secured Credit Cards

If you have a damaged credit rating, or no credit, a secured credit card may be your ticket. These Visas and MasterCards offer people who can't get regular credit cards the opportunity to begin rebuilding—or building for the first time—a good credit rating using a major credit card.

A secured card is a bankcard that's backed by a collateral deposit in a bank. You make a security deposit in the bank and keep it there for as long as you have the card. In exchange, you get a MasterCard or Visa card. Since the bank can collect from your deposit if you fail to pay your bills, it is often willing to accept customers who don't have a good credit rating. Some will even issue cards to people who have recently been through bankruptcy, as long as it has been discharged (completed).

Secured cards have had a very lousy reputation in the past. Because so many people are desperate to establish or rebuild credit, marketers and banks found it easy to exploit consumers and make a lot of money doing so. There has been a renewed interest in secured cards lately, however, and there are a number of legitimate issuers across the country.

Here's how a secured card works: You make a deposit in a savings account, CD, or another type of bank account of, say, $250.

The bank gives you a Visa or MasterCard with a credit limit of up to $250. Your deposit is "frozen"—you can't touch it until after you have closed the account.

You will be asked to fill out an application for a secured card, just as you would for an unsecured card. The bank will also likely run a credit check and evaluate your application, with more lenient standards than regular issuers. Many people erroneously think that if they are willing to put up a deposit as collateral, the account should be automatically approved. Not so. Even secured card issuers have minimum standards for accepting applications.

There are two reasons issuers review applications before issuing secured cards. First, you may go over your limit by shopping in stores that don't authorize small charges. More important, the bank really does not want to touch your deposit. They want to keep you as a paying customer.

You use your secured credit card just like a regular, unsecured card. There's nothing on the card to indicate it is different, and if a merchant calls in for authorization he won't be told the card is secured. You're expected to make monthly payments on the account, just as with any other major credit card. If you miss a few payments on your secured card, the bank will not simply take the payments out of your collateral account. Instead, you will go through the bank's collection process. The bank will generally not dip into the savings account unless it—or you—cancels the account and your bills are not paid.

When you close your secured card account, you won't be able to withdraw your deposit immediately. You'll usually have to wait as long as ninety days to allow any outstanding charges to appear on your account (just the way a bank waits for checks to clear before closing your checking account).

If you pay the bills on time each month, some issuers will "graduate" or "convert" your account to an unsecured card in about eighteen months. Others will gradually increase your credit line so that it's larger than your original deposit. While many people find that paying a secured card on time for a couple of years qualifies them for other cards, there is an obvious advantage to knowing that you will get an unsecured card in the not-so-distant future.

Choosing a Secured Credit Card

The secured card market is wide open for exploitation by quick-cash con artists. They set up a post office box, promise guaranteed credit cards "for only $35," and just wait for the mail to roll in. Some take the money and run; others send out applications for secured cards from banks with which they have no relationship.

How can you tell if an offer for a secured credit card is legitimate?

1. The name of the bank issuing the secured card appears in the advertising. In fact, Visa and MasterCard require marketers to name the issuing bank in all advertising. If you see an ad for a secured card and no bank name is listed, stay away from it. The deposit you send may help finance someone's new Ferrari.
2. It doesn't promise a "guaranteed" major credit card. There is no such thing as a guaranteed bankcard. Some cards may be easy to get, and some banks may approve 95 percent of applications, but there are factors (like an unpaid federal tax lien on an applicant's credit report) that will cause even secured card issuers to reject applications.
3. The security deposit is held in a bank account that is federally insured. If a bank issues a secured card and the deposit is not federally insured, it doesn't mean the program is not legitimate. But do you really want to take a chance with your money?

The Price You Will Pay for Good Credit

Secured credit cards are generally not cheap, although they are getting better and better as competition heats up. A couple of banks are offering special secured cards at rock-bottom prices to encourage good customers to switch their savings accounts to the same bank that issues their credit cards. There are currently only

a few banks offering these programs, however, and they are usually not offered to people with damaged credit.

If you have bad credit, you may not qualify for a cheap card.
You may pay high annual fees, expensive finance charges, and
penalty fees (late fees, overlimit and bounced-check fees), if you
don't manage your account well. Still, some cards are much better than others, so it's worth shopping around.

Here's what to look for in a secured card program:

Interest Rate or Finance Charge: This is the "commission"
you pay to the bank in exchange for borrowing money. Finance
charges on secured cards are usually high—in the 18 to 24 percent range—but lower-rate cards are out there.

Interest Earned: Some secured card programs require you to
deposit your collateral account in a savings account where it will
earn interest on all or part of the balance. Others allow you to
make your deposit in a CD or money-market account.

Find out how much of the balance will earn interest. For example, some programs don't pay interest on the first $500 of your
savings deposit. In addition, the rate paid on the amount above
$500 may be less than what you could earn in a savings account
in your own bank.

In the past few years, some issuers have started offering *better*
interest rates on savings deposits than most people can get at
their local bank. Some programs are so attractive that people are
actually taking their money out of the bank and parking it in one
of these accounts, even if they don't need a secured card.

Secured card issuers may tell you that the interest earned on
the savings account "offsets" the finance charge. In other words,
even if you're paying 21 percent interest on purchases, you're
earning 5 percent on your collateral deposit, so your real interest
rate is 16 percent (21 percent minus 5 percent). That, however, is
like saying if you have your car loan at the same place as your
checking and savings accounts, the interest you earn on your savings account reduces the interest on your car loan. (This is not to
be confused with some banks that *do* offer lower rates to customers who hold multiple accounts at their bank.) A high interest rate is a high interest rate, period.

Fees: In addition to annual fees, which may be quite high, some banks also charge application fees or processing fees. These are one-time fees charged to you when you open the account. Some issuers will require you to pay these fees up front with a check or money order, others will put them on your first bill. *Make sure these fees are refundable if you are turned down for the card.*

A few banks make you pay the processing fees, then tell you several weeks later whether you have been rejected or accepted for the card. If you are turned down, they send you a refund check for the fees you paid. Presumably the bank is trying to make money off the float of your money. Even though you didn't buy their product, you gave them an interest-free loan of $35 or $65, or whatever the fees were, for six weeks or so. Personally, I think any bank that needs to engage in those kinds of practices is questionable.

Late fees, overlimit fees, bounced-check fees, etc., can add up. If you don't check these fees out before you sign up for the card, make sure you do after you have the card in hand. A $10 late fee may not sound like much, but if you have a habit of sending out your bills at the last minute, several late charges can add up.

Grace Period: Like unsecured bankcards, most cards offer an interest-free grace period—the amount of time you have to pay off your balances *in full* to avoid finance charges. And like unsecured cards, you don't need a grace period if you're a credit user—someone who carries a balance from month to month. If you do pay off your credit card bills in full most or all of the time, you should choose a card with a grace period, especially since secured cards tend to be expensive. If you don't understand how grace periods work, be sure to read the section on credit card costs in Chapter Three before choosing a card.

When I was working at Bankcard Holders of America in 1987, we had a hard time coming up with even ten secured card issuers for our secured credit card list. All of the banks on that original list are no longer around or issuing cards. There are now, however, over one hundred issuers of secured cards nationwide, and the number continues to grow.

Lists of secured credit cards are available from CardTrak, Consumer Action, and Myvesta.org (formerly Debt Counselors of America).

Your credit union is another place to look for a secured Visa or MasterCard. While credit unions usually do not have formal secured card programs, many are willing to help their members build a credit rating by holding a savings deposit and extending a loan equal to that deposit.

See the Resources section for more information on secured cards.

Building a Credit Rating

Before signing up for a secured credit card, make sure your good payment history will be reported regularly to at least one of the three major credit bureaus—better yet, to all three. Your whole purpose for obtaining a secured card is to use it to obtain unsecured credit cards. If the secured card is not listed on your credit report, then you are wasting your time. Credit references that do not appear on your credit record will do you little good when applying for unsecured credit.

You also want to make sure that the issuer doesn't report the credit history on your secured card differently than an unsecured card. Issuers are being encouraged to "flag" secured accounts when they report them to the credit bureau. That way, anyone who gets your credit report will automatically know the account is secured.

There are some issuers that will not report their customers' accounts as secured, and I personally think that's the way it should be. Issuers are likely to count against people with secured cards, just like they do people who have loans with finance companies. But just because you have a secured card doesn't mean you have credit problems. Some people get these cards because they have no credit after moving here from another country or paying cash all their lives; others get them after a divorce in which their ex-spouse demolished their credit rating; some people even get them because the interest rate on the savings account is better than they could get elsewhere.

Getting a Mortgage After Credit Problems

One of the questions that frequently come up when I do radio talk shows is, "Can I get a mortgage if I've been through bankruptcy or had other serious credit problems?" The answer is "yes." But how?

Keep in mind that you're more likely to get approved for a mortgage if you can show that your bankruptcy or other credit problems were due to unusual circumstances that don't apply now (a divorce or illness, for example) and you've since put your financial life in order.

For conventional loans, you'll have a better chance of getting approved for a mortgage if your bankruptcy has been discharged (completed) for at least four years and you've reestablished credit. For FHA loans, lenders will usually want to see that your bankruptcy has been discharged for at least two years and you've reestablished credit. If you filed Chapter 13 (where you've paid back some of your debts), you can apply for a mortgage after you've completed at least one year of payments under your repayment program, and you've received approval from your trustee to add the mortgage to your debt.

Here are some specific suggestions for getting a mortgage when you have less-than-perfect credit:

1. Work with a mortgage broker. Robert J. Bruss writes a syndicated real estate column. He frequently runs letters from readers who thought there was no way they could get a mortgage because they had credit problems. Often they were able to get a loan by working with a mortgage broker. Brokers typically work with several different lenders and can "shop" your application with those that are more flexible.

2. Get a "lower-grade" mortgage. A regular, no-problem mortgage loan that fits the guidelines of mortgage investors such as Fannie Mae or Freddie Mac is usually considered an "A" quality loan. But if your application doesn't make you eligible for an "A" loan, you may be able to get a "B," "C," or even "D" loan through a number of lenders.

These loans usually cost more. They carry higher rates and points in most cases, and you'll have to make a larger down payment, but you'll get a mortgage. Then, after you've paid on time for a while and the negative information has dropped off your credit report, you can refinance at a better rate. Ask a couple of good mortgage brokers or your real estate professional for information on these loans.

3. Buy a house from someone who's willing to "carry back" the mortgage. For example: An older couple has paid off their mortgage and wants to move to a sunnier climate. You offer to make payments—including interest at the prevailing interest rate—to them instead of to a bank. Since mortgage interest rates are often higher than what the sellers could get on their own by parking their money in a bank account, they may be more than willing to strike a deal. It's perfectly legal—a real estate attorney can draw up the paperwork for you. It may require a bit more shopping than if you were preapproved by a mortgage company for a loan, but it's certainly a good option to consider.

On the Road to Good Credit

The advice in this chapter may frustrate some people. They believe there must be an easy, quick way to get rid of their bad credit record. Take heart. For years Bob Bouza ran the secured card program for Key Federal Savings Bank, one of the oldest secured card programs in the business. He told me he closed out as many secured card accounts as he opened each year. His customers, who weren't able to get an unsecured card before signing up for his program, were closing their accounts because the secured card reference gave them the credentials to obtain an unsecured card elsewhere.

A study by the Credit Research Center at Purdue University showed that even bankruptcy is not always the credit death sentence that it's portrayed to be. Their study showed that people who have been through bankruptcy get credit 65 percent as often as the general population. While most of the new credit obtained by former bankrupts is through finance companies and retailers, it is still a new start.

Most people who have been trying for any period of time to improve their credit say they'd be willing to do almost anything to clear it up. Arm yourself with the information in this book and start rebuilding your own credit history—and save a lot of money in the process!

CHAPTER FIVE

Get All the Credit You Deserve

Are you applying for your first credit card and want to make sure your application is approved? Are you a woman about to marry, and wonder whether to put the bills in your name and your husband's or keep them separate? Perhaps you're older and you've paid cash for everything all your life, and are now finding it difficult to get a single credit card.

In this chapter, I'll examine the special credit circumstances of older Americans, college students, women, people in the military, immigrants, and first-time credit applicants. I'll give each specific strategies to help get and keep the credit they deserve.

This chapter isn't only for people in one of those groups, though. I'll start by walking you through the loan application process, and show *everyone* how to improve their chances for getting the loans they want. I'll also warn you about the *big* problems that can result if you cosign a loan for someone else.

How to Apply for Credit and
Get the Loan You Want

Nobody likes rejection, and rejection from a bank or credit card company is no exception. Millions of people are rejected for credit cards and loans every year. Bankcard issuers often approve only 40 to 50 percent of the applications they receive. That means, for some lenders, more people are turned down than are approved!

What can you do to improve your chances of getting approved for credit cards and other loans? Whether this is your first time applying for credit, or if you already have credit, here are some techniques you can use to make sure your credit applications get you the credit you deserve. And if you are turned down, I will explain how to turn a rejection letter into a loan.

Step #1. Do Your Homework. Most banks won't give out information about their credit standards. It almost seems as if they would rather waste the time and expense of considering applicants who won't qualify than tell consumers up front what will get them turned down for the card, but they'll usually state privacy or security reasons.

In Chapter One, I discussed what types of qualifications lenders look for in an application. Beyond that, you should always try to determine from a card issuer as much information as possible about their credit criteria. Do they, for instance, accept applicants from your state or local area? Will they reveal their minimum income requirements? Do they look more favorably upon customers who have existing banking relationships with them? Do they have a department that handles reapplications from consumers who are turned down for reasons they believe are unfair?

If you have unusual credit circumstances, such as past credit problems, you may want to try calling the credit department before you apply to see if your application will even be considered. Don't expect someone to tell you whether or not you will be approved. Most customer-service representatives are told to encourage everyone to send in applications—after all, they don't make the decisions (and may not even know the criteria for acceptance). You may get some helpful feedback, however, if you explain exactly what the problem is and tell them you don't want to waste their time with your application if you are not the type of customer they want.

Do not waste your time, or damage your credit record, by applying for credit through banks where you are certain not to qualify. (If you just completed a bankruptcy, for example, you're probably not going to get a low-rate credit card.) Remember, every time you apply for a loan, you are creating another inquiry on your credit file. Too many inquiries in a short period of time can mean an automatic rejection for other loans.

Step #2. Be Complete. Fill out your credit application as completely as possible. If your application is not complete, some creditors will ask you for the missing information. This simply adds extra time to the process.

You can actually get rejected for failing to list some of your debts on your application. I've seen people turned down for "undisclosed debts." This means the credit report revealed loans that weren't listed on the application, and the creditor may have suspected they were trying to hide something. If you have seen your credit report, you will know which accounts appear on the report. Be sure you list them on your application.

Some applications are "mini-aps"—short applications requiring nothing more than your name, address, Social Security number, and perhaps one or two credit references. Unless you are filling out one of these applications, be as complete as possible. Note that most creditors will not require you to list utilities, medical bills, or legal bills on applications.

It's a common misconception that an application makes or breaks a loan, especially in the case of credit cards or revolving loans. Creditors usually put more weight on the information in credit reports, and simply use applications to "fill in the gaps." Applications help update the information on the credit report, and will often provide information about income, assets, and employment that may not appear on credit reports.

Don't just scribble in some basic information on your application, thinking the lender will get the rest from your credit report.

Some creditors view gaps of information as an indication of potential fraud—especially if vital information, such as a Social Security number, is missing. While most lenders will just ask for the missing data, you never know which ones will just turn you down.

Step #3. Be Truthful, but Not Modest. Do not lie on a loan application. Lying can leave you open to legal action if you don't make your payments on time. If you later go through bankruptcy and a lender can show you put false information on your application, you may not be able to include that debt in your bankruptcy.

Beyond lying, however, there is room for you to present yourself in the best possible light. If you have real estate or tangible assets, make sure you list what you believe to be their current value, not the price for which you bought them. Be sure to include valuable jewelry, furs, stocks and bonds, and other assets when possible, if they will boost your net worth. When you write down your credit accounts, be sure to list their current outstanding balances, not the original amount of the loan. If you have income from a part-time job, regular overtime, or investments, feel free to go ahead and list it.

Step #4. Keep Records. Save copies of your credit applications. Not only will this make filling out subsequent applications faster, it will also help you to be consistent on each application you fill out. Just like a prospective employer doesn't like to see unexplained gaps in a resume, lenders don't like to see inconsistencies or missing information in credit applications or credit files. With so much credit fraud today, mistakes on an application can cause a lender to wonder if you are who you say you are.

Your Credit Application Rights

The Equal Credit Opportunity Act (ECOA) is the law that governs the credit evaluation and application process. According to the ECOA, lenders are required to tell you, within thirty days of receiving all the information necessary to process the loan, whether your application was accepted, rejected, or incomplete.

That does not mean you'll always get a final answer within thirty days, since the lender can have a few extra days to get your credit report, or to verify your employment or other information.

It takes an issuer anywhere from one and a half minutes to several weeks to evaluate an application and decide whether to issue a card. On average, card issuers make credit decisions in a week, but it is likely to take a couple of weeks before you receive a card in the mail.

If you don't hear something within thirty days, be sure to call and find out what's happening with it. (You did save a copy, right?)

What If They Say "No"?

Rejection letters are called "adverse action letters." Under the federal Equal Credit Opportunity Act, lenders have to tell applicants in writing when their applications have been rejected. Some rejection letters are easy to read and understand, but many are confusing and give little information about what to do after you've been turned down.

Two important pieces of information have to be included in rejection letters:

- The specific reasons the applicant was turned down for credit;
- The name and address of the credit bureau that supplied a credit report, if one was used in the decision.

While the Equal Credit Opportunity Act requires creditors to tell you the specific reasons you were turned down for credit, they *don't* have to tell you *in* the rejection letter. If they want, they can tell you how to contact them to get those reasons (usually by calling a toll-free number or writing to a certain address). If you get a rejection letter that doesn't list the reasons you were turned down for the loan, be sure to contact the creditor immediately, since by law you have only sixty days to do so.

The reasons you were rejected have to be specific: "You do not have a sufficient number of revolving accounts" or "Your credit report shows late payments in the past," for example. If your rejection letter doesn't offer one to three specific reasons why your application was not approved, or if it only mentions that information about your credit history was obtained from a certain credit bureau, then you have *not* been supplied with specific reasons for the rejection. Some of the reasons for rejection I have seen that do not appear to meet the requirements of this law have included: "your qualifications do not meet our standards" or "information in credit report" or "credit history."

You may have to scrutinize the rejection letter pretty carefully to figure out if you have been given adequate reasons for rejection. I reviewed a rejection letter for a woman who had been turned down because the creditor claimed she "did not meet our credit qualifications." Immediately I assumed the creditor had not met its legal obligation to supply the specific reasons for rejection. When I looked closer, though, I noticed that on the back of the letter was a paragraph telling customers that they had the right to contact the creditor to get their specific reasons for rejection if they wanted them.

Even when you are supplied with the reasons you were turned down, that information may not be of much help to you. There are a couple of reasons for this:

- **The ECOA only requires creditors to tell you the *main* reasons you were turned down.** Most creditors choose to list only two or three reasons why you were rejected, when in fact there may be many more.
- **The ECOA allows creditors to tell you the reason for rejection in general terms—even if it is not meaningful to you.** For instance, your "length of time at residence" could be a reason for rejection. You may not have any idea how the length of time you have been at your current address affects your application for a credit card. A more helpful response would be, "Our experience shows that people who have moved more than twice in the past five years do not pay their bills on time as often as people who have not moved recently." But that's probably not what you'll get.
- **Creditors are sometimes afraid to be specific.** Some

card issuers provide reasons for adverse action that are as vague and general as possible (within legal guidelines) on advice of their legal departments, which are afraid of lawsuits from consumers who are wrongly turned down.

- **Credit scoring systems are so complicated that it is often difficult to determine why applicants were turned down.** The factors in credit scoring systems are often interactive. For example, your score for "length of time at address" may depend on your age as well as your number of credit references. Trust me, after sitting through several credit scoring seminars, when they say it's difficult to figure out exactly why someone was turned down, they mean it.

Suppose you have moved three times in the past year and have no major credit cards. If you are forty-five years old, the creditor may turn you down for a card, since its experience with other customers is likely to show that people of that age who do not have stable addresses and strong credit references are not very good credit risks. If you are only twenty-two years old, however, that same issuer may offer you a credit card. After all, people in that age group may not yet have had a chance to build credit references and are more likely to move frequently. In this case, what would be the main reason for rejecting the forty-five-year-old person's application: age, length of time at residence, or number of credit references?

The Fair Credit Reporting Act requires the lender to tell you in your rejection letter which bureau supplied your credit report if you were turned down because of information in your file. If you contact the credit bureau within sixty days of being rejected for credit, you can find out for free what your credit report says.

Always order this free copy of your credit report. You may find your credit report reveals inaccurate or incomplete information about your financial profile. You may be able to correct it and get the loan you want.

DON'T GIVE UP! You don't have to take an initial credit rejection as the final word. Always find out the reasons you were turned down and order a copy of your credit report. If you think the reasons for which you were turned down are inaccurate or misleading, say so.

First, call the customer-service number and find out if the card issuer has a person or department that handles reapplications. If it does, that's a good sign that the issuer takes reevaluations seriously and has procedures for considering second-time applications.

Take this opportunity to make a good second impression. Write a letter explaining why you should get the card. If the information in your credit file is inaccurate, file a dispute with the credit bureau and enclose a copy of the dispute letter with your reapplication letter. (Some lenders only want you to reapply after your credit report has been corrected.)

Be sure to address the specific reasons you were rejected. For instance, if you were turned down due to an excessive number of bankcards, you may state that you are willing to close a couple of accounts to get this card. If you were turned down because you have been at your job for less than a year, you may want to show the creditor that you have been in your field for a longer period of time. (If you can show them that this job is a step up, it may help your case.) Remember, you are trying to persuade the creditor that it will not be making a bad decision by issuing you a card.

If the card issuer seems reluctant or uninterested in your reapplication, you may have a difficult fight ahead of you. Some creditors have been advised by the companies that sell credit scoring services *not* to reevaluate applications, since they believe those consumers who are initially rejected do not make good customers. If you really believe you deserve the card or the loan, you must play hardball.

Try to determine first if you legitimately have a chance at the loan. If you have been rejected due to late payments and your credit history accurately shows a history of slow payments because you overspent yourself into a financial crisis a couple of years ago, you probably won't qualify for the loan. On the other hand, if the late payments on your report were due to a nasty divorce, and you've always paid your bills on time since, you may have a better chance of getting the card.

Now write a careful letter, which you are going to send as part of your reapplication. Also send a copy to the legal department of the bank—to the attention of the "compliance officer," the person responsible for making sure the bank follows federal laws. Be sure to remain calm and straightforward in this letter. While you will be putting the lender on the defensive, you don't want to be offensive. In your letter, explain why you believe the reasons for which you were denied credit do not indicate your creditworthiness; then ask the creditor to take into account whatever additional information you have.

Here's an example of how this can work: I assisted a consumer who had been turned down for a credit card by a large national bank. His rejection letter listed two reasons for rejection: negative experiences by other creditors and lack of experience with the type and amount of credit requested. He ordered a copy of his credit report and sent it to me.

I was baffled by the rejection. He made a decent income, had had a stable job for several years, and had a number of credit references, including a Visa card paid on time for three years. Equally surprising, he had no negative marks on his credit file. Not one account reflected a late payment.

I wrote to the bank's legal department challenging their conclusion and asking them how, specifically, they had arrived at their decision. I also questioned the accuracy of their reasons for rejection. I never received a direct reply to my letter. Instead, I received a letter stating that they had reevaluated their position and decided to issue a card.

What Happens When Your Account Is Closed?

There are other times when a creditor must tell you why adverse action was taken on your account. If you ask for an increase in your credit line and the creditor refuses to give it to you, you must be told the specific reasons you were not approved for the increase. If your credit report was used as a basis in that decision, they have to tell you the name and address of the credit bureau, so you can order a free copy of your report.

If a creditor closes your account, or makes unfavorable changes in the terms of your account (raises the interest rate, for example), you must be told within thirty days the reasons why. This rule does not apply if the creditor closed or changed the terms on all or most of the accounts similar to yours or if the change was anticipated (a teaser rate expired, or you triggered a penalty rate because you were late with payments, for example).

If you applied for credit and received an offer, but it was not on the same terms or in the same amount for which you applied, you can refuse to accept it. In that case, the creditor would be required to supply you with the specific reasons you did not receive the credit you wanted. An example of this would be if you applied for a gold card with a $5,000 credit line, but instead received a standard card with a $3,000 credit line. If you accept the standard card and use it, the creditor doesn't have to tell you why you didn't qualify for the gold one. But if you refuse to accept the standard card, and don't use it, the creditor must tell you within ninety days why you didn't get the gold card.

Creditors don't have to give credit to anyone who wants it, but they must evaluate applications fairly and without discrimination. If you are having trouble getting credit because you don't fit into normal credit profiles, it's important that you make the effort to get the credit you want. Once you have one or more major cards under your belt, pay them on time and you will likely find that you will get more offers for cards than you can handle.

First-time Credit Applicants: Cosigning

Of all the credit complaints I hear, troubles resulting from cosigning probably top the list. While most people who cosign for someone else genuinely want to be helpful, it's not unusual for them to pay a steep price for their kindness—for years to come. Here are just a few of the real-life stories I've heard:

- During a refinance of their home, parents discovered that their credit had been ruined because their son's car was repossessed. They had cosigned the car loan and didn't even know he had been late on payments, much less lost the car.
- A mother cosigned a credit card for her daughter while she was in college. Eight years later, her daughter was

divorced and the mother was stuck with bills her daughter's now-ex-husband had run up on that card.

- A pastor cosigned for a car loan for a parishioner trying to get back on his feet and instead got stuck with a gas-guzzling SUV when the payments weren't made.
- A young woman cosigned a credit card for her boyfriend and was sued when he defaulted—long after the relationship was over.

If someone asks you to cosign a loan, you may be tempted to help, especially if it's a relative, boyfriend, or girlfriend. Please read this section first before you decide to go ahead with it.

When you cosign for a loan, you are signing a legal contract that holds you responsible for the entire debt. If the person for whom you cosigned does not pay the loan, or makes payments late, it can—and probably will—be reported on your credit record as well. If the person for whom you cosigned does not pay the loan and the lender places the account for collection, it is very likely that the collection company will try to collect from you as well. If any information about the cosigned loan is reported on your credit report, another lender reviewing your report will treat the cosigned account as if it were your own. And, if the information is correct, it will stay on your credit report up to seven years, and chances are slim you will be able to get it removed from the report. (Are you *still* considering cosigning?)

If information reported about the loan is negative, and counted against you when you apply for another loan, it will probably do you no good to explain to the lender that "it is not your account." Legally, you are liable for any debt for which you cosign. Even if the account is paid on time each month, you may find that another lender will take into account the amount of the cosigned debt when determining if you have too much credit already. The lender wants to be sure that if you must pay the cosigned debt, you will still be able to pay your own debts as well.

If you are seriously considering cosigning a loan for another person, ask yourself these questions:

1. Does the person for whom I am cosigning have a good reputation for paying bills on time? Am I willing to risk

     damage to my credit report if this person is not respon-
     sible about making the payments?

2. Can I make the monthly payments *for the entire life of*
    the loan if the person for whom I am cosigning stops
    paying or is no longer able to pay?

3. Is the amount of the loan for which I am cosigning large
    enough to count against me when I apply for my own
    credit elsewhere?

If someone asks you to cosign because they have no credit history, suggest alternatives such as a secured credit card for building credit. If you are being asked to cosign for someone who does
not have a high enough income to qualify for the loan, you will
be doing them a favor by refusing to help them get in over their
head with debt.

Another option is for you to borrow the money and put the
person you want to help on the loan as a cosigner. In most cases,
the lender does *not* have to notify the cosigner if the bills aren't
being paid on time, so you may find your credit record ruined before you have a chance to make amends.

If, instead, you are the primary borrower, the bills will come
to you. If the cosigner doesn't pay, you'll at least be able to make
the payments and protect your credit rating. You will be helping
the cosigner build his or her credit rating, as long as the account
is reported to the credit bureaus. Just keep in mind, of course,
that the debt *is yours* if they don't pay.

In case you're wondering, there is a difference between cosigning a loan and applying with someone else as a joint applicant. Generally, if you cosign for someone, they have to be able to
qualify for the loan based on their own income and credit qualifications. When you apply as a joint applicant (which is typical
with credit cards), the creditor will generally use information
from both applicants when deciding whether or not to make the
loan. As far as your credit report goes, both can help (or hurt).

If you have already cosigned for someone who is not making
the loan payments on time, you might consider making the payments yourself and asking the other person to pay you directly.
You may want to arrange a legal contract to enforce this arrange-

ment. Don't forget: Contracts between you and the person for whom you cosigned do not change the fact that you had a contract with the lender previously. The lender can still collect from you. The best alternative, if possible, is for the other borrower to pay off the loan with a new loan from another lender.

It is also a good idea to talk with your lawyer before cosigning, since state laws regarding a cosigner's liability vary.

Women and Credit

Despite the economic and occupational gains by women in the past decade, many women still face financial hardship that makes it difficult to get credit in their own names. Full-time homemakers, single mothers struggling on a modest income, or divorced women whose husbands screwed up their credit ratings can find it difficult to get credit in their own names. We may have come a long way, baby, but we still have a long way to go.

In 1974, Congress passed the Equal Credit Opportunity Act (ECOA) to halt creditors' blatant discrimination against women and other minorities. The ECOA prevents creditors from discriminating against applicants on the basis of race, color, religion, national origin, sex, marital status, or age. Before the ECOA became law, creditors often asked women to find a husband or male family member to cosign for a loan, asked details about a women's childbearing plans, and canceled a woman's individual credit as soon as she married.

The ECOA doesn't guarantee credit for women or anyone else. What it does guarantee is that a creditor will use the same criteria for judging credit applications from women and minorities as it does other applicants. The ECOA provides women with several protection measures designed to prevent discrimination:

You Are Entitled to Credit in Your Own Name if you qualify for the loan. You can't be asked to get a spouse or another person to cosign just because you're married or female. In fact, these are the only circumstances under which a lender can ask for information about your husband:

- He will use the account.
- It is a joint account he will share with you.
- You are using his income to qualify for the loan.
- You are listing alimony or child support as income.
- You live in a community-property state (see next page) or are listing property located in a community-property state.

By law, you can have accounts under your own name or you can share accounts with a spouse or another person. If you are sharing an account, the payment history on the account must be reported under both of your names.

Creditors Must Give Fair Consideration to Your Income, even if it is part-time income, or comes from public assistance, child support, or alimony. That doesn't prevent a creditor from considering how stable that source of income is, however. For example, if you rely on alimony as a substantial portion of your income, and your husband has a history of failing to pay it, the creditor could turn you down for insufficient income.

A Creditor Cannot Take Your Cards Away simply because you get married, divorced, or are widowed, provided you continue to qualify for the loan. If your accounts were joint accounts, and your creditor has information (probably from your application) that you may not have the qualifications to handle the account on your own, the creditor may request that you reapply for the loan. If that is the case, your account cannot be closed or frozen during the reapplication period.

You Can Keep Your Personal Life Personal: Lenders can't ask your gender or marital status on an application for an unsecured loan (credit cards, overdraft lines of credit, or personal loans). In fact, if you don't want to, you don't have to check those boxes on loan applications where it asks if you prefer to be called Ms., Miss, or Mrs.

If the loan is secured, you can be asked if you are married, unmarried, or separated. The lender is not supposed to use that to discriminate against you. The only time you must reveal your gender is when you apply for a home loan—you will be asked your gender for government monitoring purposes, and if you don't want to reveal it, the loan officer will find it out based on "observation."

Community-Property States: Exceptions to the Rule

Throw out a lot of the above when it comes to community-property states. Since most of the property you own in a community-property state is his too, creditors have a lot more freedom in asking for information about your marital status and—if you have one—your spouse. They aren't supposed to discriminate against you based on that information, but I can't say that it's impossible for them to do so.

If you live in one of the community-property states—Arizona, California, Idaho, Louisiana, Nevada, New Mexico, Texas, Washington, or Wisconsin—and think you may have been discriminated against, call your state attorney general's office for information on credit rights and community property laws in your state.

Maintaining an Excellent Credit Record

At some point, you'll probably have to decide for yourself whether to share accounts with your spouse and what name(s) to maintain credit under. Although there is no "best" way to build an excellent credit record, here are some guidelines:

Newly Married: Minimize Your Exposure

In the glow of nuptial bliss, it is hard to imagine fights over financial matters. But the fact is, couples fight over money more than any other issue. And the majority of complaints I hear from women involve ex-spouses ruining their credit.

Don't rush out and sign on to all his accounts and put him on all of yours. Keep some to yourself. If you put all of your accounts in both your names, there's a serious financial risk if your marriage runs into trouble. It only takes one of you to close all the accounts, leaving the other one stranded with no credit. Don't forget, too, that if your husband is irresponsible and doesn't pay the bills on your shared accounts on time, *your* credit record will also carry the damage—for seven years.

If you have managed fine with your own credit, you may be surprised when you are married to find creditors look at you differently. It is not a form of reverse discrimination but a reflection of your new economic picture. For example, your income may remain steady, but creditors may be less willing to lend you money. Why? All the large debts you carry with your husband—the mortgage, both car loans, and joint credit accounts—will be weighed against only your income if you are applying for your own credit. It's another good reason for carrying at least some of your own credit into your marriage.

If you change your name when you get married, it's up to you whether to change it on your credit accounts. The ECOA allows you to have credit in your birth-given surname, your married surname, or a combination of both. You may want to consider keeping your accounts in your own name regardless of a change in marital status. To avoid confusion later, use the same name for legal and professional purposes.

If you decide that you can't live without your spouse *or* his name, notify the three major credit bureaus and all your creditors of the change. Never use *only* your husband's name for credit purposes. Charlotte Price may have a credit history, but Mrs. Wilbur Price won't: The latter indicates only the wife of Wilbur Price (and he could have several in his lifetime).

Married Since the Mid-1970s or Before: Get Your Own Name

Surprisingly, there are still a number of women who are nonpersons when it comes to credit. These women use credit cards, pay the bills, manage the household budget, but have nothing to show for it. They are riding on their husband's credit reputation. What happened? Years ago, the husband got a couple of credit cards and requested extra ones for his wife. These cards probably even have her name on them.

The key point here is that his wife never filled out and signed the other half of the application as a *cosigner* or *joint applicant*. If she had, she legally would be equally responsible for the bills, but since she didn't, she truly has no credit on that account. The account may show up on her credit report, but she will be listed as an "authorized user," which means she can use the account but has no liability for it. That status may or may not help as far as building a solid credit history is concerned.

How do you go about building a credit history if you've been using your husband's for years? First, call the creditors that issued the cards you use. Ask for an application to become a joint applicant on the account. Sign up on a couple of accounts. Adding your name to one bankcard and one department-store card should be sufficient for credit-building purposes. Creditors will then be required to list the account as a joint account in your name as well as your husband's.

After six months or so of being listed on the accounts together, you can try for your own credit card accounts. If you can't get a credit card in your own name because you don't have a verifiable income of your own, you may be able to qualify for a secured credit card. Review Chapter Four if you are interested in trying this route.

Newly Separated or Divorced

A distressed father called me a while back seeking advice for his daughter. She had recently divorced, and at the divorce hearing the judge had divided the bills between her and her husband. The judge stipulated in the divorce decree that each spouse was responsible for certain bills. Unfortunately, some of the accounts they divided up in the divorce were joint accounts, and her ex didn't keep up on the bills. She was being dunned for bills she thought were his—and damaging information about those accounts was blemishing her credit file.

When you open joint accounts, you and your mate sign a legal contract holding both of you responsible for all legitimate charges on the account. The divorce decree is a legal document binding between the two people who are divorcing. It does *not* erase those previous contracts between you and other creditors.

It doesn't matter to the creditor whether the husband or wife made the charges, and it doesn't matter who offered to pay for them during the divorce. The creditor can and will try to collect from whoever seems willing or able to pay. Remember, too, that if you don't close out accounts when you separate or divorce, your former spouse can run up large bills, take off, and "forget" to pay them—leaving you holding the bag.

You may be able to arrange new, individual lines of credit for each of you with the same lenders and transfer mutually agreed upon balances to those new accounts. You won't be removing your responsibility from the debts that already exist, but you can protect yourself from having to pay new charges.

Some creditors will tell you that you'll have to pay off the entire account before they'll put it in just one person's name. If that's the case, at least close the account from further charges. I do have to warn you: This can get tricky. Some creditors will tell you that you can't close an account without your ex's permission. You should insist, however, that while you understand your responsibility for current charges, you refuse to be responsible for new charges. Send a letter stating your desire to close the account via certified mail, return receipt requested, and keep a copy. You may also want to get the address for the legal department of the issuer and send a copy to the compliance officer there (the person in charge of complying with federal credit laws). They'll get the message that you are serious, and if you went to court, you may have good evidence that you made every effort to close the account.

If either spouse cannot qualify for credit cards on his or her own, at least try to consolidate your debts on a couple of credit cards, or get a personal loan for a fixed amount. Put the cards in safekeeping where neither one can reach them to use them to charge.

What if it's too late? Your ex has already defaulted on loans you held together. There's no easy solution. If your spouse can't make the payments, and you don't make the payments, your credit rating will be damaged. If you can't afford to make the payments, though, what are you supposed to do?

You may want to try to settle with the creditor—agreeing that by paying a smaller amount than the total balance, they'll take your name off the account. (Myvesta.org may be able to help you with this. See the Resources section.) You may want to pay the bills yourself and then go after your ex for the money. Or you may be forced into bankruptcy, which leaves your ex-spouse holding the bag (and leaves you with a ruined credit rating). None are great options—just make sure you get a good attorney to help you sort through them and make the best decision you can under the circumstances.

Don't forget: If those joint debts don't get paid, both of your credit ratings will be harmed. Check every month to make sure your spouse is paying the proper share on time. If you want to keep your distance, handle this through your attorney.

Also be aware that if your spouse files bankruptcy and includes joint debts you held together, you may be injured in two ways. First, if he files a straight Chapter 7 bankruptcy discharging his debts, the creditors will then come after you for payment since they can't touch him. (This is true even if he agreed in the divorce to pay them.) Secondly, whether he files Chapter 7 or Chapter 13, accounts included in the bankruptcy may be noted as "included in bankruptcy" on the credit report. In effect, his bankruptcy may appear on your credit file along with those individual accounts and severely hurt your credit.

Keep in mind that I'm only talking about joint accounts. If your ex had a Visa in his name only, you will generally not be responsible for any of the bills he ran up on his own. If you were just an "authorized user" on his account, and not a joint applicant or cosigner, lenders usually can't come after you for payment.

Divorced with Bad Credit: Get Rid of His Credit

If your spouse's lousy bill-paying habits hurt your credit record, you may have some relief. If the reasons you were rejected are accurate, but you feel they do not accurately reflect your credit standing, the Equal Credit Opportunity Act, Regulation

B section 202.6(b)(6) gives you the ammunition to fight back. This section of the law states:

> "To the extent that a creditor considers credit history in evaluating the creditworthiness of . . . applicants . . . a creditor shall consider . . . (ii) on the applicant's request, any information the applicant may present that tends to indicate that the credit history being considered by the creditor does not accurately reflect the applicant's credit-worthiness . . ."

What does this mean? It means that, legally, a creditor must take into account any evidence that shows that your credit report does not truly reflect your credit qualifications. Most creditors won't pay much attention to this law unless you make them. If you think you have a good case, be persistent.

What type of evidence can help you? Suppose, for instance, you can show that before your marriage you always paid your bills on time, and that the only accounts with negative marks are shared accounts (maybe you can even produce canceled checks showing he paid those bills). It may not sway some creditors, but if you are confident and assertive about your legal rights, you may be able to convince at least one of them to give you a card.

Note that it's very unlikely that you will be able to persuade the *credit bureau* to remove negative information about joint accounts simply because it was linked to a spouse's payment history. You may, however, be able to convince the creditor that reports the information to drop it. For more information about dealing directly with creditors, see Chapter Four.

Widowed: Protect Yourself

As a widow, you probably will have a great deal of paperwork and problems to deal with. Handling credit issues is just one more thing to add to that list. In particular you'll want to address any of the following issues that apply to your situation:

Settling Unpaid Separate Accounts: If your husband had accounts that were in his name only and you do not live in a community-property state, you should not be held liable for those bills. You may, however, find that the creditor wants to try to collect from the estate. Whether they will actually do so depends on the size of the debt, the size of the estate, and how likely it is they will be able to collect. Give them the name and number of the executor of the estate, if possible, who can then take the burden of dealing with them off your shoulders. The creditor will also likely want a copy of the death certificate.

Handling Joint Accounts: You will have to continue to pay on joint accounts. Again, the lender may ask you for information to prove you can still handle the accounts, but even if they close them, you will be required to pay on them until they are paid in full. If your spouse left you with large debts and little ability to pay them back, you may need to contact an organization like Myvesta.org for help, or even consult a bankruptcy attorney.

Getting Your Own Credit: If you have not established credit on your own, you'll want to make sure you do. Consider a secured card if you don't have other options.

Opting Out: You'll need to notify the three major credit reporting agencies of your spouse's death by sending them a copy of the death certificate. Sadly, some people use personal information from recently deceased people to commit credit fraud, and you don't need that aggravation on top of everything else. It's also a good idea to submit your spouse's information to 1-888-5OPT-OUT to prevent prescreened credit offers, as well as to take his name off direct mail and telemarketing lists (see Chapter Eleven).

Every Woman

Review your credit file annually. Confirm that the information it contains is accurate, complete, and up-to-date. Considering the importance of the information in your credit file, it's smart to review it regularly. If you find errors, write to the credit bureau and ask them to correct them. If you find that some of the accounts you share with your husband are listed on his file and not on yours, write to the creditor who holds the account and remind them that the ECOA requires that joint accounts be reported in both names.

College Students: Pick a Card—Any Card

Here's an excerpt from a letter I received from the parent of a college student:

> In August, my then-18-year-old son left for college. Shortly after enrolling at his college, he received three credit cards through the mail from various banks. One of the cards had a credit limit of $1,500, one had a credit limit of $500, and another had an $800 limit. All had access to cash through a PIN number.
>
> When he went away to college, my son had established no credit whatsoever in his name. His income was $45 per week, which he earned working at his dorm cafeteria. On an income of $180 per month, he was granted a limit of $1,500 by one of the companies. Following these same guidelines, my husband and I should be able to get a credit card limit of $45,000 based on our income!
>
> My son is now in his fourth year of college and is in debt $2,000 to these credit card companies. I am not excusing his foolishness. However, I feel that the biggest fault lies with the company that would grant this credit. His life has now become a nightmare of constant phone calls from bill collectors—what little amount he can afford to pay doesn't seem to make a dent in the bill with their exorbitant interest rates. I do feel these credit card companies are like vultures preying on young and vulnerable students who are away from home for the first time.

Seem extreme? Maybe—but it isn't the only letter like that I've received. Credit is extraordinarily easy for students to get, and both parents and students need to know what they're up against.

If you're a college student and you want a credit card, you'll have your choice of plastic. You don't have to have an income or even a parent's signature to get a card. All you do is sign on the dotted line, and the plastic is in the mail. More than half of students carry credit cards, and some even get cards *before* they get to school.

Why are credit cards so easy for students to get? Issuers woo college students early, knowing that most cardholders will keep their cards well after graduation. It's hard to find new customers in today's market, and every year there's a new batch of students who are more than willing to take a card (or two, or three).

But wouldn't students be a bad risk—especially if you consider most don't have the income to pay back large credit card debts? The credit card companies say no, and one reason is that parents are often willing to step in and pick up the tab if their kids fall behind on bills.

Despite the dangers, though, I do think it's a good idea for students to get one major credit card in college. If not, they'll probably find it really tough to establish credit once they've graduated. Their application will be thrown in with everyone else's, and the fact that they haven't been on the job for a couple of years and don't have any major credit cards will make it that much more difficult to get the first one.

So, if it's a good idea to get a credit card in college, which *one* should a student go for? (One is enough!)

American Express: Though American Express cards are traditionally thought of as the "prestige" plastic, they aren't available only to people with a lot of money. College students are one of AmEx's marketing targets, and college students who hold an AmEx card get special treatment from the company, including offers for discount merchandise, cheap airfare, or other perks.

American Express prides itself on customer service and they market this service to customers, especially to parents of students who worry about their children away from home. Although they would prefer that the price of their card not be compared with that of other major credit cards, a personal card (a.k.a. Green card) does carry a $55 annual fee, which may be too expensive for some students. Plus, there's the danger with a charge card that a student will spend more than he or she can afford to pay back and end up with a late payment on a credit report for the next seven years.

College students who want an AmEx card may decide to go with a Blue card instead. That way, they can make smaller payments if they have to, and it doesn't carry an annual fee.

Visa, MasterCard, and Discover: These applications litter the dormitories and classrooms of every campus in America. Major credit cards are usually easy to get—a student need only show that he or she is a student and indicate some type of income, whether from a part-time job, allowance, or a savings account.

Over the years, the terms on these cards have become more competitive and some can be quite decent. Some campuses may limit the amount of marketing on campus by issuers. If that's the case, it's possible for a student to shop for a good deal at Web sites like cardtrak.com or creditcardmenu.com.

Department-Store Cards: A number of department stores, including Sears, JC Penney, and Filene's, offer cards to students. Department-store cards can only be used in one store, which may keep a student from overspending. On the other hand, these cards generally charge very high interest rates, so a several-hundred-dollar balance can take a long time to pay off if you make only the minimum payment each month. Most department stores report cardholders' payment histories to credit bureaus, but these cards are not always as strong a reference as a bankcard.

Gasoline Cards are often easy to get, even for students. They require payment of the entire balance in full each month, although some offer revolving credit for car repairs and tires. Most gasoline card programs don't report payment histories regularly to credit bureaus, so they may not be of much use as a credit reference.

Easy Does It

Many parents shudder at the thought of their children getting a walletful of plastic, and with good reason. There is a temptation to let the bills pile up when in college—thinking that you can pay them after you graduate and start making "real money." Finding a job and a place to live after graduation can be tough enough, though. Worrying about paying a lot of bills will only make it more difficult.

Also, keep in mind that when you graduate, there'll be a lot of expenses draining your budget—a deposit for an apartment, car payments, utilities, and bills for new furniture or moving, for example. One study found that students would have to earn nearly $39,000 after college to support their debt payments and living expenses. That's a lot of dough for most new college grads! The first couple of years after you graduate may be some of the most challenging financially, so it is smart to keep your credit lines free for essential charges. If you do graduate with a pile of debt, you may find yourself back with Mom and Dad for longer than you'd like.

Parents—Talk to Your Teens

Parents are usually more worried about their kids getting credit cards than the students themselves, so here are some tips for them:

Share Your Credit Card Experience: While they've often seen you pull out the plastic to charge something, your kids have probably never seen the bills. Sit down with them and go over a credit card statement. Explain the finance charge, grace period, and minimum payment. If you've recently paid off debts, or if you're trying to do so now, show how much it's costing you, and why it's so difficult to get ahead when you only pay the minimums due.

If Your Kids Enjoy Computer Games, Give Them the Banker's Secret Credit Card Software: Let them see for themselves that it will take over twelve years and $1,115 in interest to pay off a $1,000 bill at 18 percent if they just pay the minimum. Then encourage them to look at a few "what if?" scenarios, where they'd send in more. Just a quarter a day, $7.50 a month, will save them almost seven years and $592. (See the Resources section for more information.)

Set Limits Before They Head Off to School: David Hunt, president of AT&T Universal Card Services, gave his daughter a credit card when she went off to college and told her she could only use it for emergencies. His definition of an emergency? "If you can eat it, drink it, or wear it, it's not an emergency."

Explain What Will Happen If They Run Up Bills They Can't Pay: Will you be willing, or able, to bail them out if they can't pay? Lay out the consequences.

Let Them in on Real Life's "Permanent Record Card"—That All-Important Credit Report: Explain that late payments will show on their credit report for seven years, which could ruin their ability to rent an apartment, obtain a mortgage, buy a car, get affordable car insurance, or even get a job—if they fall behind.

Of course, the best way to teach smart credit management is to practice it! For more information on college students and credit, see the Resources section.

Older Americans and Credit Cards

Some time ago, I participated in a trade show for people aged fifty and older. The booth featured credit information geared toward seniors. Only a few hours into the show, I found that most of the attendees didn't want to hear our pitch. Proudly, they declared that they had no need for credit because they always paid cash for *everything*. Indeed, quite a few older people don't use credit cards at all because they were raised with the belief that taking on debt is a sign of poor financial responsibility.

Older Americans with a "pay as you go" attitude are right to be wary of credit. Paying large amounts of non-tax-deductible interest to credit card companies can certainly be a waste of money and a poor financial choice. It is wrong, however, to assume that credit cards themselves are "bad." Anyone who shuns credit cards completely is ignoring the fact that credit cards are not only a way to get credit, but are also a convenient payment tool. Credit cards can benefit older Americans—or anyone else—for several reasons:

Credit Cards Are Convenient: They make mail-order and telephone shopping a breeze.

Credit Cards Are Safe: For those who don't like the idea of carrying a lot of cash, or who prefer not to make frequent trips to the bank, credit cards can be a useful alternative. If your plastic is lost or stolen, the most you can lose is the first $50 of unauthorized charges. If your wallet or purse full of cash is stolen, however, chances may be slim that you will recover your money.

Credit Cards Provide Emergency Buying Power: If your heater breaks down and you don't have the money to pay for a new one, a credit card can finance the purchase until you have the time to pay it back. Even if you do have the money to pay the bill, you may want to pay by credit card rather than making a trip to the bank to withdraw the money to pay the bill.

Credit Cards Offer Protection: Suppose you do have the heater replaced, and two weeks later it conks out. If you paid for the new heater by cash or check, you must deal directly with the merchant to try to repair the problem. If you paid by credit card, you can notify the card company of the problem and refuse to pay the bill until the company fixes the heater properly.

Credit Cards Travel Well: You can travel without credit cards, but it can be a hassle. Hotels and car-rental companies hesitate to make reservations or rent autos to customers who can't offer a major credit card as a deposit. Carrying credit cards on trips also means you can carry less cash, and will have access to money when you need it.

If you are in your fifties or older and don't have a credit card, you may be surprised at how difficult it can be to get the first one. Those who have paid cash all their lives, have paid off cars and

homes, have a large net worth, or have excellent retirement benefits may be shocked to find out they can't get a major credit card.
Why? Because of the old catch-22 of "it takes credit to get credit."
What can you do if you are trying to get your first credit card
when you're older?

Age Discrimination

Creditors have been prohibited from discriminating against
older Americans since the enactment of the Equal Credit Opportunity Act (ECOA) in 1975. The ECOA, the same federal law I just
discussed under the section "Women and Credit," makes it illegal for a creditor to turn someone down just because they are over
age sixty-two.

*You Can't Score Lower Because You're Sixty-two Years Old
or Older:* If a lender uses a scoring system to evaluate credit applications, and age is a factor in the system, anyone age sixty-two
or over must be given a score at least as high as the best score
available to anyone under age sixty-two. For example, suppose
a creditor uses a scoring system and awards ten points to applicants thirty years old or younger, twenty-five points to anyone between the ages of thirty and forty, and twenty points to
anyone over forty. In that system, anyone age sixty-two or older
must be given at least twenty-five points or more for age—a score
at least as high as that for anyone under age sixty-two.

*The ECOA Requires Creditors to Count Income from Pen-
sions, Annuities, or Part-time Jobs When Evaluating Applications:* Income can be a particularly difficult hurdle for credit
applicants who are retired. You may own a home free and clear,
have a nest egg in the bank, or own valuable stocks and bonds. At
the same time, your income may be only a fraction of what you
earned when working full time. In other words, you have plenty
of money, but your cash flow is low. Since most card issuers' systems are set up to accept only those applicants whose income
meets or exceeds a certain level, you may find yourself denied
credit time and again.

The ECOA Protects the Cards in Your Wallet: Creditors are not allowed to require you to reapply for a loan, change the terms of your account, or close your account simply because you reach a certain age or retire.

You Don't Need Insurance to Get Credit: Under the ECOA, creditors are not allowed to reject you for credit simply because at your age you are not eligible for credit life, health, accident, disability, or other credit-related insurance.

These rules don't mean you will automatically be given credit if you are over sixty-two years old. Creditors can also take into account the adequacy of collateral offered if your remaining life expectancy is shorter than the length of the loan *and* the cost to the creditor to take back that collateral could exceed the equity available.

For instance, a creditor might refuse to grant a sixty-five-year-old applicant a 5 percent down, thirty-year mortgage. A creditor cannot make that kind of decision arbitrarily, however. An applicant's individual qualifications must be taken into account. If a creditor decided that all applicants over the age of sixty-five must pay higher down payments than younger applicants, the creditor would likely be discriminating against older applicants.

Getting Your First Card If You Are Older

"I don't understand it," the man says to me over the phone. "I've always paid cash for things all my life. I do have a house I've paid off, and several cars and a boat that they lent money to buy—and I paid them off on time. After all that, no one will give me a credit card with a lousy $2,000 limit. Everyone keeps turning me down for a credit card because they say I have no credit history."

His is the classic example of "it takes credit to get credit." What do you do if you find yourself in the same situation? Here are a few options:

1. *Try Your Bank:* Visit the bank where you have your checking and savings accounts. Make an appointment with a loan officer or the branch manager and find out if

you are eligible for one of their credit cards. If they do not offer the type of loan or card you need, ask them for some specific suggestions for building a credit history.

2. *Start Small:* Next, you may want to try a department store that you frequent. If you do not have any negative remarks on your credit history (late payments, etc.) you will probably find it easy to get a department-store credit card. When you do apply for credit, do not sell yourself short: List all sources of income, such as retirement pay and Social Security. If you think a creditor is unfairly refusing to give you credit because of your age or circumstances related to age, try contacting the legal department of the bank and speak with the attorney in charge of making sure the bank follows the Equal Credit Opportunity Act. If that attorney is not helpful, you may want to contact the Federal Trade Commission (listed in the Resources section) for more information on your credit rights.

3. *Get a Debit Card:* If you just want a card for convenience or traveling, a Visa Check Card or MasterCard MasterMoney card may work just as well as a credit card. You can use these cards anywhere that Visa or MasterCard is accepted, and you won't have to worry about paying the bills since the money's deducted straight from your account. Read the warnings about debit cards in Chapter Three before you go this route.

As I mentioned earlier, older women frequently have difficulty establishing their own credit because they have used their husband's credit all their lives and have failed to establish credit on their own. If you have been married and using your husband's credit cards since before June 1977 (even if the cards bear your own name), carefully read the previous section on "Women and Credit" to determine if you need to build your own credit rating.

Credit Card Fraud and Older Americans

One of the most popular targets of swindlers are older Americans. In part, it is because the senior population as a whole controls over 60 percent of the net worth of all U.S. households. Older people, because of high living expenses and smaller incomes, may be willing to risk even a small life savings in an investment that will help them or their spouse live the rest of their life in comfort. Many mailing houses will sell lists of names, addresses, and telephone numbers of older Americans, which hucksters then use to target them for marketing.

It is important to understand that these con artists are often very slick. Their offers may not sound suspicious, and they are often backed by glossy brochures and sophisticated sales pitches. They use very high pressure sales tactics. It's heartbreaking to hear of the ways thieves have made their fortunes by stealing people's life savings. Fraud is a real threat to older Americans' financial security and should not be treated lightly. Be sure to take a look at the section on credit fraud in Chapter Eleven for more advice on protecting yourself.

If You Are in the Military

For those in the military and their families, trying to get credit cards can be a frustrating experience. Americans employed by the army, air force, navy, or marines often find it difficult to get credit because they don't fit into many of the traditional profiles of credit applicants. They might move frequently, their income may be low (although it may be boosted with housing allowances and other benefits), and they often live overseas.

If you are having difficulty getting credit, be sure to give yourself credit for all income on your application. In addition to your salary, add any regular additional income, such as per diem pay or housing allowances. If any of your income or benefits are tax-free, note that point as well.

One credit executive I know claims that APO boxes are the primary reason military personnel are turned down for credit cards. He says that the fraud associated with APO boxes is so high that creditors would rather turn down those applicants than risk sending cards. If you are stationed overseas, get a post office box in your hometown or, better yet, list a trusted relative's address on your application. Using that address for all credit purposes can give you the added bonus of a stable address if you move.

Also, be sure to check with your credit union. Not only do they often have special evaluation standards for members, most credit union cards carry very low rates and fees.

If you still can't qualify for a credit card, consider a secured card. By depositing several hundred dollars as collateral for the card, you will be reducing the bank's risk. See Chapter Four for more information about secured cards.

Soldiers and Sailors Civil Relief Act of 1940

The Persian Gulf War in 1991 alerted service people to this obscure, almost-forgotten law (abbreviated SSCRA), originally passed by Congress to provide protection for individuals entering or called to active duty in the military service. The law protects active-duty service members from unfair evictions or foreclosures, high interest rates, and default judgments.

The act usually includes:

1. All service members on extended active duty, whether inductees, regulars, members of the National Guard, Reserves, or volunteers, serving with the army, navy, air force, marine corps, or coast guard.
2. All officers of the Public Health Service detailed for duty with the military services.
3. All persons who are training or studying under the supervision of the United States preliminary to induction in the military service.
4. All former citizens of the United States who serve with the Allied forces of our allies during wartime.
5. All persons who have been ordered to report for induction.

In some cases, dependents of service people may also be eligible for benefits.

Reservists and members of the National Guard are protected under the SSCRA while on active duty. The protection begins with the date of entering active duty and generally terminates within thirty to ninety days after the date of discharge from active duty.

It is important to note that you can apply for protection under this law whenever you go into active military duty. It is not applicable only during wartime.

Here are the main provisions of the act. (There are additional provisions that relate to courts and legal action.) This is a *general* discussion of the act. For details and complete information, it is important to contact your judge advocate's office (JAG office) or legal staff on your base.

Terminating Leases

If you are called to active duty and must terminate a lease on an apartment or home, the act gives some relief. To be eligible for the termination provisions, the lease must have been executed by the service member *before* entering active duty, and the property must have been occupied by the member or dependents.

To terminate a lease, you must give the landlord *written* notice any time after receiving your orders to report for active duty, or after entering active duty.

For month-to-month rentals, your termination is effective thirty days after the first date on which the next rental payment is due, subsequent to the date when the notice of termination is delivered. For example, suppose your rent is due on the first of the month. You mail your notice of termination on August 1. Your next rental payment is due September 1. Thirty days after that date (the date when the next rental payment is due) is October 1—the effective date of termination.

For all other leases, termination is effective on the last day of the month following the month in which proper notice is delivered. For example, suppose you have a yearly lease and you give written notice of termination on July 20. The effective date of termination would be August 31—the last day of the month following the month in which notification is given.

You are required under law to pay rent only for those months before your lease is properly terminated, and if you paid in advance, you must be given a prorated refund of the remaining amount. If you paid a security deposit, that must be returned when you terminate the lease.

Home Evictions (Rental Properties)

While a service member is on active duty or has received orders to report for active duty, and if the rent doesn't exceed $1,200 per month, a landlord is not allowed to evict the service man or woman's family from their home without first getting a court order authorizing an eviction. If the landlord does try to get court permission for an eviction, the judge hearing the case must determine if the service member's military service has affected his or her ability to pay the rent. If so, the judge can stay (halt) the eviction proceedings for up to three months. This provision applies to property rented before *or* after entry into active duty.

Maximum Interest Rate

The interest rate on any financial obligations—including home mortgages, credit card debts, and auto loans—incurred *prior* to entering active duty is capped at 6 percent per year during active duty.

This protection does not apply to debts incurred after one enters military service.

This protection is not automatic; the creditor can go to court and try to prove that the ability to pay a higher rate of interest is not materially affected by the service member's entering active duty. If successful, the military person may lose this protection on that loan.

Mortgage Protection

Service members are protected from foreclosure on their homes, as long as the following conditions are met:

- Protection is sought on a loan secured by a mortgage, trust deed, or other security in the nature of a mortgage on either real or personal property,

- The obligation originated before the service member entered active duty,
- The property was owned by the service member or a family member prior to entering active duty,
- The property is still owned by the service member or a family member at the time protection is sought,
- The ability to make the payments is materially affected by the service member's active duty obligation.

Installment Contracts

A service member who entered into an installment contract to purchase real or personal property before going on active duty is protected under the SSCRA if his or her ability to make payments is "materially affected."

- The service member must have paid, prior to going on active duty, a deposit or installment under the contract.
- The lender or vendor is then prohibited from exercising any right or option under the contract to rescind or terminate the contract, to repossess the property if payments are not made, or to breach the contract, *unless authorized by the court.*

Note that many of these provisions depend on whether the service member's ability to make payments is "materially affected" by entering the service. It is up to the court to decide this on a case-by-case basis. The court must compare the service person's financial condition before going on active duty to his or her financial condition while on active duty.

Entrepreneurs

If you own your own business, you probably know a lot about credit. Most likely, you have sat across the desk from many loan officers, filled out financial forms until you could do it in your sleep, and juggled bills when business was slow. Credit cards are one of the most important tools for self-employed business people. They provide quick and easy cash (without having to beg and plead with a loan officer), they can be an excellent record-keeping tool, and they require relatively low monthly payments.

Credit cards can sometimes be difficult to obtain if you are self-employed, however. Self-employed people are traditionally considered risky. One study showed, for example, that one in five people who filed bankruptcy were entrepreneurs.

If you are self-employed and want to obtain credit cards, you have to know how to apply for them. The challenge here is to make yourself look as "normal" and "stable" as the rest of the bill-paying public. Here are some tips:

1. ***Don't Name Your Business After Yourself:*** A business carrying your name is a dead giveaway that it's your own.

2. ***Hire Yourself as an Employee of the Business and Pay Yourself a Salary:*** If you call yourself president or owner of the company, understand that the lender may dig deeper to find out if you are self-employed. If you put an employee—perhaps the office manager or someone in charge of the books—in charge of verifying employment information in your organization (and you are honest about your salary with them), it will appear as if you work in a normal nine-to-five position. I am not advocating stretching the truth here—I am simply suggesting that you set it up to make it easier for you to get credit.

If you need extra credit, one of the first places to ask is your current card issuers. If you have paid your bills on time (even just the minimum monthly payments), many card issuers will be more than happy to raise your limits. Although most card issuers will often pull your credit report to determine that you haven't fallen into credit problems, the check is often perfunctory.

Immigrants

While lenders may not turn applicants down because of race or national origin, they can consider permanent residency or immigration status when deciding whether to extend credit. A lender might turn someone down for a credit card if they are not a citizen if they think it would be difficult to recover their money if the person left the country. If an application asks whether you are a United States citizen, call the lender first to determine if it considers noncitizens for loans. If not, check with another lender. Not all of them have this requirement.

PART TWO

CUT YOUR DEBT

CHAPTER SIX

Weighing In: Do You Carry Too Much Debt?

According to a news story that ran in 1995, a sixty-nine-year-old Denver woman died leaving behind a $90,000 credit card debt. Although she only earned $840 a month, she had thirty-seven credit cards—and investigators found she had thousands of dollars worth of credit still available on them.

Americans love credit. When times are good, we use credit to finance a lifestyle that's just around the corner when the bonus comes in or the stocks pay off. When the economy is slower, we're almost chastised for not spending more and getting America up and running again. After watching this industry for some time, I am no longer surprised by ever-increasing amounts of consumer debt or rising bankruptcies. There seems to be no ceiling to the amount of debt we can accumulate.

What's far more interesting than the numbers, however, are the personal stories. Having been there myself more than once, I know how easy it is to justify carrying debt, and how hard it is to finally acknowledge that "enough is enough."

In this chapter, we'll look at several ways of determining whether you have too much debt. Each one has its pros and cons, so choose the one (or more) that you feel comfortable with. The most important thing you can do right now is to take an honest look at your situation and decide whether it's time for change.

Are You in Credit Trouble?

There are a number of ways to determine if you have too much debt. In this chapter, I'll cover three of the most common methods: debt/income ratios, current ratios, and the "comfort level" method.

Debt/Income Ratios

Comparing your income with your outgo (your bills) is one of the most widely used methods for analyzing if you have too much debt. Bankers have for many years used debt/income ratios when deciding whether to approve loan applications. The debt/income ratio is usually figured on a monthly or annual basis.

A monthly debt/income ratio provides a good snapshot of how strong your financial situation is on a day-to-day basis. Since the weakness of the monthly debt/income ratio method is that it overlooks long-term loans that may threaten your overall financial stability, I'll also discuss the "current ratio" later.

To figure your debt/income ratio, gather your most recent credit billing statements. If you don't receive a monthly statement for some bills—your car loan, for example—call the creditor for your current balance. This is very important. Your rough idea of your balance may be completely different from what you actually owe.

Now, as I show in the following table, list all your bills in one column. In a second column, list your monthly payments. In a third column, list the total amount you still owe on those bills. (Be sure to list your current outstanding balance, not the original amount of the loan.) Don't include your utilities or taxes as debts here.

Revolving debts, such as credit cards, do not have fixed monthly payments. You may want to find out from your card issuer how your monthly payments are calculated. Otherwise, estimate that your monthly payments are 2.5 percent of the total amount you owe. (To figure the monthly payment on that basis, multiply the total due by .025.) Here's an example:

MONTHLY/TOTAL BILLS

Lender:	Monthly payment:	Total owed:
Car loan	$250	$ 6,700
Credit union MasterCard	$ 95	$ 1,900
Bankcard Visa	$ 20	$ 1,000
Dr. Sharp	$ 20	$ 175
Department-store card	$ 15	$ 225
Totals:	$400	$10,000

Next, determine your monthly income. Start with your annual gross income (income before taxes). Add any additional, steady income you receive, such as alimony, Social Security benefits, or interest from investments. *Do not* include overtime or bonuses unless they are guaranteed. If you earn an hourly wage instead of a salary, take an average weekly paycheck and multiply that figure by fifty-two (weeks) to determine your gross annual income. You can then divide that figure by twelve to determine your monthly income.

MONTHLY INCOME

Annual gross income:	$17,000
Alimony or child support:	800
Social Security or government pay:	
Interest/investment income:	
Regular overtime (if guaranteed):	200
Other income or support:	
Total annual income:	18,000
Divided by 12	÷ 12 =
Total monthly income:	1,500

Next, divide your monthly debt payments by your total monthly income. The answer is your monthly debt/income ratio.

The number you end up with will be a fraction. Debt/income ratios are expressed as percentages, so move the decimal point on the number over two places to the right. Here's an example:

MONTHLY DEBT/INCOME RATIO

400 ÷ 1500 = .26 or 26%
Monthly debt payments ÷ monthly income = debt/income ratio

What Does It Mean?

Here's what your debt ratio means. (I am assuming here that you included a mortgage payment. If you don't have a mortgage payment, then these numbers should include your rent or the monthly payment you expect to pay, including taxes and insurance, if you buy. If you don't pay rent or have a mortgage, but you are falling into these categories, then you can assume your debt level is high.)

36 Percent or Less: A debt ratio of 36 percent or less is generally considered healthy. You would not have trouble getting a mortgage with that debt ratio (provided you qualified on income and credit history, of course). The higher your debt ratio, the more risky your situation.

37 Percent to 42 Percent: You will probably find it easy to get credit cards, but it may be more difficult for you to get other types of loans. If you want a mortgage, you may still qualify for a VA or FHA loan, but some lenders will expect you to pay a higher rate or reduce some of your debt first. It would be a good idea to pare down your debt now, while it is manageable.

43 Percent or More: You may be keeping up with the bills, but your debt ratio is definitely on the high side. Financial difficulties are probably right around the corner if you don't start taking action.

50 Percent or More: Read the next chapter and plan a strategy for reducing your debt before it gets too far out of hand.

Most mortgage lenders, by the way, follow the "28/36 percent" rule when evaluating debt/income ratios. That is, to qualify for the mortgage, your monthly house payment debt (including taxes and insurance) should not exceed 28 percent of your gross income. Your total monthly debt payments—housing plus all other revolving and unsecured debts—should not exceed 36 percent of your gross monthly income. (Notice that only leaves 8 percent for nonmortgage debts.) FHA and VA loans and some first-time-buyer programs are more lenient, with acceptable ratios as high as 41 percent. If you can't meet those debt ratios, you may be required to put up a higher down payment, take out an unconventional mortgage (such as owner financing), or pay some of your debts before you can qualify for the loan.

Current Ratio

The main problem with the debt/income ratio method is that it can provide a false sense of security. Since many credit cards require only a very low minimum monthly payment, it may appear that you can afford the monthly payments even though your total debt is unmanageably high, and would take *forever* to pay off. That's why figuring your current ratio is important. It will give you an estimate of your overall net worth; how much you have accumulated compared to how much you owe. This ratio is also sometimes called a "liability/asset" ratio or "debt/equity" ratio.

Liabilities are what you owe. When you figured your debt ratio above, you listed your liabilities, so that work should be done.

Assets are what you own. They can include cash; money in your savings, checking, or other bank account; securities such as stocks and bonds; real estate; valuable jewelry, furs, or art; automobiles; cash value of life insurance policies; and pension benefits.

For each asset, determine the current market value of the goods. For example, if you list your car as an asset, check the blue book value to determine how much it is currently worth. If you are having difficulty determining how much something is worth, your insurance company may be able to help you, or you can check ebay.com or the classified section of your newspaper to get an idea of how much similar merchandise is selling for.

FIGURING YOUR CURRENT RATIO

Total Assets

	Current Value:
Bank account:	
Cash in savings:	$ 550
Cash in checking account:	$ 200
Money market account:	
Certificates of deposit:	
Home:	$45,000
Other real estate:	
Stocks and bonds:	
Company stock:	$ 500
Corporate, municipal, utility bonds:	
Mutual funds:	
IRA account:	$ 2,250
Private pension:	
Profit-sharing plan:	
Life insurance cash value:	$ 500
Automobile:	$ 8,000
Antiques and art:	
Jewelry/furs:	
Silver:	
Other assets:	
Total assets:	$57,000

Total Liabilities

Lender:	Total Owed:
Car loan	$ 6,700
Credit union MasterCard	$ 1,900
Bankcard Visa	$ 1,000
Dr. Sharp	$ 175
Department store card	$ 225
Mortgage	$20,000
Total liabilities:	$30,000
Current ratio:	

$$30,000 \div 57,000 = .52 \text{ (or 52\%)}$$

Total liabilities ÷ Total assets = Current ratio

To determine your current ratio, divide your total liabilities by your total assets. To express that number as a percentage, move the decimal two places to the right.

If your current ratio is:

30 Percent or Less: Your long-term debt position is healthy. You may want to make an appointment with a financial planner or accountant to explore investment opportunities and to make sure you are maximizing tax deductions.

31 to 50 Percent: Most financial advisors would consider a current ratio in this range stable, although as you get closer to 50 percent, it's more questionable. You may benefit from reducing your debts. It is especially important to pay off debts you have incurred on depreciating assets—like car loans or credit card spending for everyday expenses. Think of it this way: You may be able to manage your monthly payments, but over the long term you are giving your lenders a lot of money (in interest) that could be working for you, instead of for someone else.

51 to 75 Percent: Take a good, hard look at what you can do to increase your assets and decrease your debt. First reduce unsecured debt with high interest rates, then make sure you have an emergency savings account equal to your living expenses for three to six months. The next chapter will give you a place to get started.

76 Percent or More: Read the next chapter, then make an appointment with a credit or financial counselor for help (see the Resources section).

The Comfort Level Formula

The following questions are often used by financial counselors to help people identify habits that may indicate a debt problem. Be honest with yourself as you read and answer the questions on this list.

Do you put off paying your bills each month because you are worried that you won't have enough money to cover them?

Do you usually or frequently make only minimum monthly payments on your loans?

Have you paid your rent or mortgage late because you don't have enough money to pay when it is due?

Are you charged to the limit on several or all of your credit cards?

Do you sometimes find your credit card purchases denied because you are over the limit or behind on payments?

Do you frequently charge things intending to pay them off later—but then find you don't have enough money at the end of the month to do so?

Are you juggling bills each month just to get by?

Do you use credit cards to finance purchases of everyday expenses, such as food, gas, or rent?

Have you used a cash advance from one credit card to make a payment on another card?

Have any of your credit cards been canceled by the issuer because you didn't make payments on time or were chronically charging over the limit?

Do you avoid letters, calls, billing statements, or collection notices from creditors?

Have your utilities been turned off, or have you been threatened with shut-off notices, because you fell behind on your payments?

Have you written checks knowing they were going to bounce?

Do you frequently write checks for more than the balance in your account, knowing your overdraft line of credit will cover them?

Do you often use your credit cards to pay for items you know you really can't afford?

When you feel depressed or bored do you go shopping?

Are you afraid someone is going to find out how far in debt you are?

When you are out with a group of people, do you ever pay for meals or entertainment with your credit card and then ask your friends to pay you their share of the bill with cash?

Do you often use your credit cards to pay for meals or entertainment for friends or business associates because you want to impress them?

Are you usually unsure of your financial worth at any time?

Is your credit rating damaged because of late payments?

Are you denied credit because of previous late payments or because you have too much credit already?

Do you worry when you apply for credit that you will be turned down because you have too much debt?

Must you borrow money from friends and relatives because you can't get a loan from a lending institution?

Have you used most or all of your savings to pay bills?

Have you been through a recent divorce or death of a spouse, which hurt you financially?

Are you underinsured because you really can't afford auto, home, disability, or life insurance?

Do you and your spouse avoid talking about money, or do you frequently argue over money matters?

Are you depressed or worried about your financial situation?

Do you find yourself in the same "money rut" from year to year?

Would you be able to survive financially a change in job, short-term layoff, or pay cut?

Do you have to supplement your income with overtime or moonlighting just to get by?

Do you need a cosigner to qualify for a loan?

If you answered "yes" to any of these questions, it is a good idea to examine carefully why you said yes. For example, if you answered yes to the question "Have you used all or most of your savings to pay bills?" because you recently had unexpected large medical expenses, it may not indicate a long-term problem. If, however, you answered "yes" because you needed the money in your savings account to pay the minimum payments on your credit cards, you may indeed have a problem.

This quiz is not quantitative. In other words, if you answered "yes" to ten questions, it doesn't necessarily mean you are in more financial trouble than someone who answered "yes" to five questions. The point of this exercise is to be honest with yourself and to start looking at the reasons you're in the situation you're in and whether it would help you to get an objective opinion from a counselor.

Now that you have an idea of how much debt you are carrying, let's look at strategies to reduce it.

CHAPTER SEVEN

Low-Willpower Strategies for Reducing Debt

In the world of financial fitness, getting out of debt is perhaps the ultimate challenge—a marathon of money management requiring discipline, skill, and endurance. But just like getting in shape physically, the rewards—more money, less stress, and great financial habits—are tremendous.

If you don't owe a lot of money, you may want to go for the fast burn and just get rid of your bills as quickly as you can. But if you're like most people, and owe a bundle, you're going to have to dig your way out the slow and steady way. If you try to go at it too fast and too hard, you'll burn out long before the bills are retired.

Either way, you're going to have to face the facts: Getting out of debt means you're going to have to find money somewhere to pay what you owe. The key to creating a successful debt-elimination plan lies in the following pages. Some of the techniques and approaches described here may apply to you, others may not. Pick and choose those that make sense for you at this time and refer back to them from time to time as your situation changes.

Strategy #1: Figure Out How You Got Where You Are

You'll never be able to get out of debt until you understand how you got into debt in the first place. Sometimes it's truly something extraordinary that sends people's finances into a tailspin: unexpected medical bills, a new child with special needs, a messy divorce, or a failed business. But often it's more like the leak that never gets fixed—eventually those little drips of money turn into a waterfall that you can't control.

What is it that's really keeping you from getting out of debt? Are your finances so disorganized you can't keep on top of them? Are you forking over cash to the kids every time you turn around? Are you living in a house that's too expensive, or driving a set of wheels (or two or three) that cost a small fortune? Do you and your spouse have no clue how much the other is spending? Are you toiling in a job that doesn't pay enough? Be honest here! The truth will catch up with you sooner or later; you might as well 'fess up with yourself now.

The purpose of answering these questions is not to assign blame, point fingers, or rub your own nose in the sand. It is important because, as Steve Rhode of Myvesta.org says, the debt itself is rarely the problem. Chronic or excessive debt is usually the symptom of something else. Those "something else's" could be:

1. Self-esteem issues: a need to "keep up appearances" or shop to feel better.
2. Addiction: For some people spending money can create a "high" in the same way using drugs or alcohol does.
3. Underearning: staying in a low-paying job, or failing to get the skills or credentials to move up; may be tied in with self-esteem.
4. Money fights: One spouse or partner may be using or abusing money as a source of power in the relationship.
5. Gambling: not just in a casino, but with business "opportunities" or get-rich-quick schemes.
6. Denial: an unwillingness to face money facts head-on.
7. Unconscious Living: living only for today, leaving the future at risk.

All of these problems can be addressed, but only when they are recognized first.

Strategy #2: Mend the Holes in Your Pockets

How many times have you taken out $50 at the ATM machine, only to discover a day later that you've spent it all—but you don't remember where? Most people have a rough idea of how they spend most of their paycheck, on things like the mortgage or rent, the car payment, and other bills. But they lose track of where all the rest of the money goes.

To get a clear picture of where and how you use your money, you must write down *every* penny you spend. For the next month, that is exactly what you will do. I'll admit, this is a pretty tedious exercise. The first time I tried it, it took four separate attempts before I actually followed through for a whole month. I tried it again recently after a change in my financial status, and again, it took two months before I actually stayed with it for a month.

If you don't do anything else I recommend in this book, do this exercise. It's amazing what you'll learn. One woman in a seminar I was giving piped up and said she had just completed a month of tracking her spending. She discovered her family had spent almost $120 a month just on pizzas! Another counselor, Karen Varcoe, told me about a client who discovered that he was spending *$160 a week* in vending machines—mostly for sodas!

One of my colleagues thinks this exercise is "too much homework" and says he would never suggest someone bother with it. I disagree, mainly because I have found it so useful myself. I also learned that research by psychologists has shown that monitoring a behavior can be a very powerful tool for changing it. Simply writing down a behavior (overspending, for example) often brings about positive changes in that behavior. In other words, if you know you're going to have to put on paper the $3 you spent for coffee and snacks at the gas station, you might decide to hang on to your money instead!

There are several ways to keep track of your spending. If you have a computer at home, you can use a personal finance program like Quicken, which allows you to create charts and graphs that show you how you are using your money. Just be sure you enter every penny—not just what you spent with checks and credit cards.

If you don't have a computer or don't want to use it, you have a couple of other options. One is to get an accountant's notebook that has seven to ten columns across the top. Across these columns list your basic budget categories. For many people, these broad categories will be:

1. **Home:** rent or mortgage, utilities (phone, electric, heat), home maintenance costs, gardening, and upkeep
2. **Food:** food you eat at home or during work hours. Dining out in the evening should probably be included under "entertainment" or maybe "business."
3. **Transportation:** subway or bus fares, car payments, car insurance, taxes and tags, gasoline, parking, tolls, and maintenance
4. **Medical expenses:** doctor bills, dentist bills, prescription medications, eyeglasses, contact lenses and solutions, health club memberships
5. **Clothing and personal care:** all clothing purchases, including pantyhose, shoes, and jewelry; cosmetics, shampoo, toiletries, and haircuts
6. **Entertainment/Recreation:** movies, videotape rentals, sports fees, music lessons, dining out, vacations
7. **Loan payments:** credit cards, personal lines of credit, or other loans, except the mortgage and car loan
8. **Miscellaneous or other categories:** You can create your own categories, or just have a "catch-all" category for anything that doesn't fit above.

These eight basic categories should cover most expenses, but you may find there are other categories you want to add. Don't worry about getting too detailed, though. The idea is just to get a basic idea of your spending patterns.

Now, for the next month, keep track of every penny you spend. If you decide to record your expenses in an accountant's notebook, you may find it necessary to carry a tiny notebook in your wallet or purse so you can record purchases as you make them. Just don't forget to transfer those purchases to your accountant's notebook when you get home.

Another alternative is to turn your check register into a spending record. I personally find this much easier than trying to remember to write down everything I spent during the day. If you carry a checkbook or can throw one in your car, this is an easy way to keep tabs on your expenditures.

Take a blank checkbook register (you can probably get one from your bank free if you don't already have one), and on each page draw vertical lines as shown below:

		RECORD ALL CHARGES OR CREDITS THAT AFFECT YOUR ACCOUNT						
NUMBER	DATE	DESCRIPTION OF TRANSACTION	PAYMENT/DEBIT (-)	✓ T	FEE (IF ANY) (-)	DEPOSIT/CREDIT (+)	BALANCE $	
			$		$	$		

MAY		RECORD ALL CHARGES OR CREDITS THAT AFFECT YOUR ACCOUNT						
NUMBER	DATE TOTAL	FOOD	HOUSING	TRANS.	CLOTHES	PERS. CARE	MED.	REC.	BALANCE $ 300 00
153	0	300.⁰⁰	590⁰⁰	360.⁰⁰	120.⁰⁰	30.⁰⁰	50.⁰⁰	80.⁰⁰	

Instead of designing your own checkbook register, you can order one that's ready to go from the Montana State University Extension Service. For each checkbook register you order, send $1 to: Check Register, Extension Publications Office, Montana State University, Bozeman, MT 59717. I've used their check registers myself, and have found them very convenient. (They come with instructions.)

Next, decide on your spending categories. You can start with the ones listed above, or create your own. List one at the top of each column. Every time you write a check, charge a purchase, or buy something with cash, you will record it in your checkbook. This includes small purchases, like a cup of coffee or a pack of gum, as well as bills and major expenditures. Following is an example of how you can use your checkbook register to record purchases:

You will notice that for each entry, you will record as many as four figures. The first number you record, on the top half of the entry line, is the amount of the purchase. You write a minus sign in front of it, since you're subtracting it from the money you have available to spend. Right below that number, on the same entry line, is a number that indicates the total you have spent so far in that spending category.

MAY	RECORD ALL CHARGES OR CREDITS THAT AFFECT YOUR ACCOUNT								
NUMBER TOTAL	DATE	FOOD	HOUSING	TRANS.	CLOTHES	PERS. CARE	MED.	REC.	BALANCE $ 300 00
153	0	300.00	590.00	360.00	120.00	30.00	50.00	80.00	
511 K-MART	5/1					−9.06 20.94			9 06 290 94
DEPOSIT	5/11								1022 98 1313 92
CASH WITHDRAWAL	5/15								50 00 1263 92

In the far right balance column, two numbers may appear. On the top half of the balance column is the amount of the check, if you wrote a check for the purchase. On the bottom half of that same balance line is the amount left in your checking account.

Sometimes you will use cash or credit cards to buy things, and it is important to keep track of those as well. To do so, write "cash" where you would normally write the check number. Then, record the amount you spent under the appropriate category. (You may want to circle the purchase amount to indicate it was a cash purchase). *Do not,* however, subtract that amount from the balance column, since it is not affecting the balance of your checking account. If you simply take cash out of your account, list it as a cash withdrawal in your check register, and subtract the amount of the withdrawal from your total balance, but do *not* list the amount of the withdrawal under any specific spending category, since you will do that when you spend the cash.

Strategy #3: Develop a Written Spending Plan

Keeping detailed records of your spending for one month will help you see where you may be frittering away your money. It won't, however, provide you with all the information you need to develop a realistic spending plan. You may have quarterly tax or insurance payments, for example, that didn't show up in last month's spending.

To get a better idea of what's realistic for each spending category, pull out old check registers, receipts, and credit card statements from last year. Tax records can also be useful. Try to figure out approximately how much you spent monthly in each of your budget categories. Don't be judgmental here; simply total the amounts you spent. (It's likely you will find that some of your money just "disappeared." Don't worry about that money. Just document as much as you can.)

Now, the most difficult part: deciding how you will spend your money each month. Examine your past spending habits, and try to develop a plan that allows you to pay your bills and have some money left over for fun.

How much you choose to spend in each of your budget categories depends on what you need and how you choose to spend your money. But keep in mind that if any expense really seems out of whack or is eating up a big chunk of cash each month, it may need to be reduced. One of the most common traps is a huge car payment for an expensive new car. When you add on the insurance and gas and everything else it takes to maintain it, a car can end up keeping you from getting ahead.

Remember: The amounts you allot for each category *cannot* total more than your income for the month, or you are going to have to borrow to make up the difference! It's likely that, in the past, the amounts spent on each category *did* add up to more than your monthly income. That's how you got into debt.

It may be helpful to start at the top: First deduct from your total monthly spending allowance enough money to cover those bills you *must* pay. Next, allot money for essential purchases, including gas, insurance, and food. Then figure in discretionary spending that you don't want to sacrifice: music lessons for the kids, an evening out a couple of times a month, or health-club dues, for example. Divvy up what's left over among the remaining categories.

As you design your plan, take a careful look at how you spent your money over the past month to see if there are any areas where you can make some relatively painless changes. Most people are genuinely surprised to find out how much money they spend frivolously. For example:

- A cup of coffee every morning at 65 cents a day: over $162 a year.
- A soda at lunch at 50 cents a day: $125 a year.
- Renting two home videos a week at $3 each: $312 a year.
- Five magazine subscriptions at $15 each: $75 a year.
- Deli lunch purchased on workdays at $4 each: $1,040 a year.

Are there some areas where you can cut back? You will have to make some sacrifices and changes to get out of debt. The reward—real financial freedom from bills—is worth it.

Ronald Wall, Ph.D., Extension Specialist in Family Economics and Management for the Cooperative Extension Service at the University of Hawaii, says, "I've never seen a credit problem that was caused by a slight variation in credit costs. Usually the problems are due to major decisions regarding when and when not to use credit. Even more important are lessons regarding the prevention of credit problems by finding noncredit solutions to big and/or tight money problems. For example, selling the family Bronco or Blazer early on may stop a potentially serious credit problem from escalating."

Make the tough choices first. Then start looking at smaller changes that may free up extra money.

If you are especially frugal when figuring your spending allowances, you may find that the amounts you allocated to each category add up to less than your income. If so, you may want to add to the amount you put toward loan payments. The more you pay on your credit cards and loans each month, the faster you can pay them off.

Don't starve yourself. When you're dieting to lose weight, you won't be successful if you cut out every food you enjoy. The same thing is true of your debt diet: If you eliminate every luxury, your diet isn't going to last very long.

Make moderate, not drastic changes if you can afford to. If you have been eating lunch out every day, for example, resolve that three days a week you will bring your lunch, and then do it. Instead of giving up your morning cup of coffee, take a small, inexpensive coffee pot to work and brew your own. Keep your goal of becoming debt-free in the front of your mind, and soon those little things you "had to have" before your debt diet will become less and less important.

If you're developing a spending plan for your entire family, you have to consider their wants and needs as well. It's very important to give each member of the family an "allowance" (even if it's small) that they can spend as they choose. Then, give them the freedom to spend their allowance as they please, with no unreasonable criticism from you.

Before you embark on your new debt diet, you'll have to enlist the support of your family and close friends. If you usually eat lunch out with your coworkers, they may feel slighted when you start brown-bagging it and staying in. Likewise, if you're used to handing money over to the kids for everything they want, they may not understand why Mom and Dad are suddenly tightening the purse strings. Or if your spouse and you have different financial priorities, you could find yourself fighting constantly about money problems. Open and honest communication can help you work together to improve your financial situation.

You'll also have to be honest with your kids about your family finances and what you're trying to accomplish. Olivia Mellan, author of *Money Harmony: Resolving Money Conflicts in Your Life and Relationships* (Walker), tells the story of one man who had his entire paycheck cashed in $1 bills. He then went home and with the family counted out payments for all the bills. When his kids saw how few dollars were left over to spend, they got the picture.

Strategy #4: Keep Your Eye on the Prize

Everyone has goals that hinge on money. They want to add an addition to the house, or take a vacation, or put their children through college. For purposes of this book, your goal should be to get out of debt or at least reduce it to a specific, manageable level. Once you have accomplished that basic goal, you can use all the extra money you'll have each month to reach other financial goals.

If you try to accomplish too many goals at once (pay off credit cards, save for children's education, buy a new car), you'll probably find yourself reaching none of them. While your goal is to get out of debt, you can also set smaller, more immediate goals that you can celebrate as you reach them. Paying off one credit card is a good example. Or keeping track of your spending for one month is another.

In terms of getting out of debt, you're going to have to decide how little debt you want to carry. Some people don't mind if they have a car payment or student loan payments; they will be content if they can just pay off their credit cards. Others despise monthly bills and want to pay off all their loans except their mortgage. Still others don't want to owe anyone a penny.

You should definitely try to pay off your credit cards, especially the high-rate ones, your car loan (since you are financing a depreciating asset), and any other installment loans that aren't used for investment purposes. After working my way out of debt, my personal view is that the less debt you have, the better. Period. Even the supposed advantages of having a mortgage are overrated, despite the fact that you may be able to deduct some of the interest. (I talk more about prepaying mortgages in Chapter Thirteen.)

The lower your debt, the more money you'll have for whatever you want to spend it on, and the healthier you'll be financially.

Strategy #5: Create a Plan of Attack

A payback plan for your debts is where the rubber meets the road. Don't even consider trying to just blindly pay back your debt as you go along. You'll need a very clear plan, one that will show you how much you'll pay, and ultimately how much you'll save.

Create a list of all your bills, balances, minimum payments, and interest rates. With that information on hand, contact all your issuers to find out if you can lower your interest rates. Once you're as low as you can go, try the software at www.zilchworks.com to create a month-by-month repayment program for all your debts.

Be your own personal trainer and tailor your payback program to your own personal style. Although the biggest savings will come by getting rid of your most expensive debts first, that approach may not work best for you. Consider your options carefully, and choose the one you feel you can stick with:

Maximum Savings: With this plan, you pay just the minimums on all your debts—except the one that carries the highest interest rate. You throw as much money as possible toward that debt to get rid of it as quickly as you can. Once that balance is wiped out, you start on the next one.

This method—paying your highest-rate cards first—is going to save you the most time and money in the long run. Let me show you an example. Suppose you have the following bills:

Card	Balance	Interest Rate	Monthly Payment	Time/$$ Total Cost Pay Off
Department-store card:	$ 750	21%	$30	64 months $1,164.12
Furniture loan:	$ 900	19.8%	$36	70 months $1,381.17
Frequent flier bankcard:	$2,000	17%	$50	170 months $4,122.48
Credit union card:	$1,200	14%	$30	106 months $1,937.85
Total:	$4,850			170 months $8,605.62

Source: The Banker's Secret Credit Card Software (see the Resources section).

It will take you fourteen years and two months to pay off those bills and cost $3,755.62 in interest alone if you just made the minimum payments on each card each month. Now let's suppose you decide to put an extra $15 a month toward your payments ($15 total, not per card) and you pay that extra money on the highest-rate card first.

Under that scenario, you pay just the minimum due on all your loans except the one with the highest rate. Then, as soon as you pay off one bill, you'll immediately start writing a monthly check for the same amount to the loan or credit card with the next highest rate. For instance, if you pay $30 a month on your department-store card, once you pay it off you can start writing an extra monthly check for $30 to your bankcard with the higher interest rate. This will create a snowball effect as you start paying off more bills.

By prioritizing the bills I listed above and adding just $15 a month to the monthly payment, your total interest will be $1,500.18 and you'll pay them all off in three years and four months. That means you'll save $2,255.44 in interest and pay off your bills a decade sooner!

This method for paying off your bills is *very* powerful. With credit cards, you usually have a minimum payment that's based on a percentage of how much you owe. So when you make a payment, the next month's minimum payment is smaller. That stretches out your debt for years. When you instead start committing a fixed amount to paying off your debts, you beat the bank at its own game and speed up the time it will take you to pay off your balance—often dramatically.

There are two secrets to this method: First, commit a fixed amount toward your loan payments each month until they are *all* paid off. Say the first month your payments total $250, including the extra money you've decided to put toward paying them off. You want to pay a total of $250 every month until they are all paid off. If you have some extra money to throw at them one month, go for it. You'll just pay them off a little faster.

Second, stop charging! If you have to use a credit card for emergencies or whatever, keep one card separate and try to pay it off as soon as possible. If you start charging on the cards you're trying to pay off, you'll find yourself digging the hole deeper.

Quick Results: If you'd like to see some fast results, don't worry about the interest rates—you're better off just getting rid of a bill as soon as you can. Choose your smallest bill and go at it with a vengeance, putting all the money you can toward it until it is paid off. Then go on to the next smallest balance, and so on.

Of course, both of these approaches assume you'll do everything you can to stop taking on new debt. You simply can't shed debt if you keep charging.

Emergency Surgery: If your situation is so dire that you're falling behind, robbing Peter to pay Paul, make sure you read the next chapter, which addresses crisis situations.

Starting Over: Sometimes the debt load is so high that there is no other choice but to file for bankruptcy and start over. On the one hand, bankruptcy isn't the easy fresh start some attorneys would lead you to believe, but on the other hand, it is necessary for many people who are overwhelmed by debts. I talk more about bankruptcy in Chapter Nine.

Strategy #6: Stay Flexible but Focused

The key to sticking to your debt diet is to remain flexible. If you need a new suit for an important job interview but your clothing budget is used up, consider "borrowing" from your recreation budget. Just don't borrow from your loan payments budget. You don't want to get back into the habit of juggling bills again.

If you find that you set unrealistic spending limits in the beginning, revise your spending plan the next month. Don't be surprised if it takes several months of adjustment before your spending categories work realistically.

If you have money left over in one category at the end of the month, roll it over to the next month to create a cushion in case a large expense pops up later in that category. And if you do overspend a little (or a lot) one month, don't give up on the whole program. One piece of cake doesn't break a diet, and a few little slips shouldn't ruin your debt diet either.

For many of us, getting out of debt is a marathon, and sticking with it can be long and difficult. You're going to hit plateaus, and emergencies that challenge your plan will crop up. It's important that you find encouragement along the way. Is there a trusted friend or relative who can cheer you along? If you are married, are you and your spouse on the same page?

Some people find a support group like Debtor's Anonymous can help tremendously (www.debtorsanonymous.org). Working one-on-one with a Financial Recovery Counselor (www.financial recovery.com) can also be a worthwhile investment. Churches often sponsor Dave Ramsey's Financial Peace University (www. daveramsey.com), a great way for people to get support. Also contact your local cooperative extension office or a nonprofit counseling agency to find out if they offer classes on debt and money management.

Check out a few books from your library for encouragement and advice: *How to Get Out of Debt, Stay Out of Debt and Live Prosperously* by Jerrold Mundis, *Invest in Yourself: Six Secrets to a Rich Life* by Marc Eisenson, et al., *Get Out of Debt* by Steve Rhode and Mike Kidwell, and *Debt-Proof Living* by Mary Hunt are all good places to start.

The financial muscle you build while digging your way out of debt will serve you well. Although the training is tough, once the bills are paid off, you'll be in great shape to achieve your goals and build wealth.

Strategy #7: Tap Your Savings

You may have noticed I didn't mention putting money in a savings account as part of your spending plan. Most money managers insist clients set aside part of their income each month (10 percent is the usual goal) in a savings account. If you are truly serious about getting out of debt, however, putting every free penny toward your bills probably makes better financial sense than setting money aside in a low-interest savings account. Here's why:

Suppose, for example, you have $1,000 that you can keep in your savings account earning 5 percent interest (compounded monthly), or you can use it to pay off a 17.8 percent credit card. In one year, your savings account will earn $51.16 in interest. Assuming you're in a tax bracket of 28 percent, that account nets you about $36.84 in income after taxes.

In the meantime, you will pay $163.88 interest on your credit card that year. If you paid off the credit card, you would forego the $36.84 in net interest on the savings account, but would avoid paying the $163.88 in interest charges, for a total savings of $127.04. Worth it? For most people, yes.

You can get the most bang for your buck by using your money to pay off expensive credit cards or loans. Putting $100 toward your 17.8 percent card is the equivalent of getting a return of more than 24 percent on your money, assuming you are in a 28 percent tax bracket.

How does this work? To calculate the equivalent return at different tax brackets or interest rates, take the bracket and turn it into a percentage (e.g., 28 percent becomes .28), then subtract from 1 (i.e., $1 - .28 = .72$). Take the interest rate on the credit card and divide it by the number you just got in the last calculation (in this case .72) and you will end up with the equivalent return on your money.

For example, using the numbers in our example, the interest rate is 17.8 percent and you are in the 28 percent tax bracket; 17.8 divided by .72 = 24.72. That $163.88 in credit card interest I mentioned above would mean you'd have to earn $227.61 before taxes (in a 28 percent tax bracket) to pay for it.

If you are afraid to use your savings to pay bills because you consider your savings account your financial security, keep your now paid-off credit card for that purpose, or get a low-interest-rate card you can lock away as security in case of emergency. If your credit cards are charged to their limits, and you have no financial cushion, don't touch your savings account until you have paid down at least one of your cards.

If you have been a free spender all your life and have never had the discipline to save, you may want to consider starting a savings habit by putting a small amount, perhaps just $5 or $10 a paycheck, into a savings account. Make sure it is a savings account that is *not* hooked to an ATM card or your checking account, so you won't be able to touch it. Once your debts start getting paid off, you'll have a lot more money to allocate to a serious savings and investment plan.

When I paid off my own credit card debt, I was amazed by how much more money I had each month. I hadn't realized how much those bills were eating up my income. Within a year or so, I had disciplined myself to the point where I was able to save every other paycheck—without feeling like a miser.

Strategy #8: Boost Your Bottom Line

Chronic debtors are also often underearners, says Karen McCall, president of the Financial Recovery Institute (www.financial recovery.com). It's not unusual for people to sabotage their own chances for financial success. I recently researched and wrote an article for *Woman's Day* magazine on the topic of boosting your earning power. In the process, I spoke to nearly a dozen women who had increased their incomes, sometimes dramatically. A common thread among all the women I spoke with was the fact that the extra money they earned was almost secondary to the way they felt about themselves after they successfully pursued their goals. An excellent book on this topic is *Earn What You Deserve* by Jerrold Mundis.

While learning to earn more can go hand in hand with getting out of debt, it works only if you use the extra money you earn to improve your financial situation, rather than just to spend more. As you're getting out of debt, don't count on a big raise to take care of all your money problems. Ultimately, the hard work you do to learn to live on what you earn now will pay off in more ways than one. More money just means more money problems, if you don't know how to handle it.

Putting More Money in Your Pockets

There are lots of ways to increase your income. You can improve your salary at your current job, or in your current field. You can take on another job. If you have a family, you can put a nonworking spouse or child to work. You can increase the amount of money you take home from your current job by using smart tax strategies, or you can invest your money to make more money.

People have written whole books on showing people how to

increase income, start a side business, or cut taxes, and I can't possibly cover all the ins and outs right here. But I will try to stimulate your brain to start thinking of ways you can put more money in your pocket—or toward your monthly bills.

Your Current Job: What's holding you back from bringing home a bigger paycheck? Your education level? Your company's size or structure? The field you're in? Or could it be because you have trouble asking for what you deserve? Your job is to find out what the problem is and try to see what you can do about it.

Training and education usually offer some of the best pay-offs. The numbers show that the more education you have, the more money you're likely to make and the less likely you are to be unemployed. Lots of companies offer educational opportunities and will pay for you to improve your on-the-job skills. Consider local community college courses if your firm won't pay for additional training. You can often find inexpensive, practical courses aimed at business professionals. In addition to improving your worth to your company, you can also boost your self-esteem by mastering a new area or skill!

Moonlighting: Don't berate yourself for not working two or three jobs to make ends meet. If you already moonlight, don't feel guilty because you hate it or are burnt out and want to quit. Moonlighting is often counterproductive, because you feel so bad or tired after working two jobs that you end up spending all the money you make on things to make you feel better. I worked a second job at a retail store for several years and ended up blowing entire paychecks on clothes, jewelry, and makeup.

There is one case where moonlighting can make a lot of sense: if you use it as an opportunity to pursue something you really enjoy doing (or think you might enjoy doing). If you love to paint and you moonlight teaching art classes, you will be doing something you like, and it can be emotionally and psychologically, as well as financially, rewarding.

A few months of flipping hamburgers after work, on the other hand, will probably leave you exhausted and frustrated. Worse yet, you may be so resentful at having to work hard with little to show for it, that you'll probably start overspending again to make yourself feel better.

If you decide to take on a second job, don't look at it as a punishment for not having enough money. Sometimes you just gotta do what you gotta do. But if at all possible, try to choose something that will let you learn a new skill, profit from a hobby, or explore a potential new career. If you've always dreamed of owning a restaurant, for example, you could moonlight as a waiter. Don't just wait on tables, though. Treat it as a research project and ask a lot of questions. You may even find you hate that business—but isn't it better to find out, rather than torturing yourself with "if only" questions?

Your Ace in the Hole: If you've ever fantasized about being your own boss (and who hasn't at one time or another?), don't be scared off by all the statistics about business failures. One of the best ways to start a business is as a small side venture—what my friends and colleagues Marc Eisenson and Nancy Castleman call an "Ace in the Hole." Their philosophy is that a small side business gives you an excellent chance to try your hand at running a business without taking a lot of risk or putting up a lot of money. In their newsletter, *The Pocket Change Investor,* they offer advice on exactly how to start your own business inexpensively. See the Resources section for details on the newsletter.

Tightening the Belt

Author and investment advisor Michael Stolper says, "My wealthy clients became rich by saving their money, not by spending it." One smart, easy way to free up more money for paying debts is to take a look at how much you spend in each area of your plan and aim to shave a small percentage—5 percent or 10 percent, for example—from each category. Rather than trying to do it all at once, I suggest that each month you focus on just one category, then brainstorm and implement your cost-cutting ideas. The next month, move on to another area.

If you have a family, you can hold a contest to see who can come up with the best money-saving ideas. Offer rewards that cost very little or nothing—a trip to the beach, or a day of being "waited on" by the family, or cooking their favorite meal, for example.

Here are some ideas from some of the major categories to get you started:

Cutting Car Costs: Whether you drive a clunker that gets you to work and back, a wagon to haul the kids to tennis practice, or a sports car that always shines like a mirror, your auto represents a big investment—probably much bigger than you realize.

The American Institute for Economic Research (AIER) estimated in 1989 that the average cost of owning and operating a standard-sized automobile over the course of your driving lifetime is over $200,000. That's just for one auto. Take a family with two or three cars, and you can easily see why automobiles are an enormous financial investment.

There are a number of ways you can save money on transportation. You could:

- Trade down to a cheaper or more fuel efficient car.
- Do your own simple auto repairs.
- Shop for cheaper car insurance.
- Start carpooling to work several days a week.
- Check tire pressure to save gasoline.
- Don't pay more for a higher-grade gasoline than your car needs (a complete waste of money).

If your spending plan revealed that a large percentage of your monthly income is going to pay auto-related expenses, research ways to cut those costs. One place to start is AIER's book, *What Your Car Really Costs*. See the Resources section for more information.

Taking a Bite out of the Food Budget: For some people, the thought of clipping coupons and buying generic is more than they can stand. Would you become a smarter shopper, though, if it meant you could put as much as $1,000 into your family's coffers each year?

As you monitor your spending for a month, you'll probably find you're spending a lot for food. You'll probably also find that short stops at the convenience store for a gallon of milk end up costing you $20 by the time you add on little impulse purchases! In fact, some 66 percent of grocery purchases are impulse purchases.

Some of the best budgeters recommend these steps for cutting your grocery bill:

- Start making shopping lists and sticking to them.
- Cook more than you need for meals and freeze the leftovers for future meals when you're too tired or rushed to cook.
- Take your lunch to work.
- Compare prices on no-name brand items.
- Consult *Consumer Reports* for the names of best-buy products. Sometimes more expensive products are so much better than the cheaper versions that they save money in the long run.
- Keep a small notebook to compare prices at your favorite grocery stores. When you see something on sale, you can refer to your list to see if it's really a bargain!
- Stock up when items you usually buy are on sale. You'll get them sooner or later, and later may mean at full price.
- Keep a running list on the refrigerator so everyone can note what they need and so you won't run to the store every time you forget something.

Become a Savvy Shopper: Try shopping sales, flea markets, and discount stores. A few really good buys, and you may be hooked on bargain hunting.

There are a number of "penny pincher" newsletters with great ideas that can help you save a bundle. I'm partial to the newsletter published by Good Advice Press. Called *The Pocket Change Investor*, it's filled with helpful, practical advice on living better for less, making smart use of your money, and running a small side business. See the Resources section for ordering information.

Taxes: It's very important to make sure that your employer is not withholding too much from your paycheck. Tax refunds may be great, but you'd save a lot more by taking that extra money with your paycheck and using it to pay down your credit cards. If you are not sure that the proper amount of taxes is being withheld from your paycheck, see your company's personnel manager or accountant. Alternatively, the IRS publishes tax tables that (maybe) can help you figure it out on your own. Call the IRS at: 1-800-TAX-FORM for the appropriate publication.

Medical Bills: If you have excellent health and dental insurance, consider yourself lucky. As we've seen lately with all the debate about health-care reform, many people don't have adequate health insurance and are forced to put off routine medical care until they face expensive major illnesses.

For many people who aren't eligible for comprehensive health coverage, unexpected doctor bills can mean bankruptcy. Surprisingly, medical-care expenses are often negotiable and doctors' fees are not always etched in stone. If you have a health-insurance policy that requires you to pay part of your bills, find a doctor who is willing to accept what your insurance pays as payment in full. Your insurance company may be able to provide a list of doctors who accommodate those requests.

Decide What's Really Important: Admit it: How many times have you gone to the shopping mall because you didn't have anything better to do? Or blown $20 at the movies because you just needed a few hours of escape? If you're really unhappy in your job, your marriage, or whatever, it may very well affect your money life. Everyone knows someone who overspends because of some other problem in his or her life.

One of the best ways to cut spending is to find inexpensive things you really enjoy doing. Take some time right now to make a list of at least twenty-five things you can do for under a couple of dollars. Again, if you have a family, make a list together. If you can't think of at least twenty-five things you like to do, then start listing things you'd like to try. Put that list on the refrigerator and consult it every time you're tempted to wander the shopping mall.

Strategy #9: Consolidate

For many people a consolidation loan is the first strategy they seek when trying to get out of debt. I put it last on my list, however, because a debt consolidation loan is often seen as the entire solution to a debt problem, rather than one strategy of several.

Debt consolidation loans can be very attractive, since they typically offer lower monthly payments. In addition, most people find that making one monthly payment can give them a better sense of where their money is going, and how much they have left to pay off.

There are a number of ways to consolidate bills. Some methods, such as switching to cheaper credit cards, are easy. Other options are more complicated and require tough trade-offs. For example, if you're a homeowner, should a homeowner take a home equity loan to pay off credit card debts? How about borrowing against your retirement plan at work? Or should you tap the cash value of an insurance policy?

Before you rush out to obtain a debt consolidation loan or a home equity loan to lower your monthly payments, ask yourself three basic questions:

1. *Is getting out of debt the real reason I want a consolidation loan?* If you want to lower your monthly payments only to put more cash in your pocket, and you are unwilling to make any changes in your spending habits, you probably are *not* a good candidate for another loan.
2. *If I obtain a new loan, am I willing to stop buying on credit?* Again, the goal of a consolidation loan should be to help you *reduce* your overall debt level. If you are going to use another loan as a cash "windfall" to begin charging new purchases, forget it.
3. *Will the new loan reduce my overall debt load?* Make sure you carefully consider the cost of a consolidation loan. If the interest rate on the new loan is equal to or higher than the average rate on your current loans, if there are expensive fees or closing costs attached to the loan, or if the monthly payments on the new loan are so

low that they stretch the length of your debt by several years, look elsewhere for help.

Here's a perfect example of someone who should not get a consolidation loan: A young man called me once seeking information about debt consolidation loans. He had a moderate income and he lived at home, so his expenses were low. After he paid his bills (which included high monthly payments for an expensive car) and other necessities each month, he had about $150 left over for discretionary spending. I explained that $150 a month did not provide much in the way of a financial cushion, and that he should try to get out of debt, rather than take out still another loan. He insisted he did not have a debt problem, that he just needed lower monthly payments so he would have a little more money to spend each month.

If you still think you are a good candidate for a consolidation loan, here are some options for you to consider:

Use Plastic

In Chapter Three, I showed you how to save money by switching to a cheaper credit card. Switching from a high-rate credit card to a low-rate card can easily save the average person at least $100 or more a year in interest, and even more over the life of the loan. If you haven't already tried to negotiate a lower rate on your credit cards or consolidated your debt onto lower-rate cards, what are you waiting for?

Once you have consolidated to a few cards and carry a reasonable amount of credit card debt, you are likely to be approved for the loans you need.

Personal Loans

Most banks offer unsecured lines of credit of several thousand dollars. Interest rates on these loans tend to be slightly lower than average credit card rates, but higher than lower-rate credit cards. If you are interested in a personal loan, check with your own bank first, since some offer better terms and easier approval criteria for their regular customers. Just like with credit cards, bankers are unlikely to extend you a consolidation loan if they think you have too much credit already. People with lots of debt, or even lots of available credit, may be considered poor credit risks, since they could turn around and charge their cards up to their limits tomorrow.

Home Equity Loans

Home equity loans require borrowers to put up their homes as collateral or security for the loan. Securing the loan with your home helps reduce the interest rate you will pay on your loan, but if you fail to make your loan payments, you run the risk of losing your home to the lender.

There are two main ways to tap into your home's equity: through a second mortgage or a home equity line of credit. Both of those loans are types of home equity loans. A second mortgage is a loan for a fixed amount. As with other installment loans, you are given the entire amount of the loan at once, and pay it back in regular monthly payments. With a home equity line of credit (HELOC), you are approved for a loan of a certain amount, and then can borrow up to your "credit limit." You can think of an HELOC as something like a credit card, since you are free to borrow as needed and your payments will be based on the amount you have actually borrowed.

Because home equity loans offer valuable tax advantages, they can be an attractive device for consolidating your debts. In most cases, you can deduct home equity loan interest on loans up to the value of your home (but not on any portion of a loan that exceeds your home's value). This only applies if you itemize on your taxes, however.

Here's an example of how a home equity loan can help. Suppose you are paying off a credit card debt of $5,000 at 19.8 percent interest. Your first year's interest would be $847—and none of that interest expense would be tax deductible. However, using the proceeds of a home equity loan to pay off this debt would offer you two advantages: 1. You could probably get the home equity loan at a much lower interest rate (I'll use an example of 10 percent), and 2. The interest you pay would very likely be tax deductible. In the first year, tax deductions on a $5,000, five-year loan at 10 percent interest would amount to a savings of $129.69*, while the reduced interest rate would save you $384.61.

Most lenders offer home equity loans equal to anywhere from 50 to 80 percent of a home's value, minus the first mortgage. Suppose, for instance, your house is now worth $125,000, and you still owe $45,000 on your first mortgage. You would usually be eligible for a home equity loan of between $17,500 and $55,000.

Some subprime lenders offer loans totaling 100 percent to 125 percent of the value of your home. These can be particularly dangerous if you need to sell your home or if home values stagnate. Being "upside down" and owing more than your home is worth puts you in a very tenuous financial position should anything go wrong.

Don't take the decision to get a home equity loan lightly, especially if you are doing it to consolidate debt. Remember that by doing so you are trading unsecured debt for secured debt. If you should run into financial problems—even temporary ones—it's a whole lot easier to put off a credit card company for a few months than it is to put off the mortgage company.

Before you put your home on the line, ask these questions:

1. **What is the loan's interest rate?** Home equity loans are often available at interest rates below other consumer loans. This makes them a good source for refinancing expensive, nondeductible consumer loans. Most home equity lines of credit carry variable interest rates, which means the interest rate will change as rates in the economy change. Higher interest rates mean higher payments, so it is very important to take into account whether you will be able to afford your payments when interest rates go up.

    Some loans feature "interest only" payments. Attractive because the payments are so low, these loans can be very dangerous, since you are not paying down the principal balance of the loan. Interest-only home equity loans are best used to tide you over in tough eco-

*This is a hypothetical example. Be sure to check with your tax advisor to determine how much you can save.

nomic times when those low payments are the only way to keep you out of a serious financial crisis or bankruptcy.

Watch out, too, for "teaser rates"—interest rates that are offered for an introductory period only. These are commonly used to lure consumers into the bank for a hard sell on a loan that can end up costing a lot more than advertised. Shop for interest rates by comparing the APR (Annual Percentage Rate).

2. **What are the fees?** Fees and closing costs on home equity loans can range from nothing to thousands of dollars. Closing costs may include an appraisal fee, a recording fee, title insurance, and a title search. Be sure to ask for a full disclosure of all fees before you sign on the dotted line.

A "loan origination fee" may be charged up front. This fee is often one "point"—and a "point" is 1 percent of the loan amount. If, for example, your lender charges one point as a loan origination fee, and you are taking out a home equity loan of $10,000, you will pay $100 for this fee. This fee usually covers the cost of preparing loan documents, packaging the loan, and other loan processing services.

3. **Is the interest tax deductible?** Generally, you can deduct the interest on home equity loans to a maximum of $100,000.

Suppose the current market value of your home is $200,000. Your outstanding mortgage is $120,000. The lender approves a home equity loan of $40,000 (80 percent of the home's value, minus the first mortgage). The difference between the market value of your home and the current mortgage ($200,000 minus $120,000) is $80,000. You could deduct interest on a home equity loan of up to $80,000 of home equity debt and still deduct the interest. Therefore, the interest on your $40,000 loan in most cases would be completely deductible.

If you are using your home equity loan to pay for educational or medical expenses, interest payments may be fully tax deductible regardless of the amount. Since the tax laws are constantly changing, be sure to check with your tax advisor before applying for a home equity loan to make sure you are aware of all the rules regarding deductibility.

If you take out a home equity loan to pay off your credit cards, be very careful. If you don't change your spending habits, you're likely to treat the home equity loan as extra income, and run up new balances on your credit cards. For that reason, you should cut up, close out, and send back your credit cards. You may even want to limit yourself to a travel and entertainment card like American Express, which you must pay in full each month. Do not take out a home equity loan that offers access by credit card. That's only asking for trouble!

A home equity loan may or may not appear on your credit report, depending on whether the lender chooses to report it. (If you don't pay on time, of course, the delinquency *will* likely be reported to at least one of the major credit bureaus.) If your home equity loan does appear on your credit record, beware: A large available line of credit, even if you don't tap all of it, may make other lenders shy away from granting you additional credit. That means your applications for other credit could be turned down simply because you have a huge line of credit available.

Life Insurance Policies

If you have a life insurance policy that offers cash benefits, you can borrow against it, up to the cash value in the policy. Interest rates, spelled out in the policy, are usually quite low. These loans are extremely flexible. You don't have to pay them back within a certain time period. In fact, you don't have to pay them back at all. The catch is, if you die before you have paid back the loan, the amount you owe will be subtracted from the total benefits before proceeds are given to your heirs. Borrowing against your life insurance policy may very well defeat the purpose of providing security for your family. If so, think twice before using one of these loans.

Retirement Plan Loans

You can usually borrow against your 401(k), 403(b), or company profit-sharing retirement plan. Loans are typically limited to 50 percent of the assets in your plan, up to a maximum of $50,000. Some companies also cap the total amount employees can borrow at a certain percentage of their salary. Interest rates on these loans are usually quite attractive. And while interest payments on 401(k) loans are generally not tax-deductible, total payments (including the interest) do go back into your 401(k), so it's not as painful as paying a bank.

Unless you use your 401(k) loan to buy your home, it must be paid back in full within five years. If you fail to make the deadline, the IRS will hit you with income taxes on the total amount of the loan, along with a penalty of 10 percent, if you are under the age of 59½. In addition, when you leave your company, you will probably be required to fork over the balance you owe immediately, or within a month or two. Again, if you can't make the deadline, you will be charged taxes on the borrowed amount and a 10 percent penalty.

The other big drawback is the interest or money you may forfeit in the long run by taking your retirement dollars out of higher-earning investments. When you borrow against these types of accounts, the interest you'll earn on your retirement plan is zero. Although you pay interest to yourself as you pay back the loan, that's not the same as earning a return from someone else by investing your money. A retirement loan taken out during a bull market can cost you thousands of dollars in retirement savings; taken out when the market drops or stays stagnant and you may come out ahead!

The terms of 401(k) loans vary widely among companies that offer them, so be sure you understand all the conditions of the loan before you borrow. Then treat this loan as seriously as any other—after all, this is your retirement security you are borrowing against.

Loans from Relatives

Borrowing money from relatives can be a wonderful solution to your problem—or a disaster. You can often borrow money from a relative at an interest rate that's far lower than what you can get from a bank. The interest rate you offer to pay your relative on the loan will typically be higher than she could earn by parking her money in a bank account or conservative investment, so she will benefit as well. Best of all, you don't have to pass any credit checks.

If you and a relative do decide to strike a deal, be certain she understands your financial situation. You should be up front about your debt load and, if possible, sign a contract agreeing not only to the terms of the loan, but also to rid yourself of all other debt until the loan is paid. Be businesslike about the loan. If you are not, you are likely to fall into the trap of not taking the obligation seriously and might be tempted to continue to take out other cards and continue to buy on credit.

If your relative generously decides to cancel the loan later, be careful. The IRS considers "forgiveness of a debt" taxable income, and you may have to pay taxes on that amount. Be sure to talk to an accountant.

Brokerage (Margin) Loans

If you hold stocks or bonds, you can borrow against them and use the money either to buy more securities, or for any purpose you choose. Interest rates on margin loans are usually a couple of points above the prime rate. For stocks, you can borrow as much as 50 percent of the market value of the security. That percentage is mandated by law, so if the value of your securities drop, your broker will demand repayment of any amount that would put you over the 50 percent limit.

Say, for example, you have stock worth $10,000 and you borrow against 50 percent of its value, or $5,000. If the value of your stock drops to $2,000, you will have to pay back $4,000 immediately, since $1,000 is the most you can borrow against $2,000 worth of stock. Margin loans are tricky and should really be used only by experienced investors.

Loans to Avoid

Pawnbrokers

When you pawn something, you turn it over to a pawnbroker in exchange for a short-term loan on a small percentage of the value. If you can't pay back the loan in time, the pawnbroker tries to sell it. If the pawnbroker sells your item for more than the loan amount, you are supposed to get the difference. The interest rates pawnshops charge are usually very high, and the terms are not very good. It's best to stay away from these types of loans altogether.

Debt Consolidation Firms and Finance Companies

"Need money? Loans: quick approval, no credit check."
"Too many bills? Cut your monthly payments in half!"
Ads like these are tempting if you're in a credit crunch. After all, you may reason, if I could just reduce my monthly payments, I could get ahead. Finance companies can be a dangerous source of loans for two reasons:

1. They often put their clients deeper into debt.
2. They can stigmatize the borrower as a poor credit risk.

There are two types of debt consolidation firms: finance companies and bill-paying services (although these names are sometimes used interchangeably). A finance company extends you a loan so you can pay off your individual bills and owe just one creditor—the finance company. A bill-paying service also pays your monthly bills, but doesn't pay off your original bills. Let's look at each:

Finance Companies will often lend money to customers who can't get debt consolidation loans from a bank or credit union because they are too far in debt. Finance companies can afford to take risks on these customers because they charge outrageously high interest rates—as high as 25 percent or more. In addition, they may charge application fees or other additional fees. They also offer very low monthly payments, which means a customer who makes the minimum payment each month will end up paying a bundle in finance charges over a long, long period of time.

This is precisely why finance companies are so dangerous. Because the payments are so low, customers believe they are getting ahead, and may be tempted to take on additional credit obligations through credit cards or other loans. The debt spiral just continues. In addition, the total amount you owe grows, often significantly, because of the loan's high interest rate. Debt consolidation loans are illegal in most states.

More importantly, finance companies can be considered negative references on credit reports. Because many people who borrow through finance companies are not able to qualify elsewhere, credit card issuers and bankers look upon someone with a finance company loan as a poor credit risk—even if all the payments were made on time.

Some finance companies advertise as if they are offering debt consolidation loans, but they are actually offering home equity loans. If you're going to take on a home equity loan, it's best to do so through a reputable financial institution, like a bank or credit union.

Bill-Paying Services can be even more dangerous than finance companies. Their advertisements make them sound like debt consolidation firms, but they're not. Bill-paying services, however, are just what their name says they are. They pay your bills each month, but they don't refinance them and they don't pay your loans off for you.

With a bill-paying service, the customer writes one monthly check to the firm, and the firm writes checks to each creditor. In addition, the customer must pay an annual and/or monthly fee to the bill-paying service. This fee could easily amount to 10 percent of your monthly bills.

It's easy to see how bill-paying services often simply add to a borrower's total debt. Worse yet, many of these firms are not regulated, and some have failed to make customers' payments on time, or have folded, leaving customers none the wiser—until collection agencies start calling.

In some states, for-profit bill-paying services are highly regulated or even illegal. Your state attorney general's office can give you more information about laws in your state.

Check-Cashing Outlets and Payday Lenders

It's Monday, and you're already short on cash, with urgent bills to pay. How will you make it through to payday on Friday? Thousands of consumers who find themselves in that situation are turning to "payday loans" to tide them over until they get their paychecks. But they're paying a very expensive price—as much as 1820 percent!

Payday loans are offered through check-cashing outlets, which can be found now in every urban area, as well as in smaller towns. This industry has grown tremendously over the past five years, racking up billions of dollars in transactions. Many of these firms even promise money over the Internet, offering to wire it into consumers' accounts overnight.

There are a couple of ways these services work. One is to simply cash checks for consumers, for a fee. Consumers who don't have a bank account are most likely to use a check-cashing service for that purpose.

When the nonprofit Consumer Federation of America (CFA) surveyed check-cashing outlets, they found fees ranging from 1 percent to 6 percent, with an average of 2.34 percent, to cash a payroll check. (That's about $10 to cash a $400 check.) Cashing a personal check at one of these outlets costs an average fee of 9.36 percent, although they ranged from as low as 1.85 percent to as high as 16 percent. (Again, on a $400 check, that average fee would be about $37.)

More expensive and dangerous than simply cashing a check at one of these places is taking a loan from one. Here's how these payday loans work: You write a personal check to one of these neighborhood check-cashing services for $150 and get, say, $125 in cash on the spot. The check-cashing company agrees to hold the check you wrote until Friday, when you get paid. At that time, you either let the company cash your personal check, you bring in cash to pay the $125 you owe, or you let the company roll it over to a new loan for the next payday and pay a new fee. While payday loans are available to consumers with bad credit, or no credit, they do typically require a checking account in good standing.

When you need cash in a hurry, the fees these places charge may seem relatively minor, but they carry unbelievably high effective interest rates. In CFA's 1997 survey of check-cashing outlets, they found effective interest rates for seven-day loans as high as 1820 percent! In many cases, these companies aren't regulated, or interest rate ceilings are ineffective. There are more than a dozen states, however, that do ban payday loans or cap their costs.

Auto Equity Scams

If your car payments are proving to be more than you can handle, but you can't sell your car because it is not worth the amount you still owe on the loan, what can you do? Some people, desperate to avoid a repossession, turn to auto equity promoters. These firms often advertise in the classified sections of newspapers, offering to "assume" loans for people who can't make their payments. They also frequently target buyers—customers who don't qualify for auto financing with regular lenders.

Here's how they operate: You can't make your payments so you "sell" to the auto equity firm. The auto equity firm turns around and "sells" or "leases" the car to someone else. You may think your responsibility for the loan is over, but in many cases it's not.

The problem is that these contracts usually do not release the consumer from his contract with the lender. The auto equity firm will often require the new purchaser to make payments directly to the lender with a certified check or make payments to the auto equity firm, which in turn will make payments to the original lender.

At no time is the original lender notified that this arrangement has taken place, because in many cases it is illegal. Most auto loan contracts don't allow a consumer to sell a vehicle without notifying the lender, much less allow someone else to assume or sublease it. After all, the lender has to protect its interest in the collateral—the car—until the loan is paid in full.

Scams of this type sometimes take on unbelievable proportions. One consumer who fell victim to this scam, for instance, didn't know that the consumer who "assumed" his loan had not bought his car until much later, when he received notices of unpaid traffic tickets on his old car. It turned out the "new owner" was still driving the car with the previous owner's license plates!

I had another friend who leased her car this way. One night she received a call from the police. Her car had been found in another state with guns in the trunk.

In other cases, auto equity firms fail to pay the original lenders. They simply take the money and run. It is important to realize that if the person who is leasing the car doesn't make timely payments, you—the original owner—will be responsible to the lender for payments.

If you are considering working with an auto equity firm, check with your state motor vehicle department to determine whether this type of firm is even legal in your state. Also check with your state or local consumer protection agency and local Better Business Bureau to find out if the company has a good track record. Whatever you do, make sure to contact your lender to find out if your contract permits someone else to take over your car loan.

Stick with It

Your debt problem will not last forever, but it also will not be resolved overnight. On average, it takes someone with a serious debt problem two to six years to pay off their loans. Don't give up! While you are working your way out of debt, try to keep a sound perspective and a sense of humor. The discipline and money-management principles you are learning now will benefit you for the rest of your life.

CHAPTER EIGHT

Deep in Debt? How to Survive a Credit Crisis

The bills are piling up, but your checking account is already overdrawn. Your clunker just breathed its last breath on the highway, and the garage wants $50 (that you don't have) to tow it to the dump. Your friendly banker is calling to find out why you haven't paid your MasterCard bill in two months. *What do you do?*

The first thing you must do, before you do anything else, is to decide you will take responsibility for your debt. That may not be an easy thing to acknowledge, but as long as you feel your debt is out of your control, you'll never get rid of it. Decide right now that you, and only you, can take responsibility for your debt. Realize that whatever the cause of your situation, finding a solution is up to you . . . *no matter how difficult or impossible that may seem.*

You're going to have to find the money to pay off your debt. Don't count on an inheritance, lottery ticket, or debt consolidation loan to erase your bills. Instead, take a good, hard look at what's going in and out to find out where you can make changes.

If you have addiction or mental health problems, you must address them first before you can realistically expect to be able to control your debt. Don't be quick to brush off the idea that you may need help that does not seem directly financial. In 2001, Myvesta.org conducted a survey that found that 49.3 percent of people with debt problems can be classified as depressed; and of those, 39.7 percent report symptoms of severe depression. In comparison, studies have shown that about 9.5 percent of the general population is clinically depressed. If you suspect that you suffer from anxiety, compulsive spending, or depression, get help for it first. Myvesta.org can provide help or referrals, or you can also talk with your physician.

If you do not have those other issues to deal with, or if you are getting help with them, you have some practical work to do. Most importantly you need to understand that you can control two things: how much you spend, and perhaps to a greater extent than you realize, how much you earn.

Step #1: Find Out How Bad the Problem Really Is. If your bills total $1,000 a month, but your income is only $950 a month, you've got a serious problem and you need to do something about it sooner or later. If you haven't done so already, go through the exercises in Chapter Seven and figure out where you stand financially.

If you don't feel as though you can face it alone, ask a trusted friend to sit down for a few hours and help you figure out your finances. A relative may also be able to help—but only if he or she can be supportive without telling you what you *should* do!

Step #2: Order Your Credit Report. If you haven't seen your credit report lately, get a copy immediately. One of the key steps to weathering a financial crisis is knowing how it will affect your credit report and your ability to get credit in the future. Refer to Chapter Two for more information on credit reports if you don't know how to order, read, or understand them.

Step #3: Figure Out if You Can Pay. Next, write down all your bills, their minimum monthly payments, due dates, and your income for the next few months. Based on the spending plan you developed in Chapter Seven, determine if you can make the minimum required payments (and have enough money to live on) for that period of time. If not, go to Step 4.

If you can make all your minimum payments, then you're in the clear—at least for the time being. You will have to watch your spending very carefully, but you should be able to get through this crisis without too much long-term damage to your credit rating or nerves. Skip to Step 9.

Don't forget to review your resources. Can you borrow against your house or your retirement plan at work? Do you have a relative who can help you out until this crisis is over? Are there things you can cut back on or give up for the time being? Again, refer to Chapter Seven for ideas.

Step #4: Get Professional Help. If you can't meet at least your minimum payments, you may need help from an organization such as a nonprofit credit counseling agency like Myvesta.org, which specializes in helping people in financial crisis, or an organization like the Financial Recovery Institute. See the section on Credit and Financial Counseling later in this chapter.

If your "outgo" is much larger than your income, and things look really bleak, consider bankruptcy. Bankruptcy is a serious step and not one I recommend lightly, but it can be a legitimate option for those who really need a fresh start. After you've finished this chapter, read the next chapter to decide if bankruptcy is an option you want to explore.

Step #5: Set Your Priorities. In a financial crunch, some bills must be paid immediately, while others may wait. For some bills, smaller payments may satisfy the creditor until you get back on your feet. (I am assuming here that you want to try to pay all your bills and don't want to sell the house or the car or any other asset that is secured by a loan.) Here are some guidelines for juggling your bills:

Bankcards: Major credit cards are valuable references on your credit report. If you are worried about keeping your credit rating intact, try to make sure they are paid on time. For the short term, don't worry about making more than the minimum monthly payment. That's all you need to pay to keep your credit record clean.

If you can't make at least your minimum payments, watch out for stiff late fees. Some issuers will raise interest rates if you are late with one or more payments, and may also raise your interest rate substantially if you are late with a payment. I've even encountered issuers who will raise your interest rate if you are late on *other* bills listed on your credit report. If you can't make at least your minimum payments, read Step #7.

Department-Store Cards that appear on your credit record: Since balances on department-store cards are often fairly low, you can probably fit the minimum payments for these into your budget. If not, most department-store card issuers will be willing to accept lower payments for a few months.

Mortgage: Your mortgage may or may not appear on your credit report each month, but payment information *will* in most cases be reported to the bureaus if you become ninety days or more late on your payments. In addition, mortgages tend to carry hefty fees for late payments, and if you miss two or more payments your lender may initiate foreclosure proceedings. Your mortgage is an important bill—try to pay it first. If you can't, refer to the section on mortgages later in this chapter.

Car Loans: Your car loan may or may not appear on your credit record, but either way you don't want to get behind in your car loan, because in some states your car can be repossessed after you've missed only one payment. If your car is worth more than you currently owe on it, you may be able to refinance your loan with lower monthly payments. If not, your lender may agree to a temporary schedule of reduced payments.

Most of the major auto financing companies (American Honda Finance Corp., Ford Motor Credit Company, and General Motors Acceptance Corp., for example) will allow a borrower with a good payment history and a reasonable repayment plan either to skip a few months' payments or refinance the loan. If you skip payments, you'll be charged a fee and the payments will be added to the end of the loan. Before you call your lender, be sure you have a realistic plan for getting back on your feet.

Child Support: Paying child support is not only the "right" thing to do; it's important as far as maintaining your credit history is concerned. By law, credit bureaus must report any information received about overdue child support, as long as it is verified by the proper agency and is not more than seven years old. Child-support payments that are late by any amount may be reported by a state child-support enforcement agency if it so chooses. A number of states are doing so.

Also, if you don't pay your child support, you may find yourself the target of one of the increasing number of programs designed to crack down on what are usually called "deadbeat dads" (although there are a few deadbeat moms, too). If you don't pay your child support, you could find your tax refund intercepted, your wages garnisheed, a lien placed on your property, your driver's license suspended, or your picture may even be advertised on a "Most Wanted" list!

If you really can't pay your child support because of a change in your financial circumstances, you'll have to go to court to see if you can get your future payments reduced.

Utilities: Obviously, you do not want your electricity or phone service cut off. Utility companies, however, may be willing to work out a modified payment schedule for a short period of time. Utilities generally don't show up on credit reports, so you probably don't have to worry about damaging your credit record if you can't pay on time. If you do pay late, you may find that in the future you will be required to put up larger security deposits for services.

Taxes: Falling behind on your taxes may create numerous problems, including penalties, interest, or damage to your credit report if the IRS files a tax lien against your property. The IRS can be tough on delinquent taxpayers. Unlike creditors or debt collectors, it doesn't have to take you to court before it garnishees your wages or seizes your bank accounts to pay past-due taxes.

If you do not have the money to pay your taxes, don't put off filing your returns. There are separate penalties for filing late and for paying late. By filing you may at least be able to avoid the former. If you can't pay what you owe, you may want to consider charging the balances to a credit card, borrowing the money from friends or family, or requesting a repayment plan with the IRS. To request a repayment plan, fill out the appropriate form (see www.irs.gov) or suggest your own payment plan with your return. If it's reasonable, you probably won't have much trouble getting it approved. Just make sure you can stick with the plan you propose!

If you can't make even reasonable payments, or you owe a very large amount, you may want to talk with the IRS about an "offer in compromise," which lets you settle for less than the total you owe. A tax accountant may be of help in this type of situation. Two other useful resources are *How to Deal with the IRS if You Can't Pay Your Taxes* at Myvesta.org and the book *Stand Up to the IRS* by attorney Frederick W. Daily.

Medical Bills: Most medical bills are not reported to credit bureaus until they are sent to collections. You can very likely work out a modified payment schedule with the doctor or hospital. Just be sure to confirm any agreements in writing and ask for confirmation that smaller payments will not harm your credit rating.

Also be sure to check your medical bills carefully to make sure you weren't overcharged for anything. It happens all the time. (It's happened to me.) There's no reason to pay for services you didn't receive.

There are companies that specialize in reviewing medical bills to see if you have been overcharged. Their fee is often a percentage of the amount they recover for you. If you have been involved in a lengthy or chronic illness, working with one of these companies may be a helpful resource.

Gasoline Cards: Most gasoline accounts are not reported to credit card companies until you are behind ninety days or more. Avoid pulling out your gasoline cards to charge gas during a credit crisis, however, since you may spend more than you would if you were paying cash.

Student Loans: Delinquent student loans can be one of the biggest credit nightmares you'll ever encounter. Dramatic increases in the cost of higher education coupled with federal loan guarantees that make it easy for students to borrow large amounts of money they may never be able to pay back meant that many adults today are struggling to make student loan payments for decades—if not longer. I've spoken to teachers, for example, with more than $100,000 in student loan debt and no hope of paying it back in their chosen profession.

Because of massive defaults on student loans in the 1980s, Congress cracked down. Student loans now are very difficult (if not impossible) to discharge in bankruptcy. There is no statute of limitations for collecting student loan debts, so they can haunt you all the way into retirement. Collection costs may be as high as 45 percent—causing an already burdensome loan to become even more expensive.

If you are having trouble paying back your student loans, you may have several options for dealing with them, none of which (except cancellation) are ideal because they just put off the inevitable. In a crisis situation, however, they are better than falling behind and having your loan placed in collections.

Deferment: Federal student loans may be deferred if you are having financial difficulties. If your loan is deferred, you will not be required to make any payments during the deferment period, and no interest will accrue during the deferment period.

You cannot qualify for deferment once your student loan is in default—so *don't wait* to apply if you think you are going to have difficulties making your scheduled payments. And be sure to make the regular payments until your request is approved.

Forbearance is also a possibility for borrowers who want to pay their student loans but can't because of financial problems. If you are granted a forbearance, your payments are decreased or postponed until you are back on your feet. The drawback is that interest continues to accrue on the loan during the forbearance period.

Some student loans can actually be canceled if, for example, you are a full-time teacher in certain areas designated as teacher shortage areas or in a designated school serving low-income families, or if you are a full-time nurse or medical technician.

For more information on deferment, cancellation, and forbearance for student loans, get a free copy of *The Student Guide*, published by the Department of Education, by calling 1-800-433-3243.

Two excellent resources are *Take Control of Your Student Loans* by Robin Leonard (Nolo.com) and *The Guerrilla Guide to Mastering Student Loan Debt* by Anne Stockwell. In addition, Myvesta.org may also be able to help settle delinquent or disputed student loan debts. See the Resources section. You may also want to get help from the Department of Education, which offers an ombudsman service for people with student loan problems (www.ombudsman.ed.gov, or call 1-877-557-2575).

Small Bills: Set aside small bills, such as bills for magazine subscriptions, book clubs, or local accounts, but be sure to contact the creditor if you think the account will be turned over to collections.

All Bills: Try not to put off any bill for ninety days or more. Some creditors write accounts off as "profit-and-loss" accounts or "charge-offs" once they are ninety days or more delinquent. A profit-and-loss mark on your credit file is a very negative mark, and if you can avoid it, do.

Try to send something—even if it is just a $5 or $10 payment—to each of your creditors to show that you are trying to pay off your debt. If you completely ignore a creditor, it is likely that the account will be written off or sent to collections. Making small payments will at least signal your creditors that you are trying to get caught up. Don't send payments to all creditors, however, if it means you will fall behind on important bills like your mortgage or car loan.

Please keep in mind that sending a smaller payment does not prevent a lender from charging off the account. If you do not make your required monthly payment, the lender may charge off the account. See Step #7 for advice about talking with your creditors.

Step #6: Decide How Much You Can Pay. Keeping these priorities in mind, figure out how much money you can afford to give to creditors each month, and prorate it according to the payments owed each creditor. Here's an example:

Bill	Monthly Payment	How Much You Can Pay
MasterCard	$40	$30
Car payment	$130	$130
House payment	$650	$650
Student loan	$75	$0 (officially deferred)
Doctor's office	$50	$10
Totals:	$945	$820

Step #7: Contact Your Creditors. Nine out of ten creditors will negotiate new repayment schedules with consumers who are having trouble paying their bills. Don't wait until you receive collection calls or dunning letters to contact your creditors. Once you've decided how much you can pay, and how long it will take you to get back to your regular payment schedule, pick up the phone and contact your creditors. If you are scared to call them, ask someone to sit with you while you dial the phone. It's easy to procrastinate on this, but the longer you wait, the less obliging the creditor is likely to be.

Call the creditor, briefly and calmly explain the situation, and propose your modified payment plan. For instance, you may offer to pay 75 percent of your normal payment for four months, and then resume paying the entire amount. *Make sure you keep a note of who you talked with, the date and time, and what was agreed.*

Don't expect your request to be accommodated graciously. But if a customer-service representative is really uncooperative or nasty, calmly ask to speak to someone who can help you. If the conversation gets too heated or upsetting, tell them you'll call back later, hang up, and call again after you've had a chance to calm down, this time asking for a supervisor.

Some lenders may try to pressure you into paying more than you can really afford, but don't give in. It doesn't do them—or you—any good to make agreements you can't possibly live up to. It's also not a good idea to use your credit cards to pay another creditor, since you're really just rearranging the problem, not addressing it.

It is extremely important to send a letter restating your agreement to whomever you spoke. In fact, it is a good idea to send that letter via certified mail, return receipt requested, so you have proof it was received. I have worked with several people who made new payment agreements with creditors, stuck to those new payment schedules, but suddenly started receiving collection calls demanding full payment because the message didn't get passed on to the "other department."

Having said all that, some creditors will not work out payments with consumers directly. Instead, they expect you to go through a nonprofit counseling agency. For some people, working through a counseling agency may be preferable anyway—unless your problem is truly short-term and you know it will be resolved soon.

Another warning: Some creditors will agree to accept lower payments, but then will consider you "late" because you didn't pay the full amount. As a result they may charge late fees, raise the interest rate, and/or report you as delinquent to the credit reporting agencies. You must insist, as part of your arrangement, that they not take any of those actions. Ideally, you want to make sure you have that in writing, or at least include that understanding in the confirmation letter you send them.

Step #8: Live Up to Your Agreement. If a creditor has agreed to accept lower payments, make every effort to keep up with those new amounts. If you can't for some reason (you are laid off longer than expected, for example, or your illness is prolonged), call the lender at the first sign of trouble. No matter how torturous it may seem, it is really important to keep in touch with your creditors throughout this time.

Step #9: Stop Spending. Cut your expenses to the bare bones and start carefully evaluating every single purchase you make. As obvious as this sounds, some people don't change their habits even when their personal finances hit rock bottom.

Dr. Ronald Wall, the financial counselor I quoted in the last chapter, sees this behavior in some of his clients. He calls it "self-contradiction"—you say you want to solve your financial problem, but you continue to overspend on things that really aren't necessary, like entertainment or clothing.

If you're really in a financial crisis, you have to make some tough choices about how you can best use your money. Stop eating out, resolve not to purchase any new clothes for several months, put vacation or home improvement plans on hold. You may even want to stop putting money into your savings account until the storm passes. Penny-pinching may be painful, but ultimately *can* prove to be rewarding. Gaining a sense of control over your paycheck can give you a sense of control over your financial crisis.

In the previous chapter, I talked about developing a spending plan. If you haven't already done those exercises, you'll want to do them now to figure out where you're spending money that could be put to better use.

Step #10: Keep Your Problem in Perspective. Millions of people go through financially difficult times every year. The debt collection business—a $40 billion-plus-a-year industry—is a testament to that fact. Like most crises, this too will pass. In the meantime, hang in there and be willing to do what you have to do to get back on track.

What Happens if You Don't Pay?

Creditors can't throw you in jail just because you can't pay some of your bills. Depending on the circumstances, though, they *can* turn over your account to collections, sue you, garnishee your wages, repossess collateral, or foreclose on your home.

If you are behind on any of your bills, the rights and remedies that the collector uses to get you to bring your bill up-to-date depends on several factors:

1. *Who is collecting the debt.* A credit card company or another lender collecting its own debts can be really tough—worse, in some cases, than debt collectors. That's because in most states they have more leeway than professional debt collectors. Debt collectors are covered by the Fair Debt Collection Practices Act, a federal law that regulates how they operate. That law doesn't cover creditors collecting their own debts.

Most creditors want to get you to pay *and* keep you as a good customer, at least at the beginning. (After all, people who carry balances are their favorite customers!) So you may be able to negotiate a reasonable compromise with a creditor until you can get back on your feet.

Collection agencies, on the other hand, have one and only one goal—to get you to pay. I'll talk more about outside debt collectors in a minute.

2. *Whether the debt is secured or unsecured. Secured debts* are debts that are backed up by collateral—property that the creditor can take if you fail to pay the bill. If a debt is secured, you will probably know it because when you took out the loan, you will have signed a "security agreement" giving the creditor a "security interest" in your property. Your collateral on a secured debt may be repossessed, or taken back, if you don't make your payments.

Many loans are *unsecured*; there is no collateral backing up the loan. Credit cards, medical bills, personal lines of credit, and student loans are examples of unsecured debts. The fact that these types of loans are unsecured doesn't mean that the creditor can't go after your property to collect. It just makes it more difficult, since they generally have to go to court first.

3. *Where you live, or where the contract was made.* State laws often govern repossessions, lawsuits by creditors, bounced checks, bankruptcy, and creditors' remedies. Sometimes a creditor can take you to court in the state where the contract was made, if it was made in a state other than where you are now living. Or if you move and a creditor has an outstanding legal judgment against you, the creditor may be able to transfer it to the state where you live and collect it under the state's laws. Robin Leonard's book, *Money Troubles* (listed in the Resources section), contains helpful charts that describe these state laws and explain how they work.

4. *Who owes the bill.* Generally, you can be held responsible for any bills incurred on any joint credit cards you hold (regardless of whether you or the other cardholder made the charges), other loans made jointly, any loans for which you have cosigned, plus your own bills. Some state laws also include a "Doctrine of Necessaries," which holds both spouses liable for debts incurred for food, clothing, shelter, or other living necessities. If you live in a community-property state, you may also be held responsible for debts your spouse runs up during your marriage.

Let's look in more detail at what can happen when you don't pay a bill.

Debt Collection

Debt collectors aren't big mean guys who break customers' kneecaps when they can't pay. Nevertheless, when you're in a financial crunch, dealing with debt collectors can be annoying or even frightening. It doesn't necessarily have to be that way.

Most collectors are professionals and conduct their business in a semireasonable (though often high-pressure) manner. There are some, though, that may use intimidation or illegal tactics to coerce consumers into paying past-due bills. The Federal Trade Commission reports that complaints about debt-collection companies are one of the top three categories by number of complaints.

Knowing your rights and what to expect from debt collectors can give you the confidence to protect yourself from illegal harassment, and to work out an arrangement that is satisfactory to everyone involved.

What Can You Expect from Debt Collectors?

If your credit card payment hasn't been received by your card issuer ten days after the due date, your credit card issuer will probably send you a friendly note reminding you that your payment is past due. If you fail to make two payments in a row, you will usually get a more serious-sounding letter requesting immediate payment of the past due amount, and the creditor may follow that up with a phone call asking you where your payment is.

If you are sixty days or more delinquent, you may find your card frozen and your account closed. Many banks are willing at this stage, however, to reopen the account if you can get back on track. Other factors that may cause a bank to close your credit line: your income goes down, or your debts go up.

Once your account becomes ninety days or more delinquent, some creditors will start "writing off" the account as a bad debt. That means that they've decided that they can't collect through normal channels, and consider your account a "bad debt." If your account has *not* been written off after ninety days, you'll face more communications from the creditor's collection department. If you still don't pay, the creditor will probably write the account off when it becomes 120 to 180 days delinquent.

After an account has been written off (also called "charged off" or a "profit and loss"), most lenders will turn it over to a collection agency. In general, the smaller the bank, the quicker they will charge off accounts (since smaller issuers are less likely to have sophisticated internal collection agencies).

If the creditor's collection department cannot collect the debt from you, it will next be turned over to an outside collection agency. A collection agency is a company in the business of collecting debts. Many collection agencies work on commission: They usually collect between a third and two-thirds of the amount they bring in for the creditor. Alternatively, some collectors or investors will "buy" bad debts for somewhere around 50 percent of the face value and try to collect for themselves.

Delinquent accounts are usually first turned over to "primary" debt collectors. These collectors try to bring in easier loans—ones that are only a few months behind. If they are successful, they receive about one-third of what they collect. If a primary collector can't get you to pay within six months or so, the loan is usually turned over to a "secondary" collector. The secondary collector tries for another six months or so to collect. If successful, the debt collector will receive a commission of up to 45 percent. If the secondary collector can't secure payment, the debt may be turned over to a third collector—the "tertiary" collector, who will earn a commission in the 50 to 55 percent range.

Credit card accounts are considered tough by many collectors, because in most cases the bank's internal collectors have already tried—and failed—to collect. For that reason, some agencies start legal proceedings very quickly on delinquent credit card accounts. Others hire lawyers to send letters threatening legal action: If you don't pay, they say, they'll turn your account over to a lawyer for legal proceedings.

Remember, paying the creditor before the account is sent to collections is beneficial both to you *and* to the creditor to which you owe the money. The creditor saves the collection fee and you avoid a collection account listed on your credit record. Although not frequently the case, creditors' internal collection agents may also earn commissions on the debts they collect. If that is the case, it is in the collector's personal interest that you pay. Make it clear to the collector that you understand how this process works, and that you are amenable to working with them.

Once your account has been turned over to a collection agency, you usually can no longer negotiate with the original lender. If you call them to discuss the debt, they'll just refer you to the collection agency.

Skipping town or trying to hide is not a particularly effective way to try to get out of paying a debt. It's hard to get lost these days! Most debt collectors rely on advanced skip-tracing techniques to find people—and they can find most people sooner or later.

Don't assume a debt has been "forgiven" if you don't hear from a creditor or collector for a while. Collections may start three, four, or five years after a debt was charged off by the bank, if it has been passed on to several collectors, or if your financial situation has improved and a collector discovers you may be able to pay.

It usually takes debt collectors about thirty days to "close a case." During that time, a collector may contact you almost a half dozen times.

Federal Protection Against Unfair Debt Collection Practices

I have heard truly outrageous debt collection horror stories. One woman I know was eight months pregnant when she was told by a debt collector that if she didn't pay by the next day, she would be arrested and thrown in jail.

Another time I listened in on a conversation while a collector told a teacher she would be served by a federal marshal in front of the children—for a debt her husband owed, but for which she was *not* legally liable. In that same call, I heard the collector repeatedly make false and harassing statements.

These kinds of practices are illegal, and have been for some time. But you must know your rights in order to protect yourself.

In 1978, Congress passed the Fair Debt Collection Practices Act to protect consumers from some of the most offensive collection tactics. The FDCPA protects debtors from harassment, public embarrassment, and unfair collection practices. It doesn't stop debt collectors from collecting debts, but it does set reasonable limits on how and when they can attempt to collect debts.

The FDCPA applies to outside collection agencies, not *internal debt collectors.* If your credit card issuer or another lender is trying to collect the money you owe them directly, then this law does not apply. (There may be state laws, however, that apply to the creditor's activities.) If your card issuer, instead of using its own name, uses a name that would make someone think it is an outside collection agency, it *would* be covered by this law.

Here are the basic provisions of the FDCPA:

Debt Collectors Can't Go Public with Your Debt

Debt collectors can't tell anyone else about your debt—not even your family members—unless they are cosigners or joint applicants on the account. If a debt collector does contact anyone else about a debt you owe, it can only be to get information about where to find you. If a collector does contact someone else to find out where you might be, they can't indicate that they're calling from a collection agency or to collect a debt you owe.

Debt Collectors Can't Call You at All Hours

They are not allowed to call you before 8 A.M. or after 9 P.M., your time. If your employer does not allow you to take personal calls at work, you can demand that the debt collector stop calling you at work. All you have to do is tell the collector you can't take personal calls at work; then they're not supposed to call you at work again.

Unfair Practices Are Prohibited

Unless the law or your contract with the creditor permits it, a debt collector cannot collect more than the amount you owe on the original debt. He can't make you pay for collect telephone calls, telegrams, or other hidden charges related to his communication with you.

Postdated checks: A debt collector can't force you to send a postdated check in order to threaten you or to initiate criminal prosecution. If you do send a postdated check, he can't deposit it or cash it (or threaten to do so) before the date on the check. In addition, if you send a check that is postdated by more than five days, the debt collector must give you written notice that he will be depositing the check three to ten days before doing so. One executive at a large collection agency suggests consumers who do send postdated checks write in red ink above the date line "VOID UNTIL DATED" as additional protection.

Don't send a postdated check to a *creditor*. (I probably wouldn't send one to a collection agency, either.) In many cases, creditors can cash postdated checks without regard to the date. Many issuers receive thousands of payments each week. They are unlikely to catch the fact that a check is postdated, but even if they do, it might be cashed anyway.

Harassment Is Illegal

The following actions are considered harassment or abuse, and collection companies are not allowed to engage in them:

- threatening to use violence or criminal means against you, your family, or property;
- using abusive or obscene language to intimidate or abuse;
- calling you repeatedly on the phone to annoy you;
- calling you and failing to identify themselves;
- publishing a list of "deadbeats."

Collectors Can't Use False or Deceptive Collection Methods to Collect a Debt

If a debt collector dressed up as a sheriff and arrived at your door demanding payment (unethical ones might go to those lengths), he would be breaking the law by falsely representing himself. Other false or misleading representations include posing as an attorney; mailing letters that appear to be from an attorney but are not; or using a false name or bogus business name when calling to collect a debt.

It is important to understand that a debt collector can't threaten legal action that by law he cannot take to collect from you, and he cannot threaten any legal action he doesn't intend to take. Collectors also can't threaten you with arrest or falsely accuse you of committing a crime if you don't pay the debt. They can't threaten to seize, attach, or sell property, or garnishee your wages, unless they actually intend to do so and have a legal right to do so.

You're Entitled to Written Notification of Your Debt

Within five days of initially contacting you, a debt collector must send you written notice of the debt and tell you: how much you owe, to whom you owe it, and what to do if you don't think you owe the debt. You then have thirty days to write to the collection agency to dispute it in writing. If the collection company claims there is a judgment against you, you can request in writing that the creditor send you a copy of the judgment. If there is *any* dispute over the amount you owe, request verification of the debt.

You Can Stop Debt Collectors

If you're sick of taking calls about a debt you can't pay, or won't pay, you can tell the collection agency to leave you alone. Under the FDCPA, you can write a debt collection agency and tell them not to contact you anymore. After they receive your letter, they cannot communicate with you *except* to tell you that they will not be contacting you further *or* to tell you they may take legal action against you (such as taking you to court).

If you decide to go this route, write to the collection agency and explain why you can't or won't pay the bill: "I can't pay anything because I'm ill and the doctor doesn't think I'll be able to go back to work for six months. I've moved in with my sister and I have no money." Or, "I've told you I won't pay this debt because my health insurance was supposed to cover it. I've sent you and the insurance company proof that it's not my responsibility and I really don't want to explain it to you again." Send your letter certified mail, return receipt requested, and keep a copy for your own records.

Tips for Dealing with Bill Collectors

A woman was told by a collection agency that her credit card company was going to sue her for fraud because she used her credit card after charge privileges had been suspended by the creditor. She didn't think that was the case, so she went back through her records, then called the credit card company to find out what they were talking about. "We don't have any intention of suing you for fraud," she was told. She called back the collection agency and told them what she had learned and accused them of breaking the law in trying to collect the debt. They didn't call her again.

Tell It Like It Is: Most debt collectors realize there are cases where they will have trouble collecting payment because the debtor just doesn't have any money to pay. Telling creditors or collectors exactly how bleak your financial picture really is may keep them from hounding you as aggressively as they would if they thought there were any chance you could come up with a payment. There may be an additional bonus: Describing your dismal financial situation in great detail may also relegate your debt to the back of a long list of debts the collector is working on.

Write a Letter: If you're too nervous, upset, or afraid to talk with a collector about your problem, write a letter. Explain your situation and propose a solution. Send your letter to the collection company immediately via certified mail, and keep a copy for your records.

Take Your Time: You shouldn't agree to a repayment schedule if the payments sound too high. It is vital that you examine your income and expenses and determine how much you can realistically afford. If a collector's offer seems unrealistic, tell her that you want to think about it for a few minutes and get back to her. Then call back with all the reasons why you can't pay that much, and propose a reasonable counteroffer.

Collectors are in the business of collecting money, and some can get pretty tough. Nevertheless, you shouldn't allow anyone to pressure you into agreeing to a repayment schedule that you really can't afford. It's going to hurt both you and the collector in the long run.

Wheel and Deal: Debt collectors are often open to creative offers for payment. For instance, you may offer to pay 75 percent of the money owed up front, if the collection company will accept that partial payment as payment in full. Other collectors may agree to moderate repayment schedules. You might also be able to ask the collection agency to remove any remarks about a collection account from your credit report in exchange for prompt payment, which they may or may not be able to do.

Keep in mind that the debt collector cannot dicker without the creditor's go-ahead, unless it has bought the debt from the original creditor. In other words, if the creditor to whom you owe the money demands that the agency collect at least 70 percent of the original debt, you won't be able to negotiate a deal that allows you to settle the debt by paying 50 percent today. But you don't know how much they have to collect, so it doesn't hurt to try to strike a deal.

The most important thing to remember when dealing with a collection agency is that it wants the cash, and it wants it yesterday. By agreeing to make a lump-sum payment immediately, you may be able to negotiate a good deal. Before you call, decide the maximum amount you are able to pay now, and don't agree to pay more. Since you are negotiating, it may be a good idea to start with a lower amount than you are willing to pay, and work up from that.

Keep Good Records: Write down details of every single conversation you have with a bill collector. Note who you talked with, when and where they contacted you, and any agreements made. Keep copies of all correspondence sent to you and from you regarding the debt. If you make any payment arrangements, send a letter to the collector outlining your agreement. *This is extremely important,* in case there are problems later. You may want to send your letter by certified mail, to make sure you'll have a record of receipt.

If you agree to settle a debt for less than the total amount owed, you will want to do two things. First, write on the check a disclaimer that states "cashing this check constitutes payment in full." In some states, that will prevent the collector or creditor from suing you for the difference between the check and the total amount of the debt.

Secondly, write a letter to the collector or creditor, and send it certified mail, return receipt requested. In that letter outline your agreement, and note that the collector has agreed to accept your partial payment as payment in full. Refer to the check you have enclosed, and reiterate that if the creditor cashes the check, it will satisfy the debt in full. It would also be a very good idea to check with your state attorney general's office or consumer protection office to determine whether creditors in your state still have the right, after cashing a check with a disclaimer, to collect the difference.

Be on Guard if you are contacted by a collection agency that seems to be using harassing, high-pressure techniques. While there are many professional collection agencies that would not break the law to collect a debt, there are also unscrupulous agencies that will do anything to get paid. Some creditors even look the other way when the collection agencies they hire engage in illegal tactics.

Pay When You Can: Avoid writing post-dated checks, and *never* write a check if you don't have the money in the bank to cover it. If the check bounces, not only will the creditor or collector hit you with a bad-check fee (anywhere from $10 to $30), the payee may also take you to court for purposefully writing bad checks—an illegal act that sometimes entitles the payee to damages of several times the amount of the check.

Catching the Bad Apples

What if you think a collection agency has done something illegal?

1. *Write a letter* outlining exactly what the agency did that you think they shouldn't have, and include as many details as possible (when they called, whom you spoke with, what they said, etc.). Send a copy of the letter to the Federal Trade Commission and your state attorney general's office or local consumer-protection office. Also send a copy to the legal department of the creditor to which you originally owed the debt. Finally, send a letter to the collection agency, certified mail, return receipt requested. Try to send it to the owner or manager if you can get his or her name.

At a minimum, you may get them off your back. If you really have a good case, you may get them to erase your bill in exchange for not suing them.

2. *Consider suing the agency* if you believe you have a strong case. If you sue a collection agency and win, you may be able to get actual damages, attorneys' fees, court costs, and punitive damages up to $1,000. You may also be able to sue the lender that hired the collection agency in the first place. Check with an attorney.

3. *Contact the ACA.* About half of the debt-collection companies in the United States belong to the American Collectors Association, a professional trade association. Members agree to conduct their business in an ethical, professional manner. If you are dealing with a debt-collection agency that claims to be a member of the ACA but seems to be engaging in unethical collection practices, you can contact the association to file a complaint against the company. For information on contacting the ACA, see the listing in the Resources section.

Going to Court

If you don't pay, a creditor or collection agency may be able to take you to court and sue you. It's helpful, therefore, to understand how lawsuits work. The person or company that sues someone is called the "plaintiff." The person who is being sued is called the "defendant." To initiate a lawsuit, a plaintiff generally will file a "complaint" with a court of law. The complaint will describe the nature of the suit. The defendant will be formally notified, by means of a "summons," that a complaint has been filed against him.

How and when you may be taken to court depends on the type of debt and state law. If your debt is a small one—in the $1,000 to $3,000 range—you may be taken to small claims court. If it is larger, or in some states if you are being sued by a collection agency, your case will probably go to your state's civil court.

Small claims court may be preferable to civil court because you don't have to hire a lawyer. You simply appear before the judge, state your case, and provide any evidence you have to back up your side of the story. It's generally a very simple, and relatively quick, proceeding.

If you are taken to small claims court, don't fail to show up at a court appointment. If you really cannot make it to your scheduled hearing, call the clerk of the court and ask to postpone the hearing. In most cases, a hearing can be postponed at least once. If you do not appear in court at the scheduled time, the judge will likely issue a "default judgment" against you, and you will have little choice but to pay.

If the creditor decides to take you to civil court, you will be served with a summons that tells you the who, what, when, and where of the complaint against you. In some states, the summons must be delivered to you in person; in other cases it may be given to a relative or left at your job, and a copy mailed to you. The summons will tell you how you are required to respond to the complaint—usually in writing. Unlike small claims court, you will probably have to hire a lawyer to defend you in civil court.

It is important that you at least *try* to settle your debts before they reach this stage. If you are taken to court and the judge determines you do owe the creditor money, a judgment will be entered against you. Even if you pay that judgment immediately, it will be placed on your credit report and seriously harm your credit record for seven years. If you don't pay the judgment, it can remain on your credit report until the statute of limitations for collecting the judgment expires: twenty years or more in some states.

There is a trade-off here, however. If you have been taken to court, your credit report probably also lists a very delinquent late payment and a charge-off and collection account. A judgment may not hurt your credit record that much more than those remarks already do.

Many court systems today offer free arbitration or mediation to decrease the number of cases that actually go to court. In arbitration, each of the parties in a dispute will explain their side of the story to an arbitrator (who may or may not be a lawyer, depending on the court), who "decides" the case. You agree before you go through arbitration to abide by the arbitrator's decision.

Mediation is more informal. You and the party that is suing you will sit down and discuss your dispute with a trained mediator, who tries to help both parties come to a mutually agreeable decision. Some creditors will be willing to go through arbitration or mediation; others won't. In some states, arbitration or mediation may be required, or may be required if you request it.

Judgments

A judgment is a court's decision about a lawsuit. Usually, if you're sued and the plaintiff gets a judgment against you, it means you owe them money. If you fail to respond to a summons or show up for a court date, the court will likely grant the creditor a "default judgment." If the creditor believes the facts of the case are straightforward, it may ask the judge to issue a "summary judgment"—a judgment without a trial. If you lose your case, the judge will simply issue a judgment against you for the amount you owe, plus any fees the creditor is allowed to collect, such as court costs or attorney fees. In most states, interest can be compounded on any amount you do not pay off immediately.

How a creditor can collect the judgment from you depends largely on state law. In some states, you will be required to go to court and reveal information about your employment or personal finances, which the creditor or collection agency will then use to try to collect from you. Creditors generally try first to garnish wages, or go after bank accounts or other liquid assets. If that fails, they may try to get a lien on your property. A lien gives the creditor a legal ownership in your property.

If you are being sued and believe that you legally don't owe some or all of the money in question, consider hiring a lawyer to assist you before you are taken to court. If you are taken to small claims court (or if you want to take a lender to court), order a copy of Nolo's book *Everybody's Guide to Small Claims Court* (see the Resources section). This reference guide will tell you what you need to do to defend yourself or pursue your case.

Wage Garnishment

When your wages are garnisheed, your employer will take a certain amount of money from your paychecks before you are paid, to pay a debt you owe. The most important fact to remember about wage garnishment (also called "wage attachment") is that in most cases, it *cannot* happen automatically. A creditor or collection agency can garnish your wages only if it has gone to court and obtained a judgment against you.

After the creditor gets a judgment against you, you will have a certain period of time (depending on state law) to either pay the judgment or set up a payment agreement. If you don't make your payments as agreed, or if you don't make any payment arrangements at all, the lender or the collection agency can go to court and get a "Writ of Garnishment" (or "Writ of Attachment of Wages") that permits them to garnish your wages.

There are limits on how much of your wages can be garnisheed. In addition to your regular wages or income, the following earnings may be garnisheed: commissions, bonuses, vacation pay, and periodic payments pursuant to a pension or retirement program. Tips, income tax refunds, unemployment, and welfare benefits are *not* subject to wage garnishment.

Only your *disposable* income can be garnisheed. Disposable

income is income left over after legally required deductions are taken out. These deductions include:

Federal income taxes

State and city income taxes

State unemployment taxes

Social Security contributions

State employee retirement deductions

In addition, only a portion of your disposable income may be garnisheed. That percentage is: 25 percent of your disposable income for the week, or the amount by which your disposable income for the week exceeds thirty times the federal minimum hourly wage, whichever is less.

Suppose, for example, your disposable income for a week is $250. The federal minimum wage is $5.15. Twenty-five percent of your disposable income is $62.50. Thirty times the minimum wage is $30 \times 5.15 = \$154.50$. $250 - \$154.50 = \$95.50$. Since $62.50 is less than $95.50, only $62.50 a week can be garnisheed from your wages.

These rules do not apply to garnishment to pay state or federal taxes. They also do not apply to Chapter 13 bankruptcy cases, where a judge may order a larger portion of your income to be withheld to pay your creditors. Finally, additional wages may be garnisheed to enforce support agreements.

In addition to the federal wage garnishment rules we've mentioned above, each state may have its own laws. State laws can only be more favorable to consumers than the federal law. In Pennsylvania, Texas, and South Carolina, for example, wage garnishment is not allowed by law. Florida doesn't allow garnishment of the wages of a head of household. It used to be that the wages of federal employees couldn't be garnisheed, but that law has been changed.

You can't be fired just because your wages are being garnisheed for one debt. If, however, your wages are being garnisheed for more than one debt, your employer may be able to fire you for that reason. (Even if you aren't fired because your wages are being garnisheed, don't be surprised if your employer is less than enthusiastic about the fact that you are in financial trouble.)

Auto Repossessions

In many states, your vehicle can be repossessed without warning. A creditor generally has the right to seize a vehicle as soon as the customer "defaults" on his loan. The definition of default varies depending on the contract and state law, but failing to make a payment on time often constitutes default.

If you are unable to make your payments on your car loan, contact your lender immediately, since you may be able to renegotiate new repayment terms or refinance the loan. If you do arrange a new payment schedule, you may be protected from further repossessions as long as you continue to meet the new payment schedule and terms. In fact, in some cases, if you consistently pay late and your lender doesn't complain, you may also be protected from a repossession, since the lender in effect has "agreed" to your "new" payment schedule.

Once a lender decides to repossess your car, it will generally give you *no* advance warning. (In some states, the lender has to tell you that you're in default and give you the opportunity to get caught up first.) "Repo men" work all hours and may even come onto your property to take your car. They can't, however, commit a "breach of the peace." A breach of the peace can include using physical violence—or even threats of violence—against you, taking your car if you object, or removing your car from a closed garage. Again, this is often a matter of state law.

After your car has been repossessed, the creditor can either keep it as payment in full or sell it. If the creditor decides to sell it, you must be notified when and where it will be sold. If it is being sold at a public auction, for example, the creditor has to inform you of the sale so that you can bid on your car. Either way, you must be given the chance to get your vehicle back. To claim the car, the creditor can often require you pay the entire balance of the loan, plus repossession costs. In some states, you can "reinstate" your loan by paying the amount you are behind, plus repossession costs.

If your creditor decides to sell your car and gets less than the amount you still owe on it, the lender may be able to get a "deficiency judgment" for the difference. That doesn't mean the creditor can sell your car to his cousin dirt cheap and then make you pay the difference. By law, the car must be sold in a "commercially reasonable" manner. Some states don't allow deficiency judgments in the case of vehicle repossessions.

When financial times get tough, some consumers simply hand their car keys over to the lender. This is called a "voluntary repossession." It doesn't prevent a lender from demanding the deficiency balance, but it may make the repossession less expensive for you by reducing repossession costs. Repossession costs can be expensive, and may include storage fees, the repossessor's fee, and a prepayment penalty if your car loan had one.

Repossessions—whether voluntary or involuntary—usually are reported to credit bureaus and remain on credit reports for seven years. Most lenders don't distinguish between voluntary or involuntary repossessions when looking at credit applications. Either way, a repossession is a very negative remark on a credit file. If a lender gets a deficiency judgment against you, it can also appear on your credit report.

If you simply can't keep up with your car payments, you may want to consider selling your car and avoid a repossession altogether. If your car is very new, or you financed most of the purchase price over several years, you may be "upside down." That means the amount you owe on it is more than the price you can sell it for. Unless you can afford to take a loss, you may be forced into a voluntary or involuntary repossession, anyway. There are some companies that will "buy" your upside-down car and lease it back to you so you'll still have wheels. This may be an option for lowering your payments, but proceed carefully. Again, at the first sign of trouble, contact your lender and see if something can't be worked out.

Your Home

For many people, their home represents their greatest source of financial security, and the thought of losing it is terrifying.

Most mortgages are serviced to conform to guidelines of several large firms: the Federal National Mortgage Association (Fannie Mae), the Federal Home Loan Mortgage Company (Freddie Mac), FHA, and VA. Most lenders will follow the servicing guidelines of these investors/government agencies when trying to collect a delinquent mortgage. The guidelines generally give lenders a number of options for helping consumers with mortgage payment problems to get back on their feet.

Mortgages are often "packaged" and sold in "pools" to investors. If your mortgage is included in one of these packages, you may find that your lender cannot work out alternative payment arrangements as easily as if you were dealing with the lender directly. That's because the guidelines on some of these investor-owned mortgages are tougher—to protect the investors.

Here's how the general mortgage collection process works:

If you miss a mortgage payment, you will likely receive a letter, or perhaps a phone call, from your lender reminding you that your payment is past due. If you don't make a payment for three months, you are in trouble. After you miss your third payment on most mortgages, your delinquency *must* be reported to a credit bureau, and the lender may start foreclosure proceedings. If you are a new borrower and have not held your mortgage very long, your lender is likely to be especially alert to *any* late payments.

Don't wait to contact your lender if you are having a difficult time paying your mortgage! Mortgage lenders really don't want to foreclose on your property any more than you want them to. They're in the lending business, not the real estate business. Nevertheless, most mortgage lenders can't ignore late payments, since the loan likely must conform to standards set by the secondary market. If you anticipate problems paying your mortgage— you've just been laid off, or you have fallen ill and will be off work for several months—contact your lender *before* you fall behind on payments.

Some lenders can offer creative financing options to keep borrowers out of foreclosure. The most important factors in working out alternative payment schedules are the borrower's attitude (are they really willing to make financial sacrifices to get payments back on schedule?), who currently owns the mortgage (e.g., Freddie Mac, Fannie Mae, or investors), and whether the borrower's financial problems are temporary or long-term. You will want to ask your lender if any of the following measures are available to you:

Forbearance: If trouble meeting your mortgage payments stems from a financial problem like large medical bills or unemployment, your lender may be willing to grant a forbearance. This allows you to make smaller payments, or perhaps suspend payments, until you are back on your feet. If your setback will be temporary, you show good faith in trying to make your payments, and your financial problems aren't due to financial "irresponsibility," your lender may grant you a forbearance. Generally, forbearance is granted for up to twelve months, although it may last up to eighteen months depending on the circumstances. (In some cases, the lender may be willing to add the amount that is delinquent to the end of the loan, giving the consumer some more breathing room.)

HUD Assignment: If you have an FHA-insured mortgage, you may be eligible for the HUD assignment program. In order to qualify, the delinquency must have been the result of circumstances beyond your control and there must be a reasonable prospect that you will be able to resume payments in thirty-six months. If you are accepted into the assignment program, HUD will become your lender and will work out a payment program for you.

Preforeclosure Sale: This option will allow you to sell your property at fair market value, if the lender agrees to accept the proceeds of the sale in satisfaction of a defaulted mortgage—even though the proceeds may be less than the amount owed on the mortgage—to avoid foreclosure. You should have this option approved as a viable alternative by the servicer before entering into a sales agreement with a buyer.

Deed-in-Lieu: Like a voluntary auto repossession, this arrangement permits you to give your home back to the lender. The benefit of this arrangement is that your credit report will not list a foreclosure, and the matter is closed so you can get on with your life.

Deed-in-lieu is becoming a more popular option with lenders. Many investors are encouraging servicers to accept deed-in-lieu. In some instances, you may receive a nominal financial incentive for selecting the foreclosure avoidance option. However, the lender will likely try to exhaust every other avenue of relief before agreeing to this option.

Loan Modification: In limited situations, the servicer may be able to modify the terms of your mortgage note to reduce your monthly payments. If you are able to resume regular payments, the servicer may be able to add the delinquency to your loan balance.

Under this scenario, your loan is refinanced, or the payment schedule is modified, in order to make the monthly payment more affordable. Your fifteen-year loan is stretched to thirty years, for example, or a fixed-rate mortgage is recast as an adjustable rate loan with lower rates in the first few years. Your lender may be willing to add the amount you are behind to the end of the loan as a "balloon payment"—one large payment you make at the end of the loan.

Be sure you understand all the financial implications of your new loan terms. While you may be desperate enough to agree to anything, keep in mind that if you cannot keep up with the new payments, you may find yourself in foreclosure in a few months anyway. Make sure the new payment schedule is something you can live with.

Temporary Indulgence: If there are unusual circumstances that have caused a borrower to get behind, the lender may grant a temporary indulgence. A temporary indulgence will be granted on the condition that the borrower will be caught up on all payments, including the amount that is delinquent, within three months. An example of a case where a temporary indulgence may be granted would be if the sale of the borrower's house was pending.

Military Indulgence: The Soldier's and Sailor's Relief Act may give those in the military some relief. For more information on this law, see Chapter Five.

Foreclosure: If all your efforts to work with the lender fail, you may be faced with the prospect of losing your home. Fortunately, foreclosures often take several months. Rather than suffer through the agony of a foreclosure, you can use this time to try to sell your home.

Be careful! If you do decide to sell, it is probably best to hire a reputable agent (perhaps one that specializes in preforeclosures) to help you sell quickly. If not, you could find yourself victimized by an unscrupulous buyer who manipulates you into a deal that costs you any equity left in your home. Watch out if the words "quit claim deed" come up at any point. Quit-claiming your house relinquishes your rights in the property but does not in itself remove you from the loan obligation. Unless you really know what you're doing, avoid this tactic.

If foreclosure is a possibility, you must carefully weigh the current value of your home against the outstanding mortgage. If you default and the house is sold for less than the amount you still owe on your mortgage, your lender can in many cases sue you to get a "deficiency judgment" that permits them to collect the difference. You may even be forced to pay the lender's foreclosure expenses.

Even worse, if you default and the lender sells your house for *less* than the mortgage amount, you may have to pay income taxes on the difference. Suppose, for instance, you bought your home for $65,000 and your mortgage balance is $50,000 when you default. If the bank sells your home for $45,000, you still owe the bank $5,000 (the difference between the mortgage balance and what it sold for). The bank may decide that it is not worthwhile to go after you for the remaining $5,000, so it forgives the debt. The IRS considers "forgiveness of debt" taxable, so you may have to pay taxes on that $5,000.

Foreclosure laws vary from state to state. In some cases, you will be given the opportunity to reclaim your home by paying the delinquent payments. In others, you will be required to bid on the property if you want to get it back. Check with your state attorney general's office for information about foreclosure proceedings in your state.

Bankruptcy: By filing bankruptcy, you may be able to keep your house, or at least stall the process of losing it. A bankruptcy attorney will usually offer a free consultation to explain your rights in your state.

Setoffs

I once received a call from a distressed consumer who had fallen several months behind on her car loan. Instead of repossessing the car, the bank took the late payments, plus fees, from the savings account she held with her grandmother at that same bank. That practice is called a "setoff" or "offset," and it is illegal in the case of credit cards.

If you have a checking account, savings account, or other funds on deposit with the same financial institution that issues your credit card, you are protected by the Truth-in-Lending Act from lenders dipping into those accounts if you don't pay your credit card bills. Credit card issuers can, however, take a security interest in any funds you have on deposit with them—a seemingly small but important difference.

If a card issuer does take a security interest in your funds, you must specifically agree to allow it to do so. A general statement in your cardholder agreement that the card issuer has a security interest in any other accounts you hold with it is probably *not* considered adequate notification of a security interest.

If you have a secured credit card, you will have to sign an agreement that the lender takes a security interest in your deposit with the card issuer. That way, if you don't pay your bills, the card issuer will have access to your deposit to pay off your bills.

Take note: Setoffs *are* generally permitted in the case of loans other than credit cards. In most cases, the lender is required to disclose its right to offset up front, so read the fine print in your loan papers to determine if you may be affected.

Credit and Financial Help

Help with a crisis or long-term credit problems is available from several sources. You may have to do a bit of research to find out which is best for you, but it will be well worth it!

Credit Counseling Agencies

Nonprofit counseling agencies have been around for a long time. They can help by examining your income and expenses, and by suggesting ways to meet your obligations. If you cannot keep up with your current bills, the counseling agency may act as an intermediary between you and your creditors. Under a typical arrangement, a counseling agency will contact a consumer's unsecured creditors, work out a repayment plan, and accept one monthly payment from the consumer. The agency then pays each of the consumer's creditors until she is back on her feet and can handle regular payments herself, completes the program, or drops out. Creditors stop contacting the consumer, alleviating one of the major stress factors of overdue bills.

The most well-known counseling agencies are members of the National Foundation for Credit Counseling (NFCC), a national nonprofit network of 1,450 member agencies designed to provide assistance to people dealing with stressful financial situations. You can find member agencies through the Web site at www.nfcc.org or by calling 1-800-388-2227. There are also independent agencies, and the Association for Independent Consumer Credit Counseling Agencies (AICCCA, www.aiccca.com) can help you find one.

Some counseling agencies do a great job; others aren't so terrific. Before choosing to work with any counseling agency, ask yourself some questions:

Am I a Candidate for a Repayment Program? Although sometimes marketed as debt consolidation solutions, these programs do not actually consolidate your debts, and they are not for people who are paying their bills on time but just want lower rates or one monthly payment. These programs are for consumers who are falling behind on their bills, are taking from one loan or card to pay another, are about to fall behind, or are seriously considering bankruptcy.

Will a Repayment Program Help Me? Traditionally, creditors have lowered interest rates, waived fees, and made other concessions so that consumers could stick with the program and get out of debt in three to six years. Lately, however, they have been cutting back on those concessions. Since most programs will charge a nominal fee per debt to handle the payments (about $4 to $7 per month per debt, or a total of about $30 per month), you'll want to make sure you're actually improving your situation, not hurting it by using one of these programs. (One counseling agency got in trouble for failing to explain to consumers that they kept the first monthly payment instead of distributing it to creditors, for example.)

Also remember that some kinds of loans aren't typically included in these plans—mortgages, auto loans, or student loans, for example, and some credit card companies won't participate either.

What Kind of Support and Education Will I Receive? Counseling agencies have for years been funded in part by "fair share," a contribution the creditors who are being paid back make to the counseling agency. With each monthly payment, for example, the counseling agency would traditionally get to keep 10 to 15 percent. I personally think that's fair. It's not cheap to run a counseling agency. (Even though they are nonprofit they still have to keep the lights on and pay salaries.)

What's happened recently is that creditors have been cutting back on fair share, in some cases reducing it to only 5 percent or not participating at all. This has made it much more difficult for counseling agencies to continue to provide quality education programs and support. Some of the more established counseling agencies have been able to make up the difference by operating more efficiently, or continuing to raise money from the United Way and other organizations. Other agencies have eliminated educational programs and do little more than try to push people into repayment programs. If you have special concerns, make sure they will be addressed. And if you need ongoing support, understand that you may have to find it elsewhere.

What Kind of Customer Service Will I Receive? When you go into one of these programs you are relying on the agency to make your payments for you. If they are sloppy or are slow in paying creditors, guess who bears the brunt of it? You do. After all, you're still legally responsible for those bills. Ask the counseling agency questions about their level of customer satisfaction and error rates, how often they pay creditors (once a month may not cut it), and who you will be able to call if there is a problem with any of your payments or creditors.

One of the questions I frequently hear is, "How will one of these programs affect my credit rating?" I think many consumers' fears about this issue are overblown. First of all, if you have a lot of debt and are falling behind, your credit rating is either damaged already or likely to be soon. Many creditors will "re-age," or bring up-to-date, accounts in a counseling program, as long as the consumer sticks with the new payment schedule. FICO no longer includes counseling in calculating credit scores.

Debtor's Anonymous

Debtor's Anonymous (DA) helps compulsive or chronic debtors get their problems under control. Modeled after Alcoholics Anonymous, they use a twelve-step support process and urge consumers to stop debting in any form. You can find out more about this approach in Jerrold Mundis's book *How to Get Out of Debt, Stay Out of Debt and Live Prosperously.* Even if you have no plans to attend DA, it's a good resource.

For more information on DA meetings in your area, visit www.debtorsanonymous.org or write: Debtor's Anonymous, General Service Board, PO Box 920888, Needham, MA 02492-0009; phone: 781-453-2743; fax: 781-453-2745.

Financial Peace University

FPU is a popular Christian approach to overcoming financial challenges and making peace with money. Created by Dave Ramsey, who went bankrupt in his twenties, The Lampo Group offers a variety of programs including FPU—a thirteen-week course where people learn with others how to take control of their finances. Dave says the average family going through the thirteen-week program pays off $5,300 in debt and puts $2,700 in savings. His book *Financial Peace* is also a bestseller. You can get more information at his site at www.daveramsey.com.

Financial Recovery Counseling

Financial Recovery counseling was created by Karen McCall, who has had years of success helping people with financial problems and issues. Karen now trains counselors who work with people over a period of time to help them transform their relationships with money and credit. Karen and her counselors have some truly amazing success stories, some of which you can read on their Web site at www.financialrecovery.com. What I like about Karen's approach is that it is ongoing and strives to get at the root of behaviors that may be holding people back—whether it's underearning, compulsive spending or debting, or a variety of other concerns.

You can also work through Karen's process in her excellent book *It's Your Money: Achieving Financial Well-Being* (Chronicle Books). If you could use the help and support of someone else, though, consider working with a counselor. It could be one of the best investments you'll make.

Myvesta.org

Myvesta.org (formerly known as Debt Counselors of America) is the nation's only comprehensive financial crisis and treatment center. Founded in 1994, the nonprofit financial crisis center has helped more than four million people through its programs and educational resources.

I've worked with Myvesta and believe strongly that they are offering unique and valuable services. They offer a variety of innovative programs that help consumers with everything from settling old debts, to working through a financial crisis, to avoiding bankruptcy. I strongly recommend you *at least* check out their Web site and the publications they offer. If you need help, you can contact them through their Web site or by calling 1-800-680-3328.

CHAPTER NINE

Bankruptcy: A Fresh Start or a Ten-Year Mistake?

Every year, hundreds of thousands of Americans declare personal bankruptcy. Let's face it—with large corporations, multimillionaires, and many average people declaring bankruptcy every day, it just doesn't carry the stigma that it used to.

Creditors have been alarmed in recent years by the dramatic increase in the number of personal bankruptcies. They insist that one of the main reasons consumers are filing for bankruptcy in unprecedented numbers is because the bankruptcy laws are lax. In other words, some bankers think that consumers take on too much debt knowing that they don't really have to pay it back.

The results of an important study of bankruptcy were published in a book titled *As We Forgive Our Debtors: Bankruptcy and Consumer Credit in America* (Sullivan, Warren and Westbrook, 1989, Oxford University Press). After analyzing data from thousands of bankruptcies across the nation, the authors concluded that:

"Bankrupt debtors are a cross section of America. There are some important subgroups in bankruptcy, but the data generally show that bankrupt debtors are not an identifiable class. They are not all—or mostly—day laborers and household maids dwelling in squalid apartments on the wrong side of the tracks. More than half are homeowners, and they work at pretty much the same jobs as everyone else . . . the financial trouble that leads to bankruptcy can be found in any community and no social or economic group is immune from it."

In addition, their study did not find widespread "abuses" of the system: They did not find large numbers of people running up large credit card bills while on vacation in Europe and then returning home to file for bankruptcy. Those cases do exist, but the Sullivan study concludes that, in the large majority of the cases they studied, bankrupts were "very sick financially, weighed down with debts far beyond their capacity to repay. A small group, perhaps 5 percent of all bankrupt debtors, might be abusing the system."

A banker's nightmare, bankruptcy can help the debtor "wipe the slate clean" and start again, or it can be a choice that haunts consumers for years to come. How do you decide whether to declare personal bankruptcy, and how do you file for it if you do? What are the differences between Chapter 7 and Chapter 13? What will you lose, and what can you keep after bankruptcy? What will bankruptcy cost you, both financially and in terms of your future ability to obtain credit and reach personal financial independence again? Here's a rundown of the facts on one of the most serious financial choices many people will ever make.

If you're seriously considering bankruptcy, there are several good resources I'd urge you to read. John Ventura, a bankruptcy attorney and consumer advocate whom I respect greatly, has written *The Bankruptcy Kit* (Dearborn, 1996). Nolo.com, the publisher of a variety of excellent legal self-help books, offers *Bankruptcy: Is It the Right Solution to Your Debt Problems?* by Robin Leonard, a simple guide to helping evaluate that choice. *Chapter 13 Bankruptcy: Repay Your Debts* and *How to File for Chapter 7 Bankruptcy*, also published by Nolo.com, are more in-depth and very helpful too. You can also get information about bankruptcy topics on their Web site. If you take the time to educate yourself, you'll feel more confident about your decision whether to file.

There are three main types of personal bankruptcy: Chapter 7 and Chapter 13 are the most common of the two. Chapter 12 is a special type of bankruptcy for family farmers. Chapter 11, which may sound familiar because it is often used by corporations, is generally not used by consumers since it is complicated and better protection is usually offered under Chapter 13.

Chapter 7 bankruptcy is commonly called "straight" bankruptcy or "liquidation." Under Chapter 7, certain types of property (such as tools of the trade, part of the equity in your home, or a certain amount of cash and clothing) are *exempt*, or protected, from bankruptcy. That's the property you get to keep. The rest of your property may be taken by the court and converted to cash, which is then divided up among your creditors. Your bankruptcy is then discharged (completed) and most creditors can no longer try to obtain payment from you, even if the total amount you owed them was not paid off.

Chapter 13 bankruptcy is often called the "wage-earner's plan." Under Chapter 13, you work out a repayment plan, subject to court approval, that allows you to pay back some or all of your debts within three years—without giving up property. A Chapter 13 plan can be stretched out to five years if a judge can be persuaded to allow it.

In general, bankruptcy is a legal procedure that:

- Gives consumers who can't possibly pay back all their debts the opportunity to wipe them out and start over.
- Helps people who are having a difficult time paying their bills the chance to work out a reasonable repayment schedule and pay off part or all of their debts under the supervision of the court.
- Prevents creditors from stripping an individual or family of all their assets when they can't pay their bills.
- May offer some breathing room for someone who is facing wage garnishment, a repossession, utility disconnection, foreclosure or eviction, and needs time to work out a reasonable schedule for repayment.

Before Filing for Bankruptcy

Bankruptcy is a serious financial step, and I do not recommend you file for bankruptcy until other options have at least been examined. I frequently hear from people who declared bankruptcy and now feel like financial failures: They can't get credit, their applications to rent apartments or homes are consistently declined, they find it difficult to travel or write checks because they don't have a major credit card, etc.

Some of these people complain that they were never really told about all the consequences of filing. Most were simply told that bankruptcy is an easy way to "start over again." One woman told me that her bankruptcy lawyer told her that she would be considered a *better* credit risk after filing, since she would no longer owe anyone any money.

Before you hire a bankruptcy lawyer, it may also be a good idea to talk with a credit counselor to see whether a repayment program can help, or with Myvesta.org about its CBA program, which is a unique alternative to bankruptcy. Again, making an informed decision is better than making a hasty decision you'll regret later.

Before deciding to file, you should also try to find a decent lawyer who can explain the pros and cons of both types of bankruptcy. Beware of someone who only tries to sell you on how wonderfully easy bankruptcy is and what a perfect solution it offers to all your problems.

Following are the basic differences between Chapter 7 and Chapter 13 bankruptcy. Of course, you'll want to check with your lawyer to make sure these rules are still current at the time you're reading this.

Chapter 7

What Happens in a Chapter 7 Bankruptcy Proceeding?

First you *file* for bankruptcy. You fill out a petition and several other forms that ask about your income, debts, and property and file them with the court. It costs about $150 to file (single or a married couple). If you can't afford the fee, you may be allowed to pay it in installments, or may even get it waived. Attorney's fees will typically run anywhere from $500 to $3,000, depending on your case. Shortly after you file, you are given a court date, and your creditors are notified that you have filed.

Many consumers are very relieved after filing. They don't have to endure nasty calls from debt collectors anymore—they can just tell them they have filed for bankruptcy. One of my friends who went through bankruptcy experienced this firsthand. One of her creditors called demanding payment. When she told him she had filed for bankruptcy, he politely said, "I hope things work out for you," and never called again.

Next, you go to court for the *"meeting of the creditors."* The name is deceptive, because creditors are unlikely to show up unless they plan to challenge your petition. Instead, you will meet with the trustee (the person the court appoints to administer your bankruptcy), who will go over your plan to determine if it is acceptable. The people I've spoken with who have been through bankruptcy tell me this meeting is very quick and easy. Often the trustee will ask a few basic questions, and you'll be out of there in a matter of minutes.

After the meeting of the creditors, the trustee will arrange to collect and sell your *nonexempt* property (I'll talk about that in a minute) and divide the cash among your creditors. If you can come up with the cash value of property you want to keep, you may be allowed to hold on to it. Or you may be able to exchange exempt property for nonexempt property.

Typically, your bankruptcy is *discharged* within three to six months of when you filed. This is the final act of the court, which clears you from your debts. You might have to go to court for a discharge hearing, but more likely you'll be notified by mail of the discharge. After your bankruptcy has been discharged, creditors generally cannot try to collect any unpaid debts from you—except, of course, for debts that weren't discharged.

What Can You Keep?

As I mentioned earlier, when you file Chapter 7, you basically "wipe out" most debts after giving up some of your property. The property you get to keep is called "exempt" property. There are basically two types of rules that determine what you get to keep: state exemptions and federal exemptions. If you live in Arkansas, Connecticut, Hawaii, Massachusetts, Michigan, Minnesota, New Jersey, New Mexico, Pennsylvania, Rhode Island, South Carolina, Texas, Vermont, Washington, Wisconsin, or the District of Columbia, you can choose whether you want to file under federal exemptions or your state's exemptions. (Federal exemptions are usually better.) California filers have two state exemption lists to choose between. Everywhere else, you can only file under the state exemption schedule.

Exemptions vary widely. If you live in Florida, for example, your entire home equity is exempt under most circumstances. In Maryland, on the other hand, none of the value in your home is exempt. Under the federal exemption, up to $15,000 in home equity is exempt. For complete lists of state and federal exemption lists, refer to any of the Nolo books I mentioned earlier in this chapter.

Under Chapter 7, you will erase most of your debts, but you'll still be responsible for:

Secured loans

Court-ordered child support and alimony

Most student loans (except in cases where it is determined by the court that paying these loans would cause undue hardship to you or your dependents)

Most federal, state, and local taxes

Debts for personal injury or death caused by intoxicated driving

Court-ordered restitution imposed in a criminal case

If you want to keep property that is not exempt from bankruptcy, you can usually do it in one of three ways:

1. *Reaffirm the debt.* Suppose you have a car on which you owe $1,200, and none of the equity in the car is ex-

empt. You need the car to get to work so you make a legal arrangement with the creditor to pay off all or part of the debt during bankruptcy. This is called "reaffirming" the debt.

2. *Pay for it.* Suppose you want to keep a family heirloom that is worth $500. If you can get cash from a friend or relative to pay for it, you will probably be able to "buy" it back.

3. *Trade it for exempt property.* In some cases, you are allowed to trade the value of nonexempt property for exempt property.

Chapter 13

You must be employed or have a regular income (such as alimony, pension, support, or government benefits) to be eligible to file Chapter 13 bankruptcy. Your secured debts can't total more than $807,750 and unsecured debts cannot total more than $269,250.

Under Chapter 13, you formulate a plan to pay back some or all of your debts. You and your attorney will design your plan based on your income and debts, but in general, the requirements are as follows:

For unsecured debts, you pay back at least as much as the creditor would have received if you had filed Chapter 7.

For secured debts, you pay back at least the amount of the claim that the creditor agrees to accept, or you surrender the collateral to the creditor.

Certain debts such as taxes and child support must be paid in full.

If any creditor or other party objects to your plan, you must commit all your disposable income for three years to paying back your debts or pay back all your unsecured debts in full.

What Happens When You File for Chapter 13?

Similar to a Chapter 7 case, you will *file* for Chapter 13 by filling out forms describing your income, assets, and debts. You will also fill out a form describing your plan for paying back your debts over the next few years. You will pay a filing fee of about $150 when you file (same for married couples). If you can't afford the fee, you may be allowed to pay it in installments, but it will not be waived.

Soon after you file, the court will notify you of the meeting of creditors, at which time you will meet with the trustee (not a judge) and any interested creditors. Unsecured creditors rarely attend this meeting, but secured creditors may, especially if they disagree with a value you've assigned property. The trustee will go over your papers and ask questions about your plan and the papers you filed.

The same day, or within a few weeks, a confirmation hearing will be set. At this time, the court decides whether to accept the plan, and if so, "rules on confirmation." Once your bankruptcy plan is confirmed, the trustee will begin payments to your creditors. (You pay the trustee, not your creditors.) During the three years or so, as long as you make your payments, you're pretty much free to conduct your financial life as you wish.

If you meet the requirements of your plan, your bankruptcy will be *discharged* and your case closed.

There are a couple of differences between Chapter 7 and Chapter 13 that you should be aware of:

Cosigners: If you have cosigners on accounts who are not filing with you, under Chapter 7 the creditor can go after them almost immediately for payment. Under Chapter 13 your creditors cannot try to collect from cosigners until after it has been determined that you will not be able to pay back the debt in full—usually that's when your case is over.

Fraud: Under Chapter 7, if a lender can show that the information you gave in your application was false, or you otherwise fraudulently obtained credit, they can try to exclude that debt from your discharge. Credit card issuers in particular are getting more and more aggressive about this, and are looking to stop anyone who might have been on a recent spending spree from just wiping out their debts. Under Chapter 13, they usually must wait until you have completed the repayment plan before they can try to demand payment of the full debt.

Waiting Period: Chapter 7 can be filed every six years. Chapter 13 can be filed as often as you want (as long as the previous bankruptcy has been discharged).

Most consumers, over 80 percent of them, choose Chapter 7 rather than Chapter 13. Unfortunately, there isn't much incentive for consumers to file Chapter 13 rather than Chapter 7. Few creditors differentiate between the two when evaluating postbankruptcy applications for credit: Either type of bankruptcy can mean an automatic credit rejection. It's true that most credit bureaus will now remove a Chapter 13 bankruptcy from a credit report seven years from the date of filing, while Chapter 7 stays on for ten years from the date of filing. Still, for some people that may not seem like a great incentive to go through a Chapter 13 plan.

Note that even if you file for bankruptcy and don't go through with it, the fact that you filed for bankruptcy will appear on your credit file for up to ten years and may harm your chances of getting credit elsewhere. Don't use filing for bankruptcy as a way to scare a creditor into agreeing to a reasonable payment schedule.

When Not to Choose Bankruptcy

While an attorney can better help you evaluate whether or not you should file, here are some guidelines for when bankruptcy may *not* be your best option:

You Are "Judgment-Proof": In the financial industry, this is a term for consumers who have little money, little property, and no joint debts. If a person who is judgment-proof were to be sued, the creditor would have little chance of ever collecting the debt. If you have nothing to lose, why bother going through bankruptcy?

You'll Lose Property You Want (or Need) to Keep: If you are considering filing Chapter 7, keep in mind that you may have to surrender property that is not exempt or pay fair cash value for it.

If you are worried about losing nonexempt property, you may want to consider filing Chapter 13 instead.

You Are Worried About Losing Your Credit Rating: It is true that bankruptcy is usually the worst mark you can have on your credit file. Even those who have paid back most of their debts under a Chapter 13 bankruptcy find themselves rejected for credit. Nevertheless, bankruptcy does not mean you can't get credit ever again. See Chapter Four for suggestions on rebuilding credit after bankruptcy.

Someone Else May Be Saddled with Your Debts if You File: If someone has cosigned one or more of your loans, or if you have joint accounts, the lender can go after the coapplicant for payment once your liability is discharged under Chapter 7. There are ways to keep a cosigner out of the picture, however, by reaffirming a debt or paying off the creditor.

Your Bankruptcy May Be Challenged: Bankruptcy courts are so clogged that most petitions go through without a second glance, much less close scrutiny. Still, your bankruptcy may be challenged if there is evidence of fraud or abuse, or if there is evidence that you could pay back your debts under a Chapter 13 plan.

Visa and Citibank are each getting particularly tough about challenging fraudulent bankruptcies through programs that help them identify and challenge petitions from people they think are trying to "beat the system." Some of the signs that may alert your creditors to potential abuse include:

Running up large bills on credit cards just prior to filing.

Taking out cash advances right before you file.

Significant changes in spending patterns.

Continuing to make credit card purchases (especially for nonessentials) after you've consulted with a lawyer about your situation.

Attempts to hide property or income from the court, including recent transfers of large assets to relatives or friends.

Fraudulent credit applications (applications that falsely overstate income or understate debts, for example).

If you are worried that your bankruptcy petition may be challenged, get a good lawyer and be up-front with her about your problem.

You'll Need to Borrow Again Soon: While most people who have been through bankruptcy can get credit again, it does usually take a while, especially to get unsecured loans. Bankruptcy can make it especially difficult to rent a home or apartment, so if you have to declare bankruptcy, move before you file.

Life After Bankruptcy

For many consumers, bankruptcy spells R-E-L-I-E-F—relief from harassment by creditors, relief from mounds of bills, relief from the fear that they won't survive. Nevertheless, the aftermath of bankruptcy is tough. Many people who have gone through bankruptcy experience a period where they feel like financial failures.

I have had several close friends declare bankruptcy in the past couple of years. These were all people who seemed to be prospering only shortly before their financial problems overwhelmed them. In a couple of cases, difficult divorces literally forced them into bankruptcy. One friend lost everything due to a failed business. In all cases, their decisions to file were made after they considered every other option for getting out of debt. After bankruptcy, they had trouble buying cars, renting apartments, and getting loans. But they have survived just fine and they don't regret their decisions to file. If bankruptcy is your decision, you'll survive, too.

Author's note: At the time this book is preparing to go to press, in the fall of 2002, Congress was once again considering major overhauls to the bankruptcy code. These changes, if passed, will make it much more difficult for consumers to discharge their debts in a Chapter 7 bankruptcy. For updates to the bankruptcy law, visit my website at www.ultimatecredit.com.

PART THREE

A LIFETIME OF GREAT CREDIT

CHAPTER TEN

Battling the Bank:
How to Fix Billing Problems

My brother opened his American Express bill and found charges totaling hundreds of dollars for plane tickets he never bought. Because AmEx sends copies of the charge slips with the bill, he immediately was able to tell who purchased the tickets—a friend of a roommate, who had apparently stolen his credit card number.

Another man wrote to me because a thief withdrew $450 from his bank account through an ATM. He reported the loss immediately, which meant the bank should have only held him responsible for the first $50 in withdrawals. The bank, however, said he was responsible for the entire amount. He read an article I was quoted in several months later and contacted me to find out if he had any recourse.

Almost everyone seems to have a credit card story, and most involve a billing error. Billing errors are common: a payment that is never credited, a bill that doesn't arrive, or a dispute over merchandise purchased with a credit card. Federal law offers a great deal of protection against billing problems—but it's important to know how and when you can take advantage of those protections.

In this chapter, you will learn exactly how to get credit card companies to quickly resolve your billing complaints. The advice in this chapter can save you a great deal of time, trouble, and money if a problem occurs. Most credit card disputes are resolved without a problem. But I've received enough complaints from people to know that isn't always the way it works. The steps for solving problems with your credit card bills I outline in this chapter can:

- Save you money when you buy a shoddy product or service with a credit card.
- Help you resolve a problem with a stubborn merchant.
- Protect your credit rating from long-term damage if your dispute drags on and on.
- Show you how to avoid the potential pitfalls of convenience checks and debit cards.

One of the major advantages of paying for something with a credit card, as opposed to cash or a check, is the protection offered by a federal law called the Fair Credit Billing Act, which covers purchases made anywhere in the world, as long as the card was issued in the United States. If you have a problem with a merchant and you paid cash, you are often stuck with the shoddy merchandise while the merchant has your money. Short of hiring a lawyer (which may be too expensive) or taking the merchant to small claims court, you may be stuck. If you paid by credit card, however, you often have legal protection that allows you to refuse to pay the charge until the problem is resolved.

If you're tempted to skip this chapter because you don't have a credit card problem right now, at least keep in mind that the minute you do have a credit card dispute, this chapter will tell you exactly how to resolve it.

Like I said before, most billing problems are resolved without a problem, but when they're not, they can be a real nuisance for several reasons:

The Bureaucracy: Billing errors often involve several parties—the merchant who charged your account, the credit card company, and perhaps credit bureaus, if information about the dispute was passed on to them by creditors. Within the credit card company, your complaint is often handled by a number of people (for "efficiency"). You can call the customer-service department several times about the same dispute and be forced to explain the whole situation again and again, perhaps with someone who lacks the knowledge or authority to resolve your problem.

The Law: One law—the Truth-in-Lending Act—governs most disputes over credit card charges. Within that statute, however, are a couple of different procedures for resolving complaints. Some billing disputes are covered by different parts of the law, while some aren't covered at all.

The Cost: Many billing errors involve a relatively small dollar amount, so it is useless to threaten the card issuer with legal action if the matter is not resolved. They really don't believe you will take them to court over a $65 charge.

A billing error is not just a mistake in addition or subtraction on your credit card bill. Many types of problems with credit card purchases can be considered billing errors. The Fair Credit Billing Act (the FCBA) is the federal law that covers billing problems.

The FCBA is part of the larger and more comprehensive Truth-in-Lending Act. Because the Truth-in-Lending Act is fairly general, Congress gave the Federal Reserve Board the authority to issue rules interpreting the law. The Federal Reserve Board's guidelines are compiled in a document called "Regulation Z." These are the rules most card issuers and attorneys use to help them follow the law. According to Regulation Z, a billing error includes the following:

- Your statement lists a charge you didn't make, or a charge you don't recognize.
- Your statement lists a charge that you made, but the amount or date of the charge is listed incorrectly.
- Your statement lists a charge for goods or services you, or someone authorized by you, did not accept.
- Your statement lists a charge for goods or services that were not delivered as agreed when you purchased them: in the wrong quantity, size, color, or delivered on the wrong date, for example.

- Credit for merchandise you returned, or a payment you made, does not appear on your statement.
- Your statement contains an arithmetic error.
- Your statement was not delivered to you—as long as you provided the creditor with a change in address at least twenty days before the end of the billing cycle.

If there is a billing error on your statement, you are allowed by law to withhold payment on the charge and ask your card issuer to investigate and resolve the matter for you if the error is legitimate.

The FCBA is very specific about how a billing error must be handled. *Never* just pick up the phone to complain about a billing problem. The law states you must put your complaint *in writing* to the card issuer.

Your letter of complaint must arrive in the card issuer's mail no later than sixty days from the date the statement containing the charge in question was mailed. Note carefully that this is *not* sixty days from the date of the disputed charge, nor is it sixty days from the statement cut-off date.

It is often difficult to determine when your billing statement was sent because many card issuers mail statements in bulk mailings, which do not include a date in the postmark. If your statement envelope bears no postmark date, you can play it safe by assuming the postmark date is the "cut-off date"—the date listed on your statement as the "close of the billing cycle."

According to the FCBA, your letter to the creditor must contain:

- Identifying information: your name and address, and your account number.
- A description of the error: the date and amount of the error, and the reason you think the charge is incorrect.

Type your letter to make sure the person on the other end can read it. Make it brief and to the point, and fit your complaint into one of the billing-error categories I listed above. Be sure to mention in your letter that you are asserting your rights under the Fair Credit Billing Act. If you want, you can ask the card issuer to send you proof of the charge—a signed sales slip, for example.

Send your letter to the correct address. Many card issuers have an address for billing errors that is *different from the one for making payments*. Your letter *must* go to the address listed on your statement as the address for "billing errors" or "billing inquiries." (The law requires this address be listed on your statement.) This is very important—*never* send a dispute note with your payment. Many payments are processed automatically. You stand a very good chance of never receiving a reply to your letter if you mail it in the envelope with your check.

To be certain the card issuer received your letter, send it by certified mail, return receipt requested. This service is inexpensive, and it's well worth the extra trouble of going to the post office. A week or so after you mail the letter, you'll receive a slip with the signature of the person who received the letter, so you will have proof that it was received within the sixty-day time period. Be sure to keep a copy of your letter and your postal receipt for your records.

Several times I have helped people in cases where the card issuer refused to resolve a billing problem because the letter of complaint was supposedly never received, or was not received within the sixty-day time period. One of my friends, for example, was disputing a charge on her credit card bill. The card issuer, one of the largest in the country, claimed it had never received her written complaint, even though she had a signed postal receipt proving her certified letter of complaint had been received, *and* a signed receipt from Federal Express proving a letter she later sent by overnight delivery had been accepted by the card company!

If for some reason you do call the card company to complain about an error, *always* follow up promptly with a letter to the person with whom you spoke, outlining your conversation. Keep a copy of the letter for your records. I cannot emphasize enough the importance of putting your complaint in writing. Even if you call and the card issuer corrects the error promptly, you may find the same error reoccurring later, and you may not be able to resolve it if you never sent a letter of dispute.

By law, you do not have to pay any charges you are disputing— or related finance charges—until the matter is resolved. You must, however, pay any charges you are *not* disputing. This can be tricky because most people do not pay their entire balance in full at the end of the month. Under the provisions of the FCBA, you are allowed to pay the minimum monthly payment figured on your balance *minus* the amount related to the dispute. Since it is nearly impossible for anyone onther than an accountant to figure a minimum monthly payment with or without the disputed amount, it's easiest to simply pay the minimum payment indicated on your statement.

Billing Error Checklist

✓ Notify the card issuer right away.
✓ Send a certified letter explaining your dispute to the address for billing errors.
✓ Request evidence of the charge if you don't recognize it.
✓ Make sure your letter clearly identifies your account and clearly describes the problem.
✓ Withhold payment on the disputed amount if you want, but not on the rest of the bill.
✓ Keep a copy of your letter for your records.

Let the Credit Card Company Do It for You

When you have properly disputed a charge, you can relax for a few weeks while the card issuer pursues the complaint for you. According to the FCBA, it is the card issuer's responsibility to conduct a reasonable investigation to determine if the charge is correct. *It is not your responsibility to prove there is an error.* This is an important distinction because time and again consumers are asked to provide extensive documentation that the charge was in error.

This certainly does not mean you should withhold proof that will help your card issuer resolve your case quickly. If, for example, you have a credit slip from the merchant for a return that never appeared on your statement, by all means photocopy the receipt and include the copy in your letter of dispute. Don't, however, be bullied into thinking you can't get a credit if you don't have irrefutable proof that you are right.

The card issuer must respond in writing to your letter of dispute within thirty days of receiving it, but need not resolve your dispute in thirty days. If the card issuer needs more time to investigate, it can send you a letter stating that an investigation is under way.

The card issuer is allowed a total of two complete billing cycles or ninety days, whichever is less, to resolve your billing problem. The ninety days or two billing cycles deadline begins *the date your letter of dispute was received by the card issuer.* Suppose, for example, your statement closing date or "cut-off date" is the 28th of each month, and you sent a letter of dispute March 15. The card issuer would have until May 28 to resolve the problem. Since your letter was received in the middle of the March billing cycle, the final resolution to the problem would be required by the end of May—two complete billing cycles later.

Resolving the Problem

The card issuer can resolve your complaint in one of two ways: by posting a correction (usually a credit) to your account, or by sending you a letter stating that the charge is correct, with an explanation of why it is correct.

If you are withholding payment on the disputed amount, the card issuer cannot try to collect it from you or report you as late to a credit bureau while the problem is being investigated. If you fail to pay charges that are *not* in dispute, though, the card issuer can—and most likely will—consider your account delinquent and report it.

Note, however, that the card issuer can "freeze" the disputed amount while the error is being investigated. For instance, if your credit limit is $1,000, and the amount you are disputing is $500, the card issuer can count that $500 as if it were an outstanding charge on your account in figuring how much credit you have available to charge against.

If a dispute is settled in your favor, you cannot be charged finance charges on the disputed amount. If you have a card with a grace period and you paid all charges except those in dispute, the card issuer cannot charge you interest on the amounts not disputed because you failed to pay the entire balance during the dispute. In other words, if you usually pay your bill on time and this time you pay everything but the disputed amount, the card issuer can't charge you interest because you didn't pay the bill in full.

If you are outside the sixty-day time limit, or if you have not followed the correct procedures, you can still request what's called a "goodwill" chargeback from your issuer. They don't have to process it, and if they do they can charge you a fee for doing so, but it doesn't hurt to try—and it might work.

Chargebacks

In the credit industry, the process of disputing a charge and receiving a credit to your account is called a "chargeback." In a chargeback, the card company sends a chargeback slip to the merchant's bank—the bank where the company that charged your account deposits its credit card sales slips. The merchant's bank then debits the merchant's account for that amount, and the merchant receives a chargeback form. The merchant is now entitled to challenge the chargeback by providing information on why the charge is valid. If the merchant is successful in countering the chargeback request, you will receive a letter from your bank stating that the charge is valid, and outlining the reasons why.

What Happens if the Card Issuer Decides You Are Wrong?

If the card issuer decides no billing error occurred, or a different error occurred, it must send you a letter outlining the reasons why no error (or a different one) occurred. If you requested documentary evidence of the charge (a signed sales slip, for example, or proof that the merchandise was mailed to you), the card issuer must provide it to you. You then have two options:

1. Pay the disputed amount plus finance charges within your normal grace period. If you do not have a grace period, the card issuer must allow you ten days to pay before issuing a negative credit report to the credit bureaus.

2. Continue to withhold payment and risk collection activity against your account.

If you decide to continue withholding payment, you *must write* to the card issuer promptly—within your normal grace period (or within ten days if you have no grace period) and state that you are going to continue disputing the charge. The card issuer can then attempt to collect from you the disputed amount. It can also report your account as delinquent, but *only* if it also reports that the amount is in dispute, sends you a notice disclosing everyone to whom that report is made (usually the credit bureaus), and promptly clears your record with anyone who received that report once the matter is resolved.

If a card issuer does not properly follow the procedures for investigating a billing error within the required time limits, you are entitled to a credit of the first $50 of the disputed charges, whether or not the charge is correct. The card issuer probably won't offer this, so you'll have to ask for it. (California residents get the entire disputed amount if the creditor doesn't respond within the ninety-day time limit.)

A word of warning: Billing error procedures do not mean you are automatically entitled to a refund of a charge just because you are not satisfied with a purchase. Buyer's remorse is not a legitimate reason for disputing a charge. If, for instance, a clothing store has a "no refunds after ten days" policy and you change your mind after two weeks and try to return the merchandise, the card company is not obligated to secure you a refund. Unless you can find a reason why you should be entitled to a refund under the billing error provisions listed above, you may not be successful in obtaining a credit on your account. That doesn't mean it isn't worth a try—many card companies will attempt a chargeback if you appear to have a legitimate gripe.

How to Stop Payment on a Credit Card

Stopping payment on a credit card charge is not like stopping payment on a check. You don't have to notify the card company before the charge slip arrives at your bank. In fact, if you call your card company and tell them a charge is coming through and you want to stop payment before it is posted on your account, you'll probably be told it can't be done. Instead, if you have a legitimate complaint, wait until you get your statement listing the charge and dispute it by following the procedures outlined above.

If you *suspect* there is a problem with merchandise you purchased by credit card, complain in writing to the credit card company immediately—even if it is simply to tell them what is going on. Don't rely on the merchant's reassurances that they will straighten it out for you. Remember, there are strict time limits on most credit card disputes.

In Chapter Eleven, where I talk about telemarketing, I explain how the scamsters will try to get around the sixty-day limit on billing errors. They'll send you some junk instead of the prize you thought you won, and then when you complain, they'll say you can't request a refund until your "trial period" of sixty or ninety days is up. By then, you may have lost your right under the federal law to dispute the charge.

My suggestion is, unless you can get a credit slip in hand, write your credit card issuer and notify them of the dispute right away. It can't hurt, and it can protect you.

Claims and Defenses

There is another way to dispute a charge, separate and apart from the billing error rules outlined above. Called "asserting claims and defenses," it falls under the "Special Credit Card Provisions" section of the Truth-in-Lending Act.

This section of the law is usually described as the one for protesting the *quality* of goods or services purchased with a credit card. In fact, though, it can cover a number of types of credit-card-related disputes. This section of the law states that whenever a person accepting a credit card fails to satisfactorily resolve a dispute over a transaction paid for by credit card, the consumer can assert claims and defenses against the card issuer.

Asserting claims and defenses essentially means that if you have a legitimate and legal complaint against the merchant who sold you goods or services you purchased on a credit card, you can usually withhold payment for the balance of the charge. If the card company cannot help you resolve the matter, and decides to take you to court to collect the disputed amount, you can use in court the same defenses against the card issuer as you would against the merchant. In essence, the card company becomes the merchant in the court case.

The rules for asserting claims and defenses are:

1. The charge must be for $50 or more.
2. The charge must have taken place in the same state as your billing address, or within one hundred miles of your billing address.
3. You must have made a good-faith effort to resolve the problem with the merchant.

The $50 and one hundred-miles-in-your-state rules don't apply if the person (or merchant) accepting the credit card:

- Is also the card issuer (a purchase made in the department store using the department store's card, for example).
- Is controlled directly or indirectly by the card issuer.
- Is controlled directly or indirectly by a third party that also controls the card issuer.
- Is a franchised dealer in the card issuer's goods.
- Controls the card issuer directly or indirectly.
- Obtained the order for the disputed transaction through a mail transaction made or participated in by the card issuer.

Unlike billing errors, there is no time limit for asserting claims and defenses. In addition, you do not have to notify your card issuer in any particular way that you are asserting claims and defenses. You can telephone, write a letter, or drop by the bank in person. The catch is, however, that *you can only withhold the amount of the charge still outstanding on your account* at the time you contact the card issuer or the merchant about the dispute.

What if you have paid part of your bill and still want to assert claims and defenses? The law is very specific here. You determine the amount still outstanding on which you can assert claims and defenses by applying payments you have made on the account so far to your balance in this order: late charges in order of when they appeared on the account, finance charges in the order they appeared on the account, and finally, other charges in the order they appeared on the account. Whatever amount is left is the amount on which you can withhold payment.

It's important here to clear up a common misunderstanding about asserting claims and defenses. For some reason, this section of the law is typically described only as a way to dispute a charge if the *quality* of goods or services is substandard. It's true that it is technically the only way to dispute charges for quality disputes. Claims and defenses, however, do not apply only to quality problems. They apply to many situations where, legally, you have a case against the merchant who sold you the goods.

If goods or services you purchased with a credit card are never delivered, you probably have a case for asserting claims and defenses. If your state has a law requiring furniture stores to deliver merchandise within thirty days of purchase or offer a refund, and your sofa doesn't show up for two months, you probably have a case for asserting claims and defenses. If you don't know if you can assert claims and defenses in a dispute, it's worth trying anyway. (Even the credit card company lawyers that I ask about this provision aren't exactly clear how it should work.)

What does it mean to make a "good-faith effort" to resolve a problem with the merchant? It simply means that you tried to resolve the problem in good faith. You don't need a letter as proof, you don't need a witness, and you don't have to go into the store to speak with the merchant directly. In one case, for example, a court upheld that the consumer had made a good-faith effort to resolve the dispute even though the merchant claimed never to have been contacted. The customer proved his good faith effort by producing payment stubs bearing notes from telephone conversations with the merchant.

The geographic limitations for asserting claims and defenses aren't always clear. For example, if you called a mail-order company in another state and ordered merchandise that was sent to you, where did the charge originate? The Federal Reserve Board, the government agency which interprets this law, claims it is a matter of state law. Some states have laws, called state "venue" laws, that do specify that purchases made by telephone or mail are deemed to have taken place at the buyer's location, regardless of the seller's location. Your state attorney general's office should be able to clarify this for you.

If you're embroiled in a dispute over a purchase you made over the telephone or through the mail, and the merchant is located across the country, you may want to try asserting claims and defenses anyway. If the card issuer refuses to place the amount in dispute because the transaction did not occur locally, counter that the transaction did originate in your home state—at your mailbox or on your telephone. In many cases, you will be right. Even if you aren't, they probably won't be familiar enough with your state's law to argue.

What happens when you assert claims and defenses? Unlike the FCBA, the card issuer is not required to follow any particular procedures to resolve the matter. It may issue a chargeback, but most likely will place the account under dispute. You then have the opportunity to resolve the problem with the merchant.

If you assert claims and defenses, the card issuer is prohibited from reporting the amount as delinquent. (The card issuer can, however, report that the account is under dispute.) This section of the law allows a card issuer to attempt to collect the disputed amount through its normal channels for collection. It's a major weakness in the law because it gives the card issuers the opportunity indirectly to damage a customer's credit rating. If the card issuer's normal channels for collection include filing a lawsuit, your credit rating could be damaged anyway, since lawsuits routinely appear on credit reports.

Some disputes may be covered by both the billing errors section of the law and the special credit card provisions. For instance, if you used your credit card to pay for goods that were never delivered, you can claim a billing error, if you write to the card issuer within the sixty-day time limit. In addition, you can assert claims and defenses if you have not yet paid that portion of the bill.

Since asserting claims and defenses is confusing and somewhat obscure, I usually try to get people to dispute charges as billing errors first. But if you run into a problem where you've waited too long, or it really is a dispute over the quality of services, or your problem doesn't fit neatly into a billing error category, you may need to take advantage of the protection offered by this part of the law.

Sticky Situations

Billing disputes aren't always cut-and-dried. One problem may arise regarding unauthorized use. Let's say you give your daughter your credit card to pay for books at school; instead she hits the shopping mall and runs up a big bill. Are the charges unauthorized and can you dispute them?

The Truth-in-Lending Act defines unauthorized use as the use of a credit card by a person other than the cardholder who does not have actual, implied, or apparent authority for such use, and from which the cardholder receives no benefit. By allowing your daughter to use the card for the first purchases, you may have given her implied authority to use the card. Some courts, however, have determined that if you allow someone to use the card for a specific purchase, and they use it for something else, the use is not authorized. Unauthorized use can be a very sticky question, however, and often is affected by state law. You may want to contact an attorney and your state attorney general's office for more information.

The fact is, though, someone is going to have to pay for those charges—either you or your daughter.

I have run into this kind of problem more than once, and very often the parent (or girlfriend, or coworker) doesn't want to pay the bill, but also doesn't want to get the person who used the card in trouble. If possible, have your daughter return what she purchased. If that's not possible, dock her allowance or work out a repayment schedule. If your card was actually stolen by your daughter (or someone you know) and you can't pay the bill, you may be required to identify them for a police report. That's a step only you can decide to take.

Another situation to watch out for is unauthorized charges that may actually be considered "authorized." For example, let's say you take your car in for repairs and the garage runs an imprint of your card through when you drop it off. The garage then goes ahead and makes repairs you didn't tell them to make. You may feel entitled to dispute those charges as unauthorized but it might not work. Under the billing regulations, charges are only considered unauthorized if the card was used without your permission *and* you did not receive a benefit. You may still be able to assert claims and defenses, though, or file a billing error dispute.

A third complaint I receive is about purchases going through on accounts that have been closed, sometimes years before. An example would be a recurring charge for a subscription or club membership, for example, or even a fraudulent charge. Consumers ask me, "How can a charge go through on an account that is closed?" The answer is that an account is never *really* closed. There's nothing in federal law, for example, that says that an account can't be charged later, and some issuers will allow charges to go through on closed accounts. (You also have to ask yourself whether you actually closed the account or just stopped using it. There's a difference.) If one of these charges is a mistake or is unauthorized, you must deal with it the same way you would deal with any other billing error.

Additional Billing Rules

Payments: If you make a payment to the address listed on your statement for payments in the manner described by the issuer, your card issuer must credit your account for the payment as of the date of receipt. If for some reason posting is delayed, you can't be charged extra interest or fees because of it.

There have been complaints and some class-action lawsuits against some issuers because consumers complained that they sent their payments well before the due date but were credited late—and late charges were imposed. If you suspect this is happening with one of your issuers, you should first dispute the fee with your issuer (most will waive one a year), and complain to the regulatory agency (see the Resources section). In the future, you'll have to either pay your bill very early, get some kind of delivery confirmation from the post office, or pay your bill with that issuer on-line.

Returns and Credits: When you return merchandise purchased on a credit card, the merchant must process the credit slip within seven business days of accepting the return. The card issuer must then post a credit to your account within three business days of receiving the credit slip.

Cash or Credit Refunds: If a merchant regularly gives cash refunds to customers who pay by cash, the merchant must also give cash or credit refunds to customers who pay by credit card, unless the merchant notifies customers at the time of purchase that it does not give cash or credit refunds.

Credit Balances: If your account shows a credit balance of $1 or more, you can write your card issuer for a refund. Within seven business days of receiving your letter, your card issuer must send you a refund for the credit balance. If a credit balance remains on your account for six months, the card issuer must try to refund you by check, cash, or money order. If you cannot be located through your last known address, however, the card issuer is not obligated to take any further action.

Lost or Stolen Credit Cards: If your credit card is lost or stolen and a thief uses it, the most you can be held liable for is the first $50 of unauthorized charges. If you notified the card issuer of the loss or theft before the card was used, you do not have to pay for any unauthorized charges on the account.

You can only be held liable for the first $50 if:

1. *The credit card is an accepted credit card.* An accepted card is one you requested or applied for; you received; and you signed, used, or authorized another person to use to obtain credit. If, for instance, someone fraudulently takes out a card in your name and uses it, you can't be held responsible for any charges on that account. Or, if—and this is very important— someone uses your card *number* (if they took it from a charge slip, for example) but *not* the actual card, you cannot be held liable for any amount of the fraudulent charges.

2. *The card issuer has provided adequate notice of your liability* if the card is fraudulently used, and has provided you with information about how to notify the card issuer in case of loss or theft. You will usually receive this notification with your cardholder agreement, although it may occasionally appear on a billing statement or on the credit card itself.

It's important to know that most issuers do not hold consumers responsible for that first $50. In fact, all major card issuers offer "zero liability" limits for fraudulent uses of their cards, so you won't be charged that $50 in any case if your card is used without your authorization and you act reasonably to dispute it. Keep in mind that with Internet purchases, where the card number but not the actual card is used, your liability for fraud is always $0 under federal law.

The rules for liability in the case of unauthorized charges do not apply only to lost or stolen credit cards. Don't overlook this section when you are trying to dispute a charge you didn't make. For instance, you may be going through your charge records at tax time and notice charges from six months ago on your account that you never made. If you try to dispute it with your card issuer to report the error, they are likely to tell you it is too late to dispute the charge. As long as the conditions for unauthorized use are met, however, there is no time limit for disputing an unauthorized charge.

No Statement in the Mail: Under the FCBA, failure to send a billing statement is considered a billing error. If you realize after one month that you haven't received a statement, call the card issuer immediately to find out where the statement has been sent. A data entry error may have occurred causing your address to be inadvertently changed.

There have also been cases involving fraud, where someone changed the address on someone else's account and then ordered merchandise by phone or mail on the card. Since the cardholders didn't receive statements, they didn't suspect anything was wrong. The bills went unpaid, and the cardholders later received calls from bill collectors demanding payment.

If you don't receive a bill, call the issuer and ask what's going on. If they say that the bill was sent or was sent to a different address, follow the procedures for billing errors, and promptly write a letter to the card issuer explaining the problem. Send your letter via certified mail, return receipt requested, and keep a copy for your records. The entire balance of the statement will be placed in dispute.

After the card issuer sends you a copy of your bill, you have the amount of time you normally have to pay a statement to pay the amount you would have paid had you properly received the statement. In other words, if you have a twenty-five-day grace period and your minimum payment is $25, you would have twenty-five days to send in your $25 payment and avoid a negative mark on your credit file.

Don't figure that just because you didn't get a bill this month you don't have to worry about paying anything! Be sure to call the card issuer immediately if you don't receive a statement. Under the billing errors rule, you have sixty days from the date the statement should have been sent to you to assert a billing error. If you wait several months and the card issuer finally sends you a bill with several months' worth of legitimate charges you failed to make any payments on, you may find your credit damaged because you didn't pay.

Unsolicited Credit Cards: It used to be common for card issuers to send out promotional mailings with credit cards included. That practice is now illegal. By law, you must request or accept a credit card before the card issuer can send you one. You can accept orally or in writing—either is legal. In addition, the card may be different than the one you requested—for example, the card you receive may have features additional to those advertised.

A card issuer can, however, send out a substitute credit card in place of a current card. In addition, unsolicited debit cards may be sent if the issuer does not allow them to be used (activated) until the consumer has requested that they be validated and the consumer's identity is confirmed. For a substitute debit card, new features may be added. For example, your ATM card could be substituted with a debit card carrying a MasterCard or Visa logo, and that card could allow purchases off-line (without a PIN).

Surcharges: An extra fee just for using a credit card is called a surcharge. They used to be illegal under federal law but that law expired some time ago. Nevertheless, the major credit card companies don't allow surcharges and in some states they are illegal. But you may find instances where you do pay an extra fee when you use a credit card—and that's not supposed to be based on the method of payment you choose. For example, if you were to purchase tickets on-line and the company that sold the tickets charged a handling fee, that would not be considered a surcharge if the fee applied to everyone who bought tickets on-line. But if they charged an extra 5 percent for purchases made by credit card, but didn't charge it if you agreed to have your checking account debited for the ticket, then it would be considered a surcharge and would not be allowed.

Convenience Checks: Cash advance checks are commonly called "convenience checks" by card companies who send them, encouraging customers to use their credit cards as cash. (My card issuers always send me a book of them around the December holidays.) They look like personal checks, but if you use them the amount of the check will be posted to your credit card account as a cash advance. Purchases made with convenience checks— even though they are drawing on the same line of credit as your plastic—are *not* covered by the billing error rules. Avoid using them to buy items. If you pay by cash advance check and there is a problem with the merchandise, you must deal with the merchant directly, just as you would with a personal check. (Note: If a convenience check is *lost or stolen*, you are not responsible for more than $50 in fraudulent charges.)

If you are making a large purchase, it's much smarter to pay by credit card rather than using the company's finance plan or a convenience check from your credit card company. The billing error rules and special credit card provisions give you leverage if there is a problem later.

Reading Your Rights: If you want to read the Fair Credit Billing Act, write the Federal Reserve Board (see the Resources chapter for an address), or your Representative in Congress and request a copy of *Regulation Z, Truth-in-Lending* and a copy of the *Official Staff Commentary on Regulation Z*. The Fair Credit Billing Act is found in sections 226.13 of the Regulation.

Tips on Resolving Your Complaints

If you follow the procedures I've outlined above, you should be able to resolve your credit card complaints quickly. There are cases, however, where a customer complains properly but the bank refuses to resolve the matter. I've seen letters from some of the largest credit card companies in the country that completely *misstate* the consumer's right to dispute a charge.

I once took out a classified ad in the *Washington Post* and they billed me several times what it should have cost me. I complained to them and they told me it would take a couple of months for me to get a refund—which could only be given by check. I wrote to my credit card company and they told me there was nothing they could do—I'd have to resolve the problem directly with the merchant. They were completely wrong.

What should you do if you think your card issuer is giving you the runaround on a legitimate billing error?

1. Find out the name of the attorney in the bank's legal department who is in charge of making sure the bank follows the Truth-in-Lending Act. (This person is often called the "compliance officer.") Send a copy of your complaint to that person, and outline why you think the bank is not properly handling the dispute.
2. Send a letter of complaint to the card issuer's regulatory agency (see the Resources section for details) and send a copy of that letter to the bank's legal department.
3. Consult with an attorney. Under the Truth-in-Lending Act, you can sue a creditor that fails to follow the law. If the creditor shows, however, that its mistake was unintentional and that procedures had been set up to avoid such errors, it cannot be held liable. If you do win your case in court, you may receive:

    a. Payment for any actual financial injury to you result-
ing from the creditor's failure to follow the requirements of the law.

    b. Twice the amount of any finance charge involved,
but not less than $100 or more than $1,000.

    c. Court costs and a reasonable fee for your attorney.

4. Consider taking the bank or merchant to small claims
court. In many cases, the bank would rather settle the
matter than pay the expense of defending itself in court.
If you want to pursue this avenue, send for Nolo.com's
excellent self-help book *Everybody's Guide to Small
Claims Court* (see the Resources section).

Debit and ATM Card Billing Errors

As I mentioned in Chapter Three, debit cards (ATM cards as
well as Visa and MasterCard debit cards) don't offer the same federal protection against fraudulent purchases and unauthorized
charges that credit cards do. If you don't catch the unauthorized
use in time, you could potentially lose all the money in your account *plus* your overdraft line of credit.

Here's how it works:

If your ATM or debit card is lost or stolen, the Electronic
Funds Transfer Act (EFTA), a federal law, requires you to notify
your bank or credit union of the loss within two business days. If
you do that, the most you can be held liable for is the first $50 of
any fraudulent withdrawals or charges.

But if you find out the card has been lost or stolen and you fail
to tell the bank within the next two business days, you could be
held liable for up to $500 in fraudulent withdrawals—but only if
the bank can prove you knew the card was gone and didn't tell
them.

What happens if you don't find out that your card's been used
until you get your statement and see the fraudulent charges? Notify your bank as soon as possible. You have sixty days from the
date that statement was mailed to you to tell the bank your card's
been used fraudulently. If you do, you will only be held liable for

the first $50 of unauthorized charges, but if you don't, and a thief uses your card after those sixty days, you could find your entire account—and any overdraft line of credit—wiped out.

Both MasterCard and Visa have created "no liability" policies for debit cards that carry their logos. Under their policies you generally won't be held liable for any fraudulent use of your personal debit card as long as you take reasonable care in protecting it. The only caveat is that it may not cover some purchases where a PIN is used, and won't cover ATM withdrawals.

The biggest problem with debit card fraud is not liability, but the "hassle factor" in cases where it takes time to get the money back into your account. If you discover that unauthorized withdrawals have occurred, you should contact your issuer immediately. Instructions for doing so will be listed in the agreement you received with the card. I'd recommend you hold on to that, but if you don't have it, just go ahead and call the bank right away to report the fraud. As with any problem of this kind, keep careful records of whom you spoke with and when.

Once you notify the issuer of the problem, they have up to ten business days to investigate and notify you of the results of their investigation. Once they determine there is an error, they must credit your account immediately. If they cannot complete an investigation within ten business days, they can provisionally credit your account within that time period and they have up to forty-five days to investigate.

Protect Your Debit and ATM Cards

✓ Don't write down your PIN number—even "disguised" as a phone number.
✓ Don't choose your Social Security number, birth date, or another "easy" number as your PIN.
✓ Save your receipts.
✓ Review your checking or savings account statement to make sure there haven't been unauthorized withdrawals.

Another potential disadvantage of debit cards is that they don't really offer stop-payment privileges. If you purchase something with a check, you can usually stop payment on the check if you contact your bank promptly. If you purchase something by credit card, and there is a problem with the merchandise, you can usually dispute the charge through your credit card and get a credit to your account. But if you purchase an item with a debit card and there is a problem, you cannot stop payment on the transaction. If there's a problem with your purchase, you will have to deal with the merchant directly—just as if you paid with cash.

Direct Debits

Most banks allow customers to set up direct transfers to cover regular payments such as utility bills, health club dues, insurance payments, etc. If you have authorized direct debit to your account and later change your mind, you must notify your bank that you want to stop payment, orally or in writing, at least three business days before the transfer. If you notify the bank orally that you want to stop payment, your bank may require you to follow up your request in writing within fourteen days. This stop-payment right doesn't apply to direct debits for loan payments to the bank that issued your debit card.

ATM Errors

What happens if the bank makes a mistake on your statement or the ATM machine makes an error? Under the EFTA, you have sixty days from the date it occurred to dispute the error. It is best to contact *your* bank (even if you made the withdrawal at another bank's ATM) immediately. Call, then follow up with a certified letter (get a return receipt) outlining what was discussed.

Once you notify the bank of the problem, they have ten business days to investigate and notify you of the results of the investigation. If the investigation will take more than ten days, the bank must credit your account for the disputed amount, and then it has up to forty-five days to investigate. If the bank determines there was no error on your account, it must send you a letter explaining why it concluded no error occurred.

Never deposit cash at an ATM. Your receipt is *not* proof of your deposit. I have heard true horror stories from consumers who have deposited hundreds of dollars in cash in an ATM machine, only to be told by the bank that their deposit envelope was "empty" when it was opened.

Also note that if there is a problem with a cash advance taken out on your credit card at an ATM, the transaction is governed by the Fair Credit Billing Act, not the Electronic Funds Transfer Act. That's an important distinction to make, since the FCBA's protection is usually the stronger of the two. So if a thief takes your Visa credit card and uses it to take out a cash advance at an ATM machine, you must dispute the charge through your credit card company.

Another tip: If your bank charges a fee for ATM withdrawals, try to withdraw the maximum daily amount, rather than taking out just $10 or $20. The fee is the same no matter how much you get, and it can really add up if you're stopping at the ATM every other day!

CHAPTER ELEVEN

Protecting Your Credit and Your Financial Privacy

One of my friends, an older woman on a fixed income, received a letter announcing she had won a sweepstakes. Her prize? $5,000 cash. All she had to do was buy some "environmentally safe" cleaning supplies. The offer looked real to her, so she responded.

All she received was a box of worthless plastic bottles, some cheap cleaning solutions, and a charge for almost $800 on her credit card. When she tried to dispute the charge, the Las Vegas–based company refused to give her a refund, pointing out that she had given her signature "authorizing" the charge.

Do you worry about giving out your credit card number when you write a check? Have you ever found charges on your credit card statement for purchases you never made—and then wondered who had been using your credit card? Or are you afraid that "junk mail" and mailing lists are getting out of hand?

Credit card fraud is a multimillion-dollar business. In this chapter, I'll warn you about the top credit card scams and show you how to protect yourself. If you've already been victimized, I'll show you how to fight back.

I'll also look at the issue of financial privacy in this chapter.

You'll learn what you can do to protect yourself from invasions of privacy and leaks in your personal information.

Credit Card and Check Purchases

How many times has a store clerk asked you to provide your phone number on a credit card sales slip? Or asked you for a driver's license and a major credit card when you were making a purchase by check—and then proceeded to write both on your check? Exactly what information can you refuse to provide when making a purchase?

When making purchases with Visa, MasterCard, or American Express cards, all you need to provide the clerk is a valid, signed card and your signature. (A signature is not even required in telephone purchases.) You do not have to provide a phone number, address, or any other additional information on a credit card sales slip—and the merchant cannot refuse to sell you the merchandise if you don't. (The exception is cash advances, which frequently require identification.)

When you're using a Discover card, merchants can ask to see other identification, but they can't write it down.

What about when you write a check? The credit card companies don't like the fact that some merchants write down credit card numbers when customers make purchases by check. They claim they can't stop the practice, however, because these are "not credit card transactions." The major credit card companies do, however, limit what merchants can do with a credit card number they get off a check to basically nothing. Merchants can't use credit cards as backups for bounced checks, and credit card information can't be used to locate customers.

In a number of states it's actually illegal for merchants to write credit card numbers on checks, and in a couple of states a merchant can't refuse to accept your check just because you don't provide a major credit card as identification.

Why do merchants write credit card numbers on checks? Some claim that credit card holders are more likely to be financially responsible, others want credit card numbers on checks to ensure that their clerks are indeed checking two forms of identification from customers. Finally, merchants may still occasionally use credit cards as backups for checks that bounce. (If a check bounces, they just fill out a credit card sales slip manually, write "signature on file" or "phone order" in place of the signature, and process it like any other card transaction.)

What can you do if you encounter a clerk who insists on writing your credit card number on your check or demands your phone number when you are making a credit card purchase?

1. Talk with the store manager or owner, not a salesclerk. The clerk has probably been told it's his job to collect that information and may have even been threatened with the loss of a job if the information is not properly collected.
2. Find out why the information is being collected. If the manager says it's "because bad-check losses are so high," ask her how collecting a credit card number reduces fraud losses—since she's not allowed to use the card to collect.
3. Explain the credit card companies' rules about using credit cards as backups for checks, or point out that the credit card companies don't allow merchants to require customers to provide personal information when making credit card purchases.
4. Express your concern about credit fraud and offer to let the clerk write down the name of the card-issuing bank and expiration date in lieu of the card number.
5. If you are making a credit card purchase and the clerk insists you provide personal information on the sales slip, ask for the name of the bank where they deposit their credit card slips. You will need the name of the merchant's bank to file a complaint with your credit card company.
6. Remind the merchant that there have been fraud cases related to collecting this type of information, and tell her that if her employees ever use your information fraudulently, she may be held liable for requiring them to collect it.
7. If all else fails, politely refuse to shop there and lodge a

complaint with the credit card company, Better Business Bureau, your local consumer-affairs office, or a local media "action line."

Minimum Purchase Requirements

Merchants cannot require you to buy a certain amount (for example, $10 or more) when you use your credit card. Minimum purchase requirements are legal under federal law, but the major credit card companies do not allow them. Visa and MasterCard's rules strictly prohibit minimum purchase requirements. American Express doesn't want its cardholders to be discriminated against, so if a merchant that accepts AmEx also accepts Visa and MasterCard, it cannot enforce a minimum on AmEx customers. If a merchant only accepts AmEx, theoretically it can have a minimum purchase requirement, but if you complain to AmEx, they'll try to persuade the merchant to change its policy. Any complaints should be lodged in the same way I described in the last paragraph.

Telemarketing Fraud

Who says snake-oil salesmen went out with gunfights and saloons? There is still a fast buck to be made off consumers hoping for an end to their financial problems forever, and there are plenty of slimeballs who are willing to take money from unsuspecting dreamers.

Many of these smooth operators take to the telephone to make their sales pitches. The telephone allows them to get someone's attention, make a fast pitch, and close the deal in a matter of minutes. It also puts the consumer at a disadvantage because he doesn't have time to think about the offer or check it out first. Credit cards have become the tool of the trade for many of these scams because they are so easy to use.

There are a couple of types of telemarketing promotions that are usually associated with fraud: sweepstakes or prize promotions and travel promotions.

Did I Really Win?

You have probably received a letter or postcard from a "Sweepstakes Claim Center" alerting you that you have won a prize. All you need to do to claim the prize is call a toll-free number. The operator explains that you have been selected to participate in a promotion and if you take part, you are guaranteed one of the following prizes: a luxury powerboat, a twelve-carat diamond ring, or a $5,000 savings bond. All you have to do is purchase a six-month supply of vitamins for $299.95.

You give the company your credit card number and wait for your winnings to arrive. First come the vitamins. They are cheap vitamins worth far less than you paid for them. Still, you figure the prize will make up for the fact that you paid so much for the vitamins. You wait some more.

When your guaranteed prize doesn't arrive, you call the company. They apologize, saying that the response has been overwhelming and they are backlogged, but you will be receiving your prize in a few weeks. They even send a confirmation, in writing, that your prize is on the way.

When you finally receive your prize, you can't believe you've been ripped off. Your join the ranks of thousands of other consumers who have been duped by prizes that turn out to be worthless. For example:

- Your luxury powerboat turns out to be an inflatable rubber dinghy with a tiny rotary "motor."
- Your $5,000 savings bond is really a *share* in a $5,000 savings bond—your share is worth about $50 or less.
- Your diamond ring turns out to be a cheap ring with a diamond chip—practically worthless.

When you call to complain, you find it hard to get through to the company. You may even find the firm has already closed shop. If the company is still around, they will probably make endless promises for refunds that never materialize. Eventually, they go out of business. You never do get your money back.

I can't even begin to describe the variations on this theme. Thousands of people have lost millions of dollars in these types of promotions. Some people have even been duped two or three times. Dumb? Not necessarily. Some of these promotions are pretty slick, and I've heard from consumers from all walks of life who have been taken.

How do they get away with such outright scams?

1. They work out of state and sell across state lines. Knowing it will be very difficult for someone to pursue a case against a company thousands of miles away, they can operate unchecked for months or years.
2. Regulatory authorities generally have their hands tied. There are many different enforcement agencies, some with limited authority, and a huge backlog of cases.
3. They change names and locations frequently. By the time large volumes of complaints begin to pour in, the scam artists are gone.
4. The sixty- or ninety-day trial period. Many of these companies know that the Fair Credit Billing Act allows you to charge back the merchandise if it turns out to be different from what you ordered (see Chapter Ten). So they ask you to try goods for sixty or ninety days, or perhaps as much as a year. If you wait until after the trial period to ask for a refund, you have forfeited your right to dispute the charges under the FCBA, and your chances of getting money back directly from the company are practically nil.

Help from the Federal Trade Commission

In 1995, the Federal Trade Commission implemented the Telemarketing Sales Rule to cut down on fraudulent telemarketing. Here are some of the protections it offers:

When They Call: Telemarketers have to say right away that this is a sales call, who is calling, the nature of what they're selling, and, if it's a prize promotion, the fact that no purchase or payment is necessary to win.

Before You Pay: The telemarketer has to disclose:

- the total cost of the goods and any material restrictions on obtaining or using them.
- the terms of any refund, exchange, or repurchase policy mentioned or, if the seller's policy is "no refunds or exchanges," a statement to that effect.
- in any prize promotion, the odds of winning, any material costs or conditions for receiving the prize, and the fact that no purchase or payment is necessary to win, and the no purchase/no payment method for entering.

More Protections: It's illegal to call someone who has asked not to be called again. In addition, the rule does not allow:

- Telemarketers calling before 8 A.M. or after 9 P.M., your time.
- Withdrawing money from consumers' checking accounts without their express, verifiable permission.
- Telemarketers selling credit repair services, recovery services ("we can get back the money you lost in the last scam"), or advance-fee loan services from seeking payment until after the services have been rendered.

If you have received a call from a telemarketer that you believe has not followed the guidelines listed above, contact the Federal Trade Commission (see the Resources section) or the National Fraud Information Center hotline.

I Want My Money Back!

What can you do if you have tried to get a refund from a company you suspect is not on the up and up, but it is past the sixty-day time frame?

1. If you paid by credit card, write your card issuer a letter of dispute—just as you would if you were in the sixty-day time frame—and request a chargeback anyway. Visa

and MasterCard say they will in some cases extend the time limits for telemarketing fraud disputes.

2. If the card issuer writes you and says it can't help you because you are out of the sixty-day time period, ask them to try to get you a refund on a "goodwill" basis. Visa and MasterCard rules may allow chargebacks past the sixty-day time period, depending on the situation.

3. Assert claims and defenses. Try to dispute the charge under the special credit card provisions (see Chapter Ten). Argue that since the charge originated in your home state, you can withhold payment. Let the bank's lawyers try to prove you wrong. (They may find you are right.)

4. Raise the roof. Write the owner of the company a very professional, typed, no-nonsense letter and at the bottom of the letter "CC:" it to your attorney, your local consumer protection office, your local television troubleshooter's office, the state attorney general's office, and/or the credit card company. That's how I managed to get a refund for my elderly friend in the example at the beginning of this chapter. Note: intimidation doesn't always work, especially for companies that receive a large volume of complaints.

5. Report your case to the National Fraud Information Center. Here's why:

Help Is on the Way!

Before you respond to any telemarketing offer, unless you are *absolutely 100 percent certain* you know the company you're dealing with is legitimate, call the National Fraud Information Center (NFIC).

The NFIC offers a toll-free hotline that will allow you to talk with professional counselors who can answer your questions about fraud (in both Spanish and English).

If you've already been taken, your complaint to the NFIC will be referred directly to appropriate federal and state enforcement agencies and consumer-protection offices—within minutes. Law enforcement agencies are able to crack down on fraudulent companies much more quickly, thanks to the NFIC database.

Call the NFIC at 1-800-876-7060.

Identity Theft

If you are the victim of identity theft, you may not find out until months or years after it happened. You may not find out until you get a collection call from a credit card company you have never heard of about late payments for a card that's not yours. Or you may apply for credit and be turned down because your credit record shows a history of late payments even though you pay on time.

Identity theft is very serious. It involves someone else using your good name to apply for credit. Someone may steal your purse and then use your driver's license and other identification to hit a number of department stores for "instant credit." Information about you may also be stolen from employee files at work, illegally obtained from credit bureaus, taken off checks you have written, or compiled through public information. People in the public eye frequently are victimized by identity theft. The results of this type of fraud are often staggering—thousands of dollars in unpaid bills outstanding in your name, creditors hounding you for payments, and a destroyed credit rating.

What do you do if you find out you are a victim of identity theft? There's no single way to straighten out your credit problems (and they will likely be severe), so be prepared for a lot of work. Here's how to tackle it:

1. Immediately contact the three major credit bureaus and request that a "fraud alert" or "block" be placed on your file. That way, anyone who accesses your file in the future will be notified of potential fraud. Warning: It may make it more difficult for you to get credit for several months. (But it shouldn't affect your ability to use your credit cards.) See the Resources section for information on contacting the three major bureaus.

2. Get a police report promptly. You may need it to convince the card issuers that you weren't on a spending spree you just don't want to pay for. If the police give you a hard time about giving you a report, be persistent. That piece of paper will be very helpful.

3. Notify card issuers about the fraud. For new accounts that have been opened under your name, they will probably want you to fill out a fraud affidavit and may want to see a police report. Go to the Federal Trade Commission's Web site, www.consumer.gov/idtheft/ affidavit.htm, and download their identity theft affidavit. It is accepted by many card issuers, credit reporting agencies, and collectors for reporting new accounts opened in your name. This single form may save you time.

4. Contact your state attorney general's office and the Secret Service. Some state attorney general's offices have white-collar crime units that investigate these types of cases. The Secret Service is charged with investigating credit fraud, but they generally won't get involved in "small" cases (what's big to you may be small to them— I've never been able to get specific guidelines). How helpful enforcement authorities will be depends on the severity of the crime and their willingness to get involved in an individual case. Some are helpful, some aren't.

5. Subscribe to a credit reporting service that will allow you to review your credit report frequently. Many companies offer this service on-line. If you have been victimized by credit fraud, you will want to know when anyone pulls your file, or when negative information is added to it. Monitor your file frequently for at least a year.

6. Keep detailed records of *everything*: your phone calls to card issuers, when you made them, who you spoke with, and what they said. Send all correspondence via certified mail and keep copies for your records. Don't assume that once the problem dies down that it is over. Since negative information can stay on your file for

seven years, you should keep all your records for that long.

7. If the theft involved your Social Security number, as is often the case, contact the Social Security Administration (SSA) at 1-800-772-1213 to verify the accuracy of your reported earnings and to ensure that your name is still reported correctly. In some cases of fraud, it is possible to get a new Social Security number, but that can create more problems than it solves. You may find any good credit history you've developed is left behind, or you may find that you have more trouble getting credit because your name, address, and other information is now matched to two Social Security numbers—a sign of possible fraud.

8. Get help. If you've been a victim of identity theft, contact the Federal Trade Commission's Identity Theft Hotline by telephone: toll-free 1-877-IDTHEFT (438-4338); TDD: 1-202-326-2502; by mail: Identity Theft Clearinghouse, Federal Trade Commission, 600 Pennsylvania Avenue, NW, Washington, D.C. 20580; or on-line: www.consumer.gov/idtheft. Ask for a copy of *ID Theft: When Bad Things Happen to Your Good Name*, a free comprehensive consumer guide to help you guard against and recover from identity theft.

An Arlington, Virginia, woman who was victimized by someone who stole her personal information and ran up tens of thousands of dollars in credit card debt under her name found it extremely time-consuming to straighten out the whole mess. She and her husband were quoted in the *Washington Post* (April 16, 1995) as recommending that anyone who's a victim of fraud should "Start calling and be tenacious. Get all of the 800 numbers you can, because it can be very expensive calling all the credit agencies and merchants." By the way, she and her husband estimate it took some one hundred or more hours to straighten out all the problems.

How to Protect Your Personal Privacy

If you're worried about the amount of information that's gathered and swapped about you, you're not alone. So much information about Americans is swapped by marketers, banks, creditors, and government agencies that many people feel they have little or no control over their own personal, and often private, information.

The collection and sale of consumer information is a multibillion-dollar business. All kinds of data about your habits may be made available to those willing to pay for it. Grocery stores can keep track of what you buy and follow up with coupons for competitor's brands. Subscribe to a magazine or join a club and your name is likely to be sold to numerous companies scouting for new customers. Even credit card companies can sell lists of their customers' spending habits.

Direct marketers are quick to point out that there's also value in all this information. Consumers benefit from the targeted offers and discounts they get. Many people are junk-mail junkies and like to get their mail, thank you very much.

The main principle that companies need to follow, and some are starting to, is that consumers should always be informed about how their information may be used, they should be given a chance to say "no,"—or better yet, say "yes"—and information collected for one purpose should not be used for another without the person's consent.

If you lean toward the side of being leery of the information that is floating around about you, use the following tips to help protect yourself. These should at least start you thinking about the ways that personal information is collected and swapped.

Be Careful When Car Shopping: Make it clear to the car dealer that you do not want your credit record checked without your express permission. A common tactic of car dealers is to get your driver's license or business card while you are discussing the deal. While you are out for a test drive, or while he is "checking with the manager," the dealer then slips to the back, punches a few buttons in the computer, and in a matter of minutes your entire financial standing is exposed.

Guard Your Social Security Number: This number accesses a wealth of information about you, including your entire credit file. Social Security numbers were intended for use only in Social Security transactions. Now, however, they are required for all kinds of transactions. In a number of states, your driver's license number is also your Social Security number. If someone challenges you about providing your Social Security number, you may want to try telling them that legally a Social Security number is only to be used in Social Security transactions. (There is no law preventing a merchant or agency from requiring your Social Security number, but there is no law that requires you to give it out.) In my opinion, going out of your way to guard your Social Security number is one of the most important things you can do to prevent fraud.

Guard Your Credit Card Account Numbers: Don't use a credit card as a means of identification. If a retailer wants you to show a credit card when you write a check, request that the number not be recorded on the check. Also avoid giving out your credit card number on the phone unless you are positive the company you are dealing with is reputable.

Consider Taking Your Name Off Mailing Lists: Some people enjoy receiving direct mail. Others call it "junk mail" and consider it a nuisance or a waste of the earth's resources. You decide, but if you do want to get your name off mailing lists, here's where to start.

> Mail Preference Service
> Direct Marketing Association (DMA)
> P.O. Box 3079
> Grand Central Station, NY 10163
> www.the-dma.org

Write to them with a list of all names and addresses under which you receive mail. It won't eliminate direct mail, but it will help.

The Direct Marketing Association also offers the Telephone Preference Service (TPS), which will remove your name from some telemarketing lists. That means fewer of those calls that always seem to come during dinner or your favorite TV show. Write to the DMA at:

Telephone Preference Service
Direct Marketing Association
P.O. Box 3079
Grand Central Station, NY 10163
www.the-dma.org

For complete information on how to cut down on direct mail (telemarketing and spam too), get the Good Advice Press booklet, *Stop Junk Mail Forever* ($4.50 post paid) by writing to them at: P.O. Box 78, Elizaville, NY 12523.

Block Your File from Prescreening: Prescreening takes place when credit card companies submit consumers' names to a credit bureau to determine if they are good prospects for their credit cards. That's how many of those offers come to you in the mail suggesting that you have an excellent credit history. To block your file from prescreening, call 1-888-50PT-OUT.

Beware of Product Registration and Warranty Programs: Many retailers and manufacturers ask customers to fill out product registration or warranty cards. Some use the information from these forms to develop product databases. Some companies use that information to follow up with additional marketing. (You buy a washer, for instance, and the next week someone calls to sell you a dryer.) Before you fill one out, ask if you can provide this information without becoming part of a mailing list. If the form requests more information than you think is necessary, include only your name and address. Understand that if you do not participate in the registration or fill out the warranty card, it may make it difficult for the company to track you down in the case of a product recall.

Ask Why Information Is Being Requested of You: A few years ago, I agreed to purchase a membership directory from an alumni-type organization to which I belong. The publisher that was compiling the book sent me a form to fill out, and requested what seemed like a lot of data from me, including information about my employment, education, and, if I recall correctly, my income. Since I am careful not to reveal too much personal information, I refused to respond to some of the questions. Nevertheless, I returned the partially completed form.

A couple of months later, I read an article in a trade paper about the publisher of that directory. It revealed that the publisher was in the business of selling detailed lists about consumers to charities, which then used those lists to prospect for donors. Where did the publisher get their information about consumers? From the directories they compiled through alumni groups and membership organizations.

If you belong to a membership organization, or other groups, ask about their policies regarding the information they collect. If they do not have a policy regarding confidentiality, ask them to develop one and publicize it.

Personal privacy is likely to become one of the most important consumer issues in this decade. Until Congress passes a comprehensive privacy law, however, Americans are going to have to protect themselves.

Your Information Up for Grabs: GLB

In the summer of 2001, consumers were deluged with privacy notices from financial services providers. It was the result of the Financial Modernization Act of 1999 (a.k.a. the Gramm-Leach-Bliley, or GLB, bill). As a result of that law, companies such as banks, stockbrokers and insurance companies can share information about you with other companies—including completely un-affiliated companies such as retailers, telemarketers, airlines, and nonprofit organizations.

The types of information that can be shared include just about anything these companies collect about you: your name, phone number, address, income, and details about your assets that you provided on an application, for example. The balances in your accounts or payment history can also be shared. And whenever you shop with your credit card, information about where you shop (and to the extent that they can tell, what you like to buy) can be fair game.

As the Privacy Rights Clearinghouse puts it, "GLB and federal regulations only keep financial institutions from disclosing your account number or access code to a third-party nonaffiliated company to use in telemarketing or direct mail marketing." Otherwise your personal information is up for grabs.

Not only is the burden on you, the consumer, to read the notices and take the time to opt out, but you don't have the right to say no to certain types of information sharing. If the information is considered publicly available (a listed telephone number, for example) or if it's used in conjunction with a joint marketing agreement between the financial services provider and another company, you can't stop it. In addition, unlike the Fair Credit Reporting Act, you don't have the right to review your information for accuracy.

If you threw away those notices (and it's hard to blame you), you may still want to contact your card issuers, bank or credit union, stockbroker, and insurance companies to ask for copies of their policies to decide if you want to opt out. If you open a new account, you should receive a notice that tells you how to opt out if you choose. You'll find more helpful information about this law at www.goodadvicepress.com and www.privacyrights.org.

CHAPTER TWELVE

VIP Credit Tips

Planning to pack the plastic on your next trip? It's probably a good idea, as long as you know the ins and outs of traveling with your credit cards. In this chapter, I'll give you some important tips for using credit cards when traveling in the United States or abroad.

Want something for nothing? Then credit cards may be just the ticket. The benefits that come with many credit cards can save you money and hassles—if you choose the right ones. Many credit card perks, however, are used so rarely that you probably shouldn't even think twice about them. In the second part of this chapter, I'll discuss the pros and cons of the most popular enhancements so you can get the ones you want and weed out those you don't need.

Have Plastic, Will Travel

The two biggest surprises that come up when people use credit cards outside the United States are: 1. that many countries simply don't have the same level of customer-satisfaction policies as we do here in the United States; and 2. that by the time your foreign charges get translated back into U.S. dollars, the cost may be different than the price you thought you paid. Let me talk about that last issue first.

Credit cards *may* cost more than you expected if you use them overseas for two reasons:

1. *Currency Conversion Rates:* When you make a purchase abroad using your credit card, you are usually making the purchase in foreign currency. In order for the charge to be posted to your account so you can pay for it, it must be converted into U.S. dollars. Here's how that process works:

When you make a purchase using a Visa or MasterCard, the merchant deposits the sales slip and, in most cases, is paid in local currency. The charge slip makes its way back to Visa or MasterCard (not the card-issuing bank), where the charge is converted into U.S. dollars. The associations make this conversion at wholesale market rates, or government-mandated rates, which are often better than you could get on your own. The conversion rate is generally *not* determined by the exchange rate prevailing on the date you made your purchase. Instead, it is typically based on the exchange rate in effect one day before the slip was processed by the association. (American Express works similarly.) This rate may be better or worse than the rate when you made your purchase.

I personally have always found that the exchange rate I was given by my credit card companies was better than the exchange rate offered by local merchants and banks. I have received a few complaints, though, from people who felt the exchange rate was worse than the prevailing rate when they made a purchase.

2. *Currency Conversion Fees:* Most credit card companies assess a *currency conversion fee*, usually 1 percent of the purchase amount. It's similar to the fee you might pay when you buy traveler's checks. Although Visa and MasterCard always assess a currency conversion fee to the card issuer, it's up to your individual card issuer as to whether or not it will pass that fee on to you. Some card issuers tack on their own fee, which means you could pay 2 percent to 3 percent more for overseas purchases. *The only way you'll know if you will be charged this fee is to call* *your card issuer before you travel and ask about their policy.* All other things being equal, you may want to use a card that doesn't charge this fee.

Since your credit card slip will be written in foreign currency, take your time and double check to make sure it's accurate—that there are no extra zeros added, for example. You don't want to be like the tourist who was charged $100 for a $1 cup of coffee! It can get confusing, since in some countries they use commas where we use periods, or vice versa (5.00 may be written as 5,00, for example).

Surcharges: My husband and I honeymooned in Cozumel, Mexico. Unlike other overseas trips, we hardly used our credit cards at all because most of the merchants charged a 3 percent to 5 percent surcharge for credit card purchases. Even though I knew surcharges weren't allowed in the United States, I thought that maybe different rules applied overseas. I wasn't too surprised a few weeks later, though, when I was speaking with a Mexican banker at a credit card conference and he told me that surcharges are *not* allowed in Mexico—or anywhere else in the world.

If a merchant tries to assess a surcharge, get as many details as possible about the name and location of the store so you can complain to MasterCard, Visa, or American Express when you return. If you must use your credit card and the merchant assesses a surcharge, make sure they write on the sales slip a breakdown of the purchase amount and surcharge, so that you can dispute the surcharge with your card issuer when you get back (see Chapter Ten for instructions).

Getting What You Paid For

You have to admit, we're fairly spoiled here. As long as you shop at a reputable store, you can probably count on getting a refund or exchange if there's any problem with merchandise you buy. Even the grocery store will often give you a refund for bad produce!

But travel overseas, and the unspoken rule is likely to be NO REFUNDS. Period. That means you want to be extremely careful that what you're buying is really what you want. And that it really is what you think you're buying. Obviously, most people have no trouble when they buy items when traveling, and in fact, credit cards are often safer to use than cash, or even traveler's checks. Yet, you'll want to be careful, since it's hard to get a refund from a merchant who's thousands of miles away—or across an ocean. Here are some guidelines:

Avoid buying expensive valuable items such as jewelry or artwork, unless you can get the authenticity and approximate value verified through an independent appraisal. I've heard from too many people who have bought valuable items overseas (especially gemstones), only to find out they were either worthless imitations, or worth much less than the merchant told them, once they got them home. If you do buy something valuable, ask the store manager or store owner to write a *complete description* of the item on the sales slip. If you're buying a diamond, for example, ask him to describe the cut, clarity, and carat weight, and sign and date it.

Familiarize yourself with customs policies before you leave. The last thing you want to do is spend hundreds of dollars on something you can't bring back into the United States. If you do buy something that's confiscated, it will be very hard (if not impossible) for you to get your money back. For information on items that may be prohibited or restricted, order a free copy of *Know Before You Go* from the United States Customs Service, P.O. Box 7474, Washington, D.C. 20044.

Get any promises about refunds or exchanges in writing. If the manager agrees to refunds or exchanges, ask her to write it *on the sales slip.*

Make sure it arrives intact. Once you buy something, you'll have to get it home. If you don't want to lug it with you on your trip, you may want to have it shipped. This can open up a whole new set of problems if you aren't careful.

Once the package leaves the store, it may become your responsibility, depending on what was arranged with the merchant. If you're having an item shipped, you'll want to: make sure the merchant packages it for shipping (to minimize the chance of damage); buy insurance for the item if it is not provided by the merchant (again, you want all agreements in writing); and get information *in writing* about how it will be shipped and when it should arrive at your home. You'll have to pay any duty or customs fees, if they apply.

Keep in mind that there is no protection for buyer's remorse. If you buy something and you later change your mind, it's up to the merchant to decide whether or not to let you exchange it or give you a refund. This is especially true in other countries, where "no refund" policies may be the unwritten rule. If you buy something and it turns out to be less valuable than you thought, you may or may not be able to get a refund through your card issuer. (Your chances of getting a refund are greatly increased if you have a complete description of the item on the sales slip, signed by the store manager, and the description is deceptive.)

Other Precautions

Here are a few other things you may want to look out for when you use your credit cards while traveling—overseas or in the United States.

Hidden Holds: When you check into a hotel or rent a car, the clerk will ask you for a major credit card. He'll then get authorization to make sure the card is good and to make sure there is enough credit available to cover the charge. At that time, a "hold" will be placed on the card: The estimated amount of your stay (plus, in many cases, some extra in case of damage or extra charges) will be "frozen" on your account.

The hold can create problems if, for instance, you are planning to pay for your hotel stay with traveler's checks and use your credit card for shopping or meals. When you get to the restaurant, you may find that your credit limit is tied up by the hotel hold and your charge for the meal could be declined.

Once a hold is placed, you usually can't remove it if you want to pay with cash or traveler's checks. The transaction is authorized through the credit card authorization system, and the hold usually remains there until either a credit card slip comes through that matches the hold, or until it "drops off" the account, in about three days in many cases.

The credit card companies have been developing better authorization systems to alleviate the hold problem. In the meantime, you should ask the clerk the exact dollar amount of the hold, so you can keep track of how much you still have free on your credit line. Also, think about using one credit card for hotels, car rentals, etc., and another one for purchases, so you won't have to worry about your purchase in a restaurant or store being declined. American Express charge cards don't have credit limits, so that may be another way to get around the problem.

You may also want to ask to have your credit limit raised before you travel, if you think you need some breathing room. I've heard that people have actually been arrested in some foreign countries for going over the limit—so you can't be too careful!

Convenience Checks: Another warning: Think twice before using cash-advance (or "convenience") checks abroad. You've already been warned that these checks may carry service charges that make them expensive. They are an especially poor choice abroad, however, because you will be dealing with merchants thousands of miles away from your home. If there is a problem with the merchandise they sold you and you paid by credit card, you may be able to dispute the charge under the Fair Credit Billing Act. If you used a cash-advance check, you lose that privilege. Cash-advance checks may seem convenient, but they are not traveler's checks. They are drawing against a line of credit, on which you will lose the float and have to pay interest. I would recommend sticking to plastic.

Accommodations: The four-star hotel you reserved a room at turns out to be a dump. Your "ocean view" is obstructed by a brand-new high rise that's still under construction. What can you do?

First, before you make reservations, ask a lot of questions. Work with a reputable travel agent, preferably someone with experience in the area you'll be traveling to. Find out if you'll have your own bathroom, shower, drinking water, etc., in the room.

Don't assume that standards for hotels abroad are the same as they are in the United States.

If you get to your destination and find your accommodations are unacceptable, ask to be moved elsewhere or get written cancellation from the hotel if you decide to leave. If they refuse, call your credit card issuer for advice. Some will tell you that as long as you can prove you stayed somewhere else, you can get a credit. Others will tell you there is nothing you can do. It gets sticky here. If you stay, you may find it impossible to get any kind of a refund once you return home, since you did use their services. If you go elsewhere, you may have an easier time since you can show that you didn't use their services—but a refund is not guaranteed.

Leave enough time for a leisurely checkout, so you can go over your bill item by item. If you gave the clerk a credit card, make *sure* you destroy the original slip if you decide to pay with cash or a check. Get a cash receipt if you pay by cash! One man I know went on a cruise and used his credit card when he checked in. He paid cash and asked for a cash receipt and his original charge card slip back. He got the slip back, but the cash receipt (written in Spanish, which he couldn't read) was not a receipt at all. The clerk then submitted another charge slip to the credit card company, and presumably pocketed the cash. The consumer had an extremely difficult time persuading the card company and cruise line that he had actually paid cash.

Airlines: A few years back, some friends and I flew to Miami on Eastern Airlines, then boarded a Cayman Airways plane to Cayman for the weekend. We spent the weekend on the beach and never once turned on a television. Imagine our shock, then, when we got back to Miami on Monday and found that Eastern had gone out of business over the weekend!

If you hold a ticket with an airline that has gone bankrupt, you can usually get a flight on another airline. (That's what we did.) If for some reason you can't, you'll probably be able to get a refund through your credit card company. Call your issuer for instructions. Usually they'll require you to send them the ticket, which you *of course* will send via certified mail, return receipt requested. Don't lose the ticket, since you may get zilch without it.

Even if you have a ticket in hand, it doesn't mean you'll get on your flight. If you show up too late, your seat may be given to someone else if the flight is overbooked. For international flights, you're often told to check in at least an hour before departure. Your travel agent or ticket seller should give you instructions on how early you need to be at the airport.

Now, for the Good News . . .

I highly recommend that you use your credit cards when you travel. The advantages, I believe, outweigh any potential problems. Here are some of the benefits of using credit cards when traveling:

1. Acceptance: Merchants may not want to take your local check, but under credit card company rules, any credit card issuer that accepts a Visa, MasterCard, or American Express card must do so without discrimination. In other words, they have to accept your credit card without regard to the location of the issuing bank.

In many countries, credit cards are just as welcome as they are here. When I went to Spain a couple of years ago, I think I used one traveler's check during the whole trip. Merchants actually preferred my plastic, and I ended up getting a great exchange rate.

2. Help in Disputes: This is perhaps the biggest advantage of using credit cards for overseas purchases. The Fair Credit Billing Act provides you with the legal muscle to fight back when the merchandise purchased on a credit card turns out to be different from what you ordered, when you are billed for the wrong amount, or when you are ripped off. As long as your card was issued by a United States–based card issuer, and you are a U.S. resident, you are covered by this law—whether your purchases were made in the U.S. or overseas.

I know of a number of people who used this law to get refunds from unscrupulous merchants. One man bought a "marble" statue in Italy, but found out when it was delivered to his home in Texas that it was only inferior alabaster. Another consumer bought an expensive jewel ring in Thailand. When the shopkeeper took it to the back of the store to "wrap" it, he switched it for a fake. The consumer didn't find out until he returned home. In both these cases, the consumers couldn't deal directly with the merchants involved, but they were successful in getting refunds posted to their credit cards—leaving the banks to deal with the less-than-honest merchants. Follow the instructions in Chapter Ten for disputing a charge.

3. *Emergency Cash:* Most credit cards offer emergency cash advances through banks or ATM networks. Be sure to check with your bank *before* you travel to determine if there are any fees for these services. Cash withdrawals through ATM machines require a PIN (Personal Identification Number), so if you haven't received one, request one from your card issuer well in advance of your departure.

Also ask about cash advance fees, which can be pretty steep. Keep in mind that your cash advance will be issued in foreign currency, so it will be converted to U.S. dollars (just like a purchase) before it appears on your statement. Some cards have limits on how much cash you can withdraw in one day, or total against your credit limit. That's one more thing to check on before you leave.

4. *Good Record-keeping:* Domestically and abroad, credit card statements provide a good record of how and where you have spent your money—especially important for business travelers who must have receipts for tax or record-keeping purposes.

5. *Float:* Overseas purchases are usually posted to the cardholder's account a few days to two weeks after they were made. If you pay off your card in full when the bill arrives, you won't pay interest—and you will have had a "free loan" during that time.

6. *Convenience:* Credit cards are almost a necessity when you travel. Some hotels won't let you rent a room without using a credit card as a deposit, and many car-rental companies refuse to rent cars to those who can't produce a major credit card to reserve it.

7. Safety: Carrying lots of cash is dangerous anywhere and especially in some countries where pickpockets target tourists as easy prey. Even abroad, the most you can be held liable for if a thief steals and uses your card is the first $50 of unauthorized charges per card—and most issuers won't even charge you that.

Be sure to make a list of credit cards before traveling, including the number to call if they are lost or stolen. (U.S. 800 numbers won't work abroad, so make sure you have a number you can call collect if you're traveling overseas.) Keep that list separate from your cards—perhaps even leave a copy with a trusted friend or relative.

8. CDW Coverage can save you money if you rent a car. Technically, it's not insurance, but it does offer free protection in case of an accident, loss, or damage to a rental car (as long as you meet certain conditions). You'll have to use your credit card to pay for the car rental and *decline the rental agency's CDW* in order to get this protection. Since the rental agencies' CDW can cost $10 to $20 per day, this benefit can really be a money saver.

Most gold and platinum cardholders receive this benefit for free. While each program varies slightly, keep in mind that most collision damage waiver programs are supplementary to any auto insurance the customer already holds, either personally or through his or her employer. These programs often do pick up deductibles, though, and may help ease a cash-flow crunch by permitting charges for damage to be billed to your card until your insurance company settles the charges.

You may not always be able to use your credit card's CDW benefit, because some merchants will not accept it. In some countries, for example, you must buy the rental agencies' CDW.

Dig out the paperwork they sent you or call your credit card company before you travel to find out exactly how the CDW coverage works: exactly what's covered, what restrictions and limitations might apply, and how to file a claim should you need to. You may also want to check with the car-rental agency when you make your reservations to determine if it will accept the CDW from your credit card.

If you do rent a car, make sure you report any problems with the car immediately, and try to get some details of the problem or resolution *in writing* from the manager of the rental agency. Also, try to let your credit card company know about the problem as soon as possible—don't wait until you get home to call them. Remember to snap a few photos of the damage for your records.

Don't wait until the last minute to drop off your car— leave plenty of time to inspect the car to make sure you won't be held responsible for any damage that could occur after you returned it.

How Many Credit Cards Are Enough?

If you travel frequently, or are planning to take a trip abroad soon, you may want to take more than one credit card.

Which two cards you choose is up to you. MasterCard and Visa are very close in terms of number of locations that accept them. American Express is accepted in fewer locations but is popular in many countries. The Discover card is not an international bankcard, so you can only use it in the United States.

Whatever you do, don't take more than you need. One reporter called me rather embarrassed about the fact that he took all his credit cards with him to Europe. When his wallet was stolen, he had a terrible time contacting department stores and other issuers of cards that couldn't even be used abroad. If you can't use the card—leave it at home!

Perks

Everyone loves a freebie, and credit card freebies are no different. How else can the popularity of a regular Visa or Master-Card that carries a $75-a-year price tag—but offers free frequent-flier miles with each purchase—be explained? Frequent-flier miles, cash-back rebates, credit card protection, and extended warranties lure cardholders to new credit cards. Some perks do benefit cardholders, many aren't worth considering, and some are clearly a bad deal.

People like perks, even though they never use some of them, or if they offer very little actual value. My general advice is: Choose a credit card on the basis of price, not perks. I realize, though, that many people are attracted to different card programs because of the bells and whistles. There are literally over a hundred different enhancements available on credit cards, but most fall into one of these categories:

1. **Rebates and frequent-flier miles** include cash rebates, frequent-flier miles, and rebates toward the purchase of certain products.
2. **Insurance** includes extended warranties and purchase insurance; disability, group health, accident, travel, life, and unemployment insurance.
3. **Travel benefits** include emergency road service, car-rental insurance, travel agents, discount travel clubs, traveler medical assistance, and legal aid.
4. **Executive services** include country-club billing, annual expense summaries, and business travel assistance.
5. **Convenience services** include credit card registration, twenty-four-hour toll-free customer-service lines, ATM cash advances, ATM locator hotlines, flexible billing dates, emergency check-cashing, and automatic minimum payments.

Despite their popularity, industry experts estimate that fewer than 3 percent of cardholders actually use enhancements. What should you look for when evaluating credit card perks?

Rebates and Frequent-Flier Miles

Rebate cards are an example of how you can get something for nothing (or almost nothing)—if you're careful. With these cards, you get some kind of benefit—frequent-flier miles, free gasoline, cash rebates, or a rebate toward the purchase of a new car or new truck, usually based on how much you spend. With a frequent-flier card, for example, you'll get one mile for every dollar you charge on the card. Here's what you need to ask before you sign up:

1. *How much am I really going to earn?* To earn a free flight on most of the frequent-flier cards, you'll have to charge at least $25,000 of stuff on the card. Since most people charge closer to $2,500 a year, it would take the average person about ten years to get a ticket!

   One of the popular cash-rebate cards promises a 1 percent rebate on all purchases—but that's only at the highest level. It actually starts out at one-quarter of 1 percent and builds *slowly* from there.

2. *How much is the freebie going to cost me?* If there's a steep annual fee on the card ($50 and up for most frequent-flier cards), factor that in to how much your "free ticket" or other benefit will cost. (A frequent-flier mile is said to be worth two cents.) The interest rates on many rebate and frequent-flier cards is very high—you don't want to carry a balance on these cards, or you'll end up paying a fortune in interest.

3. *Do I really want the benefit?* I recently read an article in the newspaper about a couple who accepted one of the auto companies' rebate cards. It earns them a rebate toward a purchase of a car through that manufacturer. They actually said in the article that they weren't planning to buy a car through that manufacturer, but now that they had the card they would! That's one of the reasons these cards exist—to encourage you to buy something you really don't want!

If you do decide to go the rebate/frequent-flier route, use the card everywhere—the grocery store, gas station, movie theaters, etc. Your miles will add up faster with small purchases. Just make absolutely, 100 percent certain that you can pay the bill in full when it arrives, so you will end up ahead of the game.

Insurance Benefits

Extended Warranties automatically double the manufacturer's warranty (usually up to a year) on purchases made with the card. They've proven to be a popular perk with cardholders, Many gold and platinum cards as well as some standard cards carry this benefit, and a few banks have extended it to other financial accounts, such as checking accounts. (Some card issuers and card companies have started cutting back on perks, so double-check the benefits before signing up for a card, if you want a particular benefit.)

Read the instructions for taking advantage of these programs, to make sure you'll be covered if you need it. Also, be sure to save your receipts and copies of the manufacturers' warranties for any purchases that may be covered under this type of program. You will need them if you have to file a claim.

Purchase Protection replaces or reimburses you for merchandise bought with your credit card if it is stolen or damaged within ninety days of purchase. This protection usually extends to gifts purchased on the card. A version of this coverage is available on some gold and platinum cards, and on some standard cards as well.

Certain items may be excluded from this protection (jewelry or furs, for example). In addition, some programs limit the amount you can claim. Keep in mind that purchase protection is supplemental to homeowner's or other insurance you have. You will probably be required to prove your homeowner's insurance doesn't cover the cost of the item before you'll be reimbursed. Also keep in mind that these programs are insurance programs and, just like with your homeowner's or car insurance, your claim may be denied if the insurance company determines your claim is not covered under the terms of the policy. Again, be sure to read the fine print!

Credit, Life, Disability, and Unemployment Insurance: Credit card insurance sounds good. A few cents each month buys you peace of mind with assurances that your credit card payments will be met if you are disabled and unable to work or if you become unemployed. If you die, credit card insurance will relieve your spouse or family of the burden of your credit card bills.

In reality, however, credit insurance often promises a lot more than it delivers. In 1997, the Consumer Federation of America (CFA) and the National Insurance Consumer Organization released a report finding that "most credit life insurance is still overpriced." CFA's executive director, Stephen Brobeck, said that "Consumers should be receiving at least 60 cents in benefits for each $1 in premiums paid, yet they actually get only 43 cents on the dollar."

The CFA study covered only credit *life* insurance, not credit card disability and unemployment insurance, and Stephen Brobeck says there have been improvements in some states. Still, I'm sure that a lot of people sign up for credit insurance without realizing how much they're going to pay and how little they may actually get from it.

Here's an example of a credit card insurance package that includes life, disability, and unemployment coverage.

Monthly premium per $100 of outstanding balance:	Translates into this much per year on $1,000 balance:
66 cents	$79.20
Except:	
6.9 cents in MA	$ 8.28
29.3 cents in MN	$35.16
29.5 cents in CT	$35.40
42.7 cents in TX	$51.24
43.7 cents in NY	$52.44
46.9 cents in NH	$56.28
55.8 cents in ME	$66.96
56.7 cents in VT	$68.04
57.3 cents in VA	$68.76
58.8 cents in IA	$70.56
59 cents in WI	$70.80
60 cents in ID, IN, MO, NJ, and WA	$72.00
63.8 cents in GA	$76.56

Monthly premium per $100 of outstanding balance:	Translates into this much per year on $1,000 balance:
64.6 cents in MD	$77.52
64.8 cents in ND	$77.76
67 cents in RI	$80.40
67.6 cents in CA	$81.12
68 cents in NE	$81.60
68.1 cents in CO	$81.72
68.2 cents in AK	$81.84
69.2 cents in AL	$83.04
69.8 cents in OR	$83.76
70.2 cents in MI	$84.24
72.1 cents in OH	$86.52
72.3 cents in SC	$86.76
73.1 cents in WY	$87.72
74 cents in AZ, IL, KY, MS, NV, PR, TN, and WV	$88.80
75 cents in LA and NM	$90.00

Notice the wide range in charges for credit card insurance. In Louisiana or New Mexico, for example, you would pay $90 for a year's coverage on $1,000 balance, but in Massachusetts, you'd pay only $8.28.

One of the main reasons credit insurance is often so expensive is that there isn't a lot of competition. The lender usually shops around for a policy that will offer big commissions to the lender—but often doesn't care whether the program offers low rates to customers. Since you buy credit insurance directly through the card issuer or lender, not an independent insurance agent, you can't really shop around for a competitive policy.

High premiums mean excellent profits to insurers and card issuers. In fact, this insurance is the single most profitable perk offered by card issuers.

Credit insurance is generally worth considering *only if* (and that's a BIG if):

- *You are uninsured because of bad health, your age, or because you can't afford it.* If your family members would be required to pay off your loans if you died, or if you have no insurance or savings to cover you if you are disabled, you may want to consider a credit insurance policy.

- *You are offered a good rate.* Compare the lender's rates with other policies, if possible. Also consider how much consumers in other states are spending for similar coverage.

Of course, if you pay off your credit card bills in full, you won't need credit insurance!

Disability insurance is very important. Considering that almost 30 percent of people now in their thirties will be disabled for three months or more before they are sixty-five, this insurance should be a part of any sound financial plan. If you find yourself unable to work, though, you will likely need far more financial assistance than what's provided in these credit card policies. You will need income for rent, food, medical bills, and other living expenses. Disability insurance should provide at least 60 percent of your current income. Money spent on premiums for credit card disability insurance is almost always better spent on a good, comprehensive disability policy.

Don't forget: If your credit cards are in your name only, your family members will *not* be required to pay them off if you die. The card issuer may attempt to collect from your estate, however. The exception, of course, is in community-property states where surviving spouses may be responsible for those debts. (Check with your state attorney general's office for more information.)

Accident Insurance provides insurance benefits if you are killed or lose limbs in an accident on a common carrier, such as an airplane or train. Very large accident insurance policies are offered free through many credit card issuers (especially on gold cards), while others will sell more to members as a "benefits upgrade." Accident insurance really is often an extra. The likelihood that you are going to be in an accident on a plane or train is very small. Most people will want to pass up this coverage if they have to pay for it.

Travel Services

Emergency Card Replacement and Emergency Cash can be very valuable if you are traveling and lose your cards. While most card issuers can have a card to you within two weeks after you report it lost or stolen, some issuers, can in most cases get a temporary card to you within twenty-four hours. Emergency cash is usually available in the form of check-cashing privileges, or ATM or bank cash advances.

These services can be lifesavers if you're traveling abroad and lose your purse or wallet. Before traveling, though, call your card issuers to find out how their emergency cash and card-replacement programs work, so that if there is a problem you will know exactly what to do to get your cards replaced quickly.

Most credit card issuers offer cash advances through ATM machines. To access cash through the machine, however, you will need a Personal Identification Number (PIN). If you haven't already received one, call your card issuer well in advance of your trip to get one. You may also want to ask for a directory of ATM locations in the state or country to which you will be traveling.

Convenience Services

Credit Card Registration: Registration services offer to "protect your cards from loss or theft," or they offer "credit card theft rewards up to $1,000." There are also several large companies offering credit card registration directly to members or through other associations. Sometimes your card issuer will offer it as a free benefit, but often you'll have to pay for it.

Although the solicitations make it sound as though you could lose thousands of dollars if your cards are lost or stolen, it's *extremely* unlikely that could happen. Under federal law, the most you can be held liable for if your cards are lost or stolen and used by a thief is $50 *per card*. There are no exceptions to this rule, except that if only the card number is stolen—and not the actual card—you cannot be held liable for a single penny of charges run up by a thief. In fact, if you notify the card issuer of the loss *be-*

fore any fraudulent charges are made, you can't be held liable for *any* of those charges.

The primary value of credit card registration is convenience. If you are on vacation and your purse or wallet is stolen, the last thing you want to do is spend hours on the phone trying to get in touch with all your card issuers. A credit card registration service can save you that hassle by doing it for you.

If you decide to pay for credit card registration, be cautious about signing up for several years' worth of services. The fees can add up, and you could find next year that one of your bankcards offers free credit card registration. Or you might be dissatisfied with the service. If you don't have a free service available and really want to sign up for one, shop around, compare prices, and try one for a year or two.

When is credit card registration a waste of time and money? When you don't hold a lot of credit cards, and when it carries an expensive fee. When you sign up for registration, you will be asked to fill out a form listing all your credit cards and their account numbers. In most cases, you will also be asked to supply the card issuers' phone numbers for reporting lost or stolen cards. By that time, you have done all the work. It will be cheaper, and perhaps smarter, to just photocopy that list and put it in a safe place. If something does happen, you can make the phone calls to the issuers yourself.

Alternatively, create your own credit card information file. Most new credit cards, as well as replacements, are sent with a piece of paper that includes a toll-free number to call if the card is lost or stolen. Keep those papers for all your cards in a spot where you'll be able to find them easily if you need them.

If, however, you get an offer for free credit card registration, take it. Filling out a credit card registration form will force you to get organized and list all your credit card information in one place. You may have used your Visa card a thousand times, but if it's stolen, you may find you have completely forgotten which bank issued the card—and where to find them.

Convenience Services: Toll-free twenty-four-hour customer-service lines, ATM cash advances, ATM locator hotlines, flexible billing dates, emergency check cashing, and automatic minimum payments are all examples of customer-service enhancements. Don't fall into the trap of thinking the bigger the bank, the better the customer service. I've seen cases where the largest card issuers that boast the best customer service flub even simple requests for assistance.

Whether your card issuer is large or small, you shouldn't settle for poor customer service. If you're not receiving the assistance you think you deserve, complain to the customer-service manager or the president's office. If you're still dissatisfied, switch cards—and let them know why.

Corporate Cards

Visa, MasterCard, and American Express all offer corporate cards (also called "business cards") targeted especially to corporate customers and to small-business owners. Just as standard cards are offered through many different issuers, Visa and Master-Card Business Cards are offered through many banks. American Express has a corporate card and an Executive Corporate Card, which is only offered to small-business owners and select top executives.

Business cards carry enhancements such as accident disability insurance, expense tracking, business seminars and information, and emergency travel services.

Corporate cards can have a big drawback, too—they don't always offer cardholders the same protection offered to individual cardholders under the Truth-in-Lending Act. As I described in Chapter Ten, credit card holders are protected under the Fair Credit Billing Act (FCBA) against billing errors and shoddy merchandise purchased on a credit card. If there is a problem with the goods or services you purchased on a credit card, you may be able to withhold payment of the disputed charge until the card issuer investigates and resolves the problem. Unfortunately, the law applies to all types of credit cards *except* corporate cards. So if there is a problem with something you bought with a corporate card, you may have to pay the charge and deal directly with the merchant.

There is one exception to this rule. If your corporate card issuer adds language to your cardholder agreement acknowledging that it agrees to follow the Fair Credit Billing Act rules for disputing charges or billing errors, you will be covered just as if you held a personal card.

In addition, the regulations regarding unauthorized use of credit cards apply to corporate cards. Just like with a personal card, you cannot be held responsible for more than $50 in fraudulent charges if your business card is lost or stolen. If you contact your card issuer regarding the loss or theft before the card is used by a thief, you can't be held liable for any fraudulent charges. *But your company may be.* If you work for a firm that employs more than ten people, a corporate card issuer can require the company or its principals to accept some of the financial responsibility if employees' cards are used fraudulently. If you're a business owner, shop several cards and banks before agreeing to that type of liability.

Credit Card Collecting

If you love the thrill of getting a new credit card in the mail, don't feel guilty. You could actually end up turning your cards into cash someday. Credit card collecting is a hot hobby that's reaping some collectors hundreds of dollars—for one card!

If you want to collect new credit cards, keep in mind that ideally you should save brand-new cards that have never been touched by human hands. (Good way to avoid charging on them.) You'll probably want to hook up with other hobbyists, and in the Resources section I note a newsletter that can help you do that.

I'm not into collecting credit cards, but I have stashed away some plastic telephone calling cards that were sent to me and I knew I'd never use, a couple of credit cards I didn't want (still in the envelopes they were mailed to me in), and an assortment of membership cards I've gotten here and there. I keep thinking maybe they'll be worth something to my grandkids. By then, they say, today's credit cards will be antiquated—instead, we'll have a smart-chip wristwatch that we can use to make all of our purchases!

A cousin to credit card collecting (and an even hotter world-wide collectors' market) are prepaid phone cards. Widely used in Europe and catching on here in the United States, these cards can be used to make long-distance phone calls or can be saved, swapped, or sold to other collectors. Again, see the Resources section for information on phone-card collecting.

CHAPTER THIRTEEN

A Lifetime of Great Credit

Putting your financial affairs in order requires patience, hard work, and a lot of self-discipline. Throughout this book, we've explored numerous methods for cutting out debt, saving money, and improving your credit record. If you have been following the advice I've offered and have improved your credit situation in just one way, congratulations!

In this chapter, I'll offer some guidelines to keep you on the right track. I'll point out some of the danger spots—including the holidays and slow economic times—that can harm a sound spending plan, and offer positive steps you can take to make smart financial planning a way of life!

Prepay Loans and Save Thousands of Dollars!

You shopped carefully for your mortgage. You compared rates and points to get the best loan. You make your regular mortgage payments on time every month and even get to deduct some interest come tax time. You think you're doing well.

In fact, by the time you pay off your thirty-year mortgage,

you'll have paid for two or three houses! Even a low-rate mortgage costs a bundle when you look at how much interest you end up paying. For example, payments on a thirty-year, $75,000 mortgage at an interest rate of 10 percent will total $237,000. Of that, $162,000—almost twice the amount borrowed—goes directly to the bank in the form of interest payments.

You can dramatically, and easily, reduce the amount you will pay over the life of your mortgage by paying off the principal more quickly. It's called "prepaying" a mortgage, and it can shave thousands of dollars off your loan. In the example above, for instance, paying an extra $25 a month could save you over $34,000 in interest, and you'd be able to burn the mortgage note five years earlier!

How does prepaying work? The original amount of your loan is called the "principal balance." On most mortgages, the lender will figure your payment by calculating interest on your outstanding balance, not the original amount of the loan. If you can reduce your outstanding balance, you'll reduce the amount of interest you pay.

All you have to do to prepay your mortgage is write out an extra check for a specific amount, say $25 or $50, and tell the bank to apply it toward your principal balance. It is a good idea to determine a fixed, reasonable amount that you will pay each month. If you don't, you may find yourself skipping these extra payments, and perhaps abandoning the program altogether. If, on the other hand, you choose an unrealistically high prepayment amount, you may find yourself short of cash between payments and using your credit cards to get by—hardly a good trade-off! The best advice is: Don't overextend yourself. Commit to making small extra payments that you can afford without a struggle and then stick to it.

Here's an example of how much you can save by making prepayments each month:

PREPAYMENT SAVINGS TABLE

Loan Amount	Pre-payment amount	8% Interest Rate $ saved (months saved)	10% Interest Rate	12% Interest Rate
$25,000	$25	$15,608 (118)	$22,617 (129)	$30,970 (141)
	50	22,058 (171)	30,786 (181)	40,647 (190)
$50,000	25	19,951 (73)	30,161 (84)	43,199 (96)
	50	31,225 (118)	45,248 (129)	61,965 (141)
$75,000	25	22,073 (54)	34,162 (63)	50,273 (74)
	50	36,473 (90)	54,180 (101)	76,126 (114)
$100,000	25	23,337 (42)	36,657 (50)	54,936 (60)
	50	39,906 (73)	60,322 (84)	86,398 (96)
$150,000	25	24,779 (30)	39,633 (36)	60,791 (44)
	50	44,149 (54)	68,325 (63)	100,545 (74)
$200,000	25	25,579 (23)	41,343 (28)	64,316 (35)
	50	46,677 (42)	73,323 (50)	109,887 (60)

This chart was reprinted with permission from Marc Eisenson's invaluable book *The Banker's Secret,* Random House, 1991. For more information, see the Resources section.

See how just a little pocket change each month can save you thousands of dollars off your mortgage and help you pay it off years earlier! If you aren't prepaying because you think you'll lose valuable tax deductions, or because you think you can't afford to prepay, or even because you aren't sure how to get started, get a copy of Marc Eisenson's *The Banker's Secret* audiotape (see the Resources section). Pop it into your tape player on the way to work, and I guarantee by the time you've listened to it, you'll be convinced you should be prepaying.

What about prepaying other loans? Most types of loans, including car loans and personal loans, can be prepaid by sending in a separate check toward principal. For reasons I outlined in Chapter Three, prepaying credit card debt is not as easy and straightforward as prepaying installment loans. You don't write an extra check to principal, as you would with a car loan or mortgage. Nevertheless, the more you pay on your credit card *and* the earlier in your billing cycle that you pay it, the quicker you will reduce your balance and interest payments.

Getting Ahead at Any Age

You can't generalize when it comes to money. Young people are often characterized as free spenders with no concept of the value of money, but you'll still find families where the children are better money managers than their parents. Older people may often be portrayed as frugal, but that, of course, is only true of some of them.

Nevertheless, there are some very broad financial challenges that many people face at different times in their lives. Knowing what those common money-management pitfalls are gives you the opportunity to plan to avoid them. Here's what to look out for:

In Your Late Teens and Twenties

- ✓ Open an IRA. Start socking as much away as possible. The time value of money makes early investments worth tons more.
- ✓ Get one—maybe two—major credit cards. Always pay the bills on time and don't charge anything you can't afford.
- ✓ Instead of being envious of people who seem to have everything, keep in mind that the bank probably really owns most of what they have.
- ✓ Ask a grandparent or older person how they managed when they were just starting out. Believe it or not, they might have some good advice—at a minimum, they'll love you for asking.
- ✓ Avoid the sometimes overwhelming urge to buy an expensive new car. Promise yourself a new car when you've saved enough to pay cash for most of it.
- ✓ Don't get into the habit of using an ATM card unless you also get into the habit of writing your withdrawals in your checkbook.
- ✓ Don't be afraid to take risks with your retirement money. In the long run, a more aggressive fund is your best bet.

Mid-Twenties to Early Thirties

Here's where you have to buckle down. A lot of big expenses usually hit during this period: buying and furnishing a house, getting married, having children. This will be the time when you can really max out the credit cards, or stay out of debt.

✓ Find out how much you'll need to start saving now to meet your retirement goals. The earlier you start, the less you need to save. (And you really don't think Social Security is going to take care of you, do you?)

✓ Build your savings account—you're going to need it!

✓ Get good insurance: health, disability, and renter's or homeowners.

✓ Learn, learn, learn! The best investments are almost always in yourself. If your employer pays for school, take advantage of it. Even just one class a semester can eventually earn you a degree.

✓ If you're the marrying type, make sure you discuss money before you say "I do." After all, money's the number-one thing couples fight about.

✓ Join an investment club. It should help motivate you to save, and you might even become an investment whiz!

✓ If you work at a company that offers a retirement plan, put as much as you can into it. If you sign up to have regular deductions taken out of your paycheck immediately, you'll never miss the money.

In Your Thirties and Forties

✓ If you don't know yet how much you need for retirement, find out now!

✓ Save, save, save.

✓ Do some career planning—do you need additional training, education, or maybe a change?

✓ Review your insurance policies every year or two. Make a couple of calls to see if you can get a better price elsewhere.

✓ Talk with a financial planner about your goals and how you hope to get there.

✓ Take a course on financial planning at your local community college.

✓ Involve your children in the family's finances at an appropriate level.

✓ Prepay your mortgage (after you've paid off your credit cards, of course).

✓ Start an education fund for your kids when they're young. Remember, the sooner you start, the less you'll need.

✓ If you have children who are sophomores in high school, start now to investigate grants, scholarships, and other free financial help for college.

In Your Fifties

✓ Review your retirement plans with a financial advisor.

✓ Review your insurance plans and make adjustments if you have to.

✓ Start thinking about how your changes in income when you retire may affect your standard of living, and how you'll adjust.

✓ Make sure you have a strong will and estate plan.

✓ Take advantage of various discounts for the fifty-five-and-over crowd.

✓ Start thinking about work you'd really enjoy when you retire from your job. Part-time income from something you love to do can make for a great transition.

✓ Don't accept an early retirement package until you've reviewed it with a financial advisor. The idea of retiring soon may sound great, but the money may not last as long as you think.

✓ Think hard about where you'd like to retire and investigate those areas carefully.

Smart Credit Strategies

Now that you have reduced your debt to manageable levels, here's a checklist of positive financial steps you can take to improve your financial self-worth:

Credit

✓ Shop Around for Credit: Check APRs, prepayment penalties, annual fees, closing costs, penalty fees, and balance calculation methods. Don't automatically go for the loan with the lowest monthly payment. Choose the loan that is the best deal for you over the long run.

✓ Pay Your Bills on Time: Once you have paid down your debt, you will have fewer bills to worry about each month. Carefully keep track of their due dates, and make sure you pay them on time.

✓ Keep Your Debts Low: Don't let your monthly credit bills get above 10 percent of your monthly income. If they do, start cutting back immediately.

✓ Monitor Your Credit Report: Once a year, or before applying for a major loan, review your credit report to make sure it is accurate, complete, and presents your financial status favorably.

Personal Finance

✓ Make Money a Family Matter: The best way to teach your children financial discipline is to set a good example. Involve your children in your family's financial matters at a level that makes sense for their age. Failing to include your children in financial planning may mean they end up making the same mistakes you did!

✓ Keep Learning about Personal Finance: When you've reduced your debt to a manageable level, you are ready to start learning advanced money-management and investment skills. You can take courses at your local university or community college. Contact your county extension service to find out if free or low-cost programs are available in your area. In addition, there are a number of excellent books that can provide sound advice on investment strategies.

✓ Develop a Relationship with Your Banker: Meeting with your bank's branch manager can be one of the smartest financial moves you will ever make. Draw up a financial statement and ask for suggestions on how you might be able to better utilize your bank's services. One of the advantages to this strategy is that if you ever find yourself with a banking or credit problem, the branch manager may become your best ally.

✓ Share Your Money-Management Skills with Others: If your local extension service or consumer-credit-counseling office provides a speaker's bureau, consider signing up and sharing your experience of getting out of debt with others. It will add to your sense of accomplishment and provide a boost to others who are facing financial troubles. You may even want to volunteer time at your local consumer-credit-counseling office, helping other consumers work their way out of debt like you did.

✓ Sign Up for Payroll Deduction: Many employers allow payroll deduction for loans or bank accounts. You can either have an extra amount of your paycheck withheld to pay off any remaining debts (see the prepayment section later) or you can set aside extra money for savings or investments. It is true that if you don't see it, you won't miss it.

✓ Put Raises, Bonuses, and Extra Windfalls to Work: Use them either to pay off debts, or have them deposited directly into your savings or investment accounts.

✓ Pay Yourself First: Sock away at least 10 percent of your income in a liquid account. Payroll deduction, if it is available to you, is a good way to painlessly set aside savings. Alternatively, write a check to your savings or investment account as soon as you are paid.

✓ Build Your Nest Egg, but don't sit on it: Once the balance on your emergency account reaches three to six months of your income, start investing the excess in more sophisticated vehicles. (Be sure to research any investments thoroughly and get professional advice before plunking your money down.)

✓ Get an Accountant: A good accountant can help you develop your money-management strategy by offering tax-planning advice.

✓ Learn to Shop with Lists: Last-minute stops at the grocery store or local convenience store often result in overspending. Make shopping lists and stick to them.

✓ Hide Your Cash Card: ATM cards are a great convenience, but they also make it easier to get your hands on money you really shouldn't spend. If impulsive cash withdrawals are draining your account, set the card aside until you can get your spending under control. Remember, we somehow managed to get by for years without ATM cards—it just takes a little more planning!

✓ Balance Your Checkbook: Few people do this, but given the amount of bounced check fees, it's important to make sure you know exactly how much money you have in your account. If you don't know how to balance your checkbook properly (it often takes a little practice to get it right), ask for help from your credit union or bank branch manager.

✓ Enjoy Yourself: If you charged yourself into a debt crisis because shopping made you "feel good," start experimenting with other ways to boost your self-esteem. Enroll in a night course at a local college, volunteer for a local charity, take up a new sport, or turn your hobby into a small business. Whatever you do, make sure it's inexpensive!

When Is It Good to Use Credit?

Credit in and of itself is not bad. In fact, using credit or credit cards can sometimes be a good financial move. If you are honest with yourself, you will often know whether your use of credit is good or bad. If you haven't developed those instincts yet, here are some guidelines:

When You Are Building Equity: Directly related to this concept is "leverage"—using someone else's money to make money. A mortgage is a good example of using debt to build equity. Most people could not afford to buy a home by paying cash. Yet a home is often the largest and most important investment many people will make, and the profits they realize after the house has appreciated (grown in value) will likely far exceed the amount of interest they paid to purchase it.

A car is at the opposite of this spectrum. Most automobiles depreciate (lose value) rapidly. Often, in the first years of a car loan, the amount owed is more than the resale value of the car. That doesn't mean you shouldn't go into debt to buy a car. It simply means that you should buy a car that won't put you into debt for too long, and that you should think twice about taking on large monthly payments for an expensive car that you may not really be able to afford. Your money will be better spent on other appreciating investments.

When the Interest Is Tax Deductible borrowing *may* make sense. In the 1980s, consumers often didn't mind carrying large debts and paying high interest rates because the interest was tax deductible. As of 1991, however, interest on credit cards and other consumer loans was no longer tax deductible. Mortgages, home equity loans, and student loans remain three of the last types of tax-deductible consumer loans, and those may face restrictions in the future.

Keep in mind that if you can afford it, it is usually better to pay yourself than pay Uncle Sam. For every dollar you spend on tax-deductible interest you get back between twenty-eight and thirty-three cents (depending on your tax bracket). But every dollar you earn is worth sixty-seven to seventy-two cents—the amount left over after taxes.

When You Can Take Advantage of Sales: The two key questions to ask before you finance a sale item on credit are:

Do you really need it?

Will the amount of interest you pay on the amount you

borrow, plus the sale price of the item, still be significantly less than if you paid full price for the item with cash?

People sometimes whip out their credit cards to take advantage of bargains, but then find they have run up large balances they can't pay off right away. By the time they do pay them off, they have paid so much interest that they might as well have paid full price in the first place.

When You Are Financing Business or Venture: Few people who start businesses have the financial means to begin without borrowing. (In many cases, they find the convenience of using credit cards far preferable to trying to beg their banker for loans.) If this is your reason for borrowing, make sure you are really ready to go into business. Do your homework, plan well, and get started.

Take Advantage of the Float: If you are disciplined enough to pay off your credit card bills in full each month, you can use your credit cards as an "interest-free loan." If you time your purchases right (by making purchases right after the closing date or cut-off date on your statement), you will have as many as fifty days to pay back the amount you borrowed. For this to work, your card should have a grace period of at least twenty-five days, and you must be careful not to cut it too close. If you slip your bill in the mail right before it is due, and it's delivered late, you could lose your entire grace period. You can then end up paying hefty interest charges and perhaps penalties.

Shop by Mail: Sending cash or a check to a faraway company you have never dealt with before can be dangerous. If the offer turns out to be less than you expected, you may be out your money. Using your credit card can be preferable to paying for something by cash. If you buy something using a credit card, you are protected under the Fair Credit Billing Act if it turns out to be different from what you ordered.

Pay for Car Repairs and Other Services: The Truth-in-Lending Act also provides protection against shoddy goods or services paid for with a credit card. You can pay for car repairs or other "iffy" services with a credit card, and by the time the bill comes due, you should have an idea of whether the service was adequate. If not, you may be able to withhold payment of the charge under the "Claims and Defenses" section of the Truth-in-Lending Act. This will give you additional leverage with the service provider (see Chapter Ten for more information).

Surviving the Holidays without a Credit Hangover

December may bring holiday cheer, but all too often it's followed by a January of bills, bills, and more bills. Just as retailers make most of their profits during the holidays, the credit card companies do the majority of their business during the fourth quarter as well.

Most people have good intentions when they overspend during the holidays. They truly want to show family members, friends, or coworkers how much they appreciate them by giving them wonderful gifts. Often, however, they focus on the cost of the gift rather than the thought behind it.

Plan Ahead: Christmas club plans offered by many banks are rarely good deals for consumers because the interest those accounts pay is rarely competitive. That doesn't mean socking away money for the holidays is a bad idea. Instead, you should try adding a specific amount each month to your interest-bearing savings account and designate it for holiday spending.

Don't wait until Thanksgiving, when stores are already hawking Christmas goods, to start frantic holiday shopping. Draw up your holiday gift list early in the year, and take advantage of season sales, trips to outlet stores, or flea markets to stock up on inexpensive gifts.

Keep Track of Your Purchases: Many people storm into the malls with a walletful of credit cards and, throwing caution to the wind, start charging their holiday purchases. It's easy to put a couple of hundred dollars on one card, a couple hundred more on another card, and pretty soon you've lost track of how much you've spent. Here's how to keep your spending in line:

Devote a page of your checkbook register to keeping track of holiday purchases. In the memo space, write down the name of the person you plan to buy a gift for. Next to that, write an estimate of how much you plan to spend on them. Then, when you make a purchase, record exactly how much you spent. For example:

Number	Date	Transaction	Payment Amount	Balance
Total Spending Budget:				$750
Visa	11/20	Mom ($150)	$125	$525
MasterCard	12/11	Jim and Sarah ($50)	$50	$475

Use the Right Cards: Unless you are certain you can pay a bill off when it comes due, don't use your department-store cards. Most carry interest rates far above the national average. Instead, use your low-interest-rate bankcard to charge most purchases.

Stick to a Few: All you need is one or two cards for holiday spending. Carrying any more than that means temptation and a hassle if your cards are lost or stolen.

Be a Smart Shopper: Be especially aware of retailers' gimmicks that encourage consumers to spend more than they can afford. Deferred payment plans that let consumers "buy now, pay later" are really popular certain times of year. In some cases, the interest clock will start ticking before the first payment comes due. Even if a purchase plan features no interest for several months, be careful. If you can't afford it now, what makes you think you can afford it later?

Rethink Gift Giving: Don't automatically scoff at the idea that a lot of your gift giving is probably unnecessary. Giving gifts from the heart, instead of ones from the department store, really can be personally and financially rewarding. Are you a talented cook? Perhaps you can hold a pre- or post-holiday brunch for friends and coworkers, instead of spending money on small gifts they won't use.

You may even be able to cut back on gifts to your family. If you have a lot of brothers and sisters, for example, you may suggest that each person draw one name and give a single, large gift to that person.

Instead of waiting till the week before Christmas to buy something and then frantically shopping, start early and buy small gifts with inspiration. Hunt flea markets for a first-edition copy of one of your father's favorite books or an addition to your sister's antique dish collection. Gifts that show some thought are likely to be appreciated far more than last-minute items.

It is not a good idea to spend money on gifts for your family or children if you can't afford it. That only gives your children the idea that Mom or Dad can buy them anything they want. Many of the expensive gifts children ask for are used for a few weeks or months, then discarded. Give your children some guidelines for drawing up their Christmas lists, and consider gifts that your children will really use for a long time.

After the Holidays: If you have planned well, you will be able to pay all your bills when they come due. If not, pay them as quickly as possible. Also, be sure to protect yourself by checking your credit card statements for possible unauthorized charges.

Shopping for Slow Economic Times

Many Americans have charged themselves into precarious financial positions. When the economy slows, as it did in late 1990 and again in 2001, many people can find themselves trapped by a tight budget. Following are some tips for making it through a tough economy.

Shore Up: If you have managed to save three months' salary for emergency expenses, boost that to six months.

Stop Buying on Credit: Period. Tell yourself the economy is in a financial "state of emergency" and you are going to protect your personal finances until it stabilizes.

Be Prepared: Consider taking out a home-equity line of credit to use *only* in case of emergencies. You may want to choose a loan with low interest-only payments, just in case you are laid off or fired, or in case your business takes a nosedive.

Take Stock: If your income is shaky, or if you anticipate large expenses in the next year, take some time to evaluate your financial situation and develop a contingency plan. What happens if you lose your job? Will you be able to pay your mortgage and other loans? Will you be able to tap the cash value of your life insurance policy, borrow money from relatives, or otherwise find a way a tide yourself over? Planning ahead is the best way to gain a sense of financial security.

Conclusion

Congratulations if you've made it this far! If you've followed just one piece of advice in this book—cutting up your high-rate credit cards, or ordering your personal credit report, or figuring out your net worth—you've taken a positive step toward a better financial future.

If you are trying to get out of debt, you definitely should be applauded for your willpower. It's tough to get out from under a mound of bills, and even harder to stay debt-free (or almost debt-free). In our spend, spend society, it's not easy to pass up something today so you will have security tomorrow.

Tell me how you're doing. I'd like to know what advice I've given in this book has really helped—or strategies you've discovered that work. See the Resources section for information on how to contact me.

Good luck, and don't forget: It's only credit!

RESOURCES

ATMs

For the location of local Plus ATMs, call 1-800-843-7587. For the location of local Cirrus machines, call 1-800-424-7787. Your issuer may also have a directory of ATM locations overseas.

Better Business Bureaus

Always call the Better Business Bureau in the area in which the company you are inquiring about is located. Get the number through directory assistance, your local BBB office (listed in the phone book), or by contacting the Council of Better Business Bureaus, National Headquarters, 4200 Wilson Blvd, Ste. 800, Arlington, VA 22203; www.bbb.org; or call 1-703-276-0100 for a referral. The council also publishes consumer-education brochures that are available through your local office or the council.

Consumer Federation of America

A highly respected advocacy organization, CFA offers booklets on saving money, buying a home, managing debts, resolving consumer complaints, etc. They're available on-line for free at www.consumerfederation.org, or you can get single copies by sending a business-size SASE to Consumer Federation of America, 1424 16th Street, NW, Ste. #604, Washington, D.C. 20036, or call 1-202-387-6121.

Counseling

Debtors Anonymous. DA provides local support groups for chronic debtors. They operate very much like Alcoholics Anonymous, and use many of the AA guidelines and principles in their program. To find if there is a group in your area, or for more information, write Debtors Anonymous, General Service Office, P.O. Box 920888, Needham, MA 02492-0009; phone: 1-781-453-2743; fax: 1-781-453-2745; www.debtorsanonymous.org.

Consumer Credit Counseling Services offer inexpensive, confidential assistance for people who are having trouble managing or paying their bills. To find the office nearest you, call 1-800-388-2227, or visit www.nfcc.org.

Cooperative Extension Service. Some cooperative extension service offices offer money-management counseling, seminars, or publications. I highly recommend them for help and referrals. To find a local cooperative extension service, look under the local government listings in your phone book or contact Cooperative State Research, Education and Extension Service, U.S. Department of Agriculture, Washington, D.C. 20250-0900; phone: 1-202-720-3029; fax: 1-202-690-0289; on-line at www.reeusda.gov.

Counseling Service Referral. Here's a number you can call, 24 hours a day, 7 days a week, to be connected with a credit counselor (from one of several agencies) for free. Lay out your situation, and they'll make some recommendations. Usually you can do it right over the phone, but many times you'll have the option of visiting their office. There's no charge for the counseling: phone 1-800-450-2469.

Financial Recovery Institute. Provides referrals to Financial Recovery counselors. Financial Recovery counseling is a structured process that helps clients transform their relationship with money. A relatively new field, it seeks to treat the "whole person," including addressing the client's history with, and emotions relating to, money. It can be very effective. Visit www.financialrecovery.com or call 1-877-913-9677.

Myvesta.org (formerly Debt Counselors of America) is the nation's only comprehensive financial crisis and treatment center. Founded in 1994, the nonprofit financial crisis center has helped more than four million people through its programs and educational resources. They are committed to helping people resolve past financial mistakes, manage current financial responsibilities, and find financial peace of mind. Its programs and services include crisis resolution, on-line bill management, bankruptcy alternatives, creditor problem resolution, debt management, and financial coaching. Visit Myvesta.org or call 1-800-680-3328.

Computer Software

There are several computer software programs that allow you to calculate how much small additional payments can save you on your credit cards and other loans. Seeing the numbers in black and white can inspire you to pay off your credit cards faster! Here are a few I recommend:

Banker's Secret Credit Card Software: IBM-compatible, includes a copy of the book *The Banker's Secret*; cost, $28.95. Order from Good Advice Press (see separate listing below).

Power Pay: IBM-compatible; cost, $20. (Make checks payable to USU Extension Service.) Order by writing Power Pay, Utah

State University, Extension Bulletin Room, 8960 Old Main Hill, Logan, UT 84322-8960.

Quicken: This software can be very useful for organizing your personal finances, including tracking your spending and investments and creating budgets. Available in retail stores or at www.quicken.com.

Zilch: One of my favorites for easy debt reduction charts, you can try this software program at www.zilchworks.com; cost, $25.

Credit Bureaus

You can order a copy of your credit report by contacting the three major credit agencies listed below. Unless you are entitled to a free copy, the cost is generally $9 (which may be adjusted annually for inflation).

Equifax
P.O. Box 105873
Atlanta, GA 30348
1-800-685-1111
www.equifax.com

Experian (formerly TRW)
Experian National Consumer Assistance Center
P.O. BOX 2104
Allen, TX 75013-2104
1-888-397-3742
Hours: 9 A.M.–5 P.M. (all time zones)
www.experian.com

Trans Union Consumer Relations
P.O. BOX 1000
2 Baldwin Place
Chester, PA 19022
1-800-888-4213 (automated system)
www.transunion.com

When you request your credit report, be sure to include your full name (including maiden name or generation, such as Junior or Senior, I or II), your spouse's name, Social Security number, year of birth, and your complete addresses for the past five years, including zip codes. Sign and date your request and include some proof of your current address, such as a copy of your driver's license or a copy of a recent billing statement. If you have been turned down for credit recently, include a copy of your denial letter.

Note these state limits on credit report prices:

California: $8 per copy

Colorado: one free copy annually

Connecticut: $5.00 for the first copy annually

Georgia: two free copies annually

Maine: $2.00 plus photocopying charges

Massachusetts: one free copy annually

Maryland: one free annually, then $5.25

Minnesota: $3.00 per copy

New Jersey: one free copy annually

Vermont: one free annually, then $7.50

Virgin Islands: $1 per copy

All others: $9 per report, plus sales tax where required

Consumer Data Industry Association (formerly Associated Credit Bureaus) is the trade association for the credit reporting information industry. They are located at 1090 Vermont Avenue NW, Ste. 200, Washington, D.C. 20005-4905; www.cdiaonline.org.

Credit Card Companies

If you have a problem with your credit card, try to work it out directly with your card issuer. If you are unsuccessful, you may want to contact the association or corporate offices.

American Express Consumer Affairs Office, American Express Company, 801 Pennsylvania Avenue NW, Ste. 650, Washington, D.C. 20004; www.americanexpress.com.

Discover Cardmember Services, P.O. Box 30943, Salt Lake City, UT 84130-0943; www.discovercard.com.

MasterCard International, Public Relations, 2000 Purchase Street, Purchase, NY 10577; www.MasterCard.com. (MasterCard has also created a helpful Web site, www.creditalk.com, with solid basic credit advice. If you have children, from teenagers through college age, check it out together.)

Visa, Consumer Relations, P.O. Box 194607, San Francisco, CA 94119-4607; 1-800-VISA-911; www.usa.visa.com. (Visa has also created Practicalmoneyskills.com, a site with helpful personal finance information for parents, teachers, students, and consumers. If you fall into one of those categories—and who doesn't?—check it out.)

Credit Card Lists

CardTrak: For $5, you can get the current issue of CardTrak, which lists low-rate cards, rebate cards, gold cards, and secured cards. More detailed lists are available, including Secured Card Report ($10); Gold Card Report ($10); and Rebate Card Report ($10). Write to CardTrak, P.O. Box 1700, Frederick, MD 21702, or call 1-301-631-9100; on-line at www.CardTrak.com.

Consumer Action, a San Francisco–based consumer education and advisory organization, offers a list of secured cards, a list of low-rate credit cards, and a variety of other helpful publications. For free copies, visit www.consumer-action.org or send a self-addressed, stamped legal-size envelope to Consumer Action (Attn: name of publication and language preferred), 717 Market Street, Ste. 310, San Francisco, CA 94103-2109.

ConsumerWorld.org is undoubtedly the most comprehensive Web site available for consumer information on a variety of topics. Bookmark this site.

Credit.about.com is an interactive education and information site designed to help people reduce debt and get smart about credit.

Credit Unions

Credit unions often offer excellent banking and credit service to their members. If you don't already belong to a credit union, contact Credit Union National Association to find out if you are eligible for membership in one. Visit www.cuna.org or send a self-addressed stamped envelope to CUNA, Box 431, Madison, WI 53701-0431.

Debt Collectors

American Collector's Association is the trade association for debt collectors. Visit www.collector.com; write ACA, P.O. Box 39106, Minneapolis, MN 55439-0106; or call 1-952-926-6547.

Fraud

The National Fraud Information Center hotline will answer questions about fraud and refer victims' complaints to the appropriate enforcement agency. Visit www.fraud.org or call 1-800-876-7060.

Credit Reporting Agencies (to report identity theft):

Trans Union
P.O. Box 6790
Fullerton, CA 92834
Phone: 1-800-680-7289; fax: 1-714-447-6034

Equifax Consumer Fraud Division
P.O. Box 740256
Atlanta, GA 30374
Phone: 1-800-525-6285 or 1-404-885-8000; fax: 1-770-375-2821

Experian's National Consumer Assistance
P.O. Box 9530
Allen, TX 75013
Phone: 1-888-397-3742

Good Advice Press

My friends and colleagues Marc Eisenson and Nancy Castle-man have helped thousands of people save money on their debts and live better for less. They publish great books, audiotapes, software, and a quarterly newsletter. They really care about help-ing people and practice what they teach. Visit www.goodadvice press.com for articles and resources. For $1 they'll send you a sample of their newsletter and a list of other Good Advice prod-ucts. To order a newsletter sample or any of the publications I've mentioned in this book, contact them at P.O. Box 78, Elizaville, NY 12523. Credit card orders only call 1-800-255-0899.

Government Agencies

Federal Trade Commission: If you have a complaint about credit bureaus, credit clinics, or collection agencies, you can complain to the FTC, either by contacting your regional office (which is listed in the Government Pages of your telephone book), visiting www.ftc.gov, or writing to FTC, CRC 240, Washington, D.C. 20580; phone: 1-877-FTC-HELP (382-4357) or 1-202-326-2222.

Helpful Publications

Automobiles: What Your Car Really Costs. Helps you buy a car that makes financial sense over the long run; cost, $6. Available from American Institute for Economic Research, P.O. Box 1000, Great Barrington, MA 01230-0100; phone: 1-413-528-1216; fax: 1-413-528-0103; on-line at www.aier.org.

College Students: Smart Credit Strategies for College Students is a thirty-minute audiotape I developed to help teens use credit to their advantage and avoid pitfalls; cost, $15.95. Available through Good Advice Press (see page 334).

Collecting Cards: American Credit Card Collectors Society will show you how credit cards can actually be profitable. Membership dues are $25 annually and include a quarterly newsletter, membership directory, catalog, and networking opportunities. Write ACCCS, P.O. Box 2465, Midland, MI 48640.

Premier Telecard is the magazine and information source for people interested in collectible prepaid phone cards. Visit their Web site at www.premier-tele.com or write Premier Publishing Group, P.O. Box 2176, Paso Robles, CA 93447-2176; phone: 1-805-227-1024; fax: 1-805-237-2530.

Complaints: Got a gripe or problem? The Consumer Action Handbook offers advice on how to handle everything from complaints about travel services to credit. It's packed with phone numbers and addresses of corporate customer-service offices, plus organizations that can help. Visit www.pueblo.gsa.gov for a free copy, or order a mailed copy for $2 by calling 1-888-878-3256.

Federal Trade Commission

The Federal Trade Commission offers a large number of free booklets on credit topics. For free copies, visit www.ftc.gov or contact Public Reference, Federal Trade Commission, Washington, D.C. 20580; phone: 1-202-326-2222; TDD: 1-202-326-2502.

Legal Guides

The National Consumer Law Center publishes for attorneys and legal counseling offices. If you need to do serious research on a credit protection law, call for a list of their manuals (each costs $100 or more). NCLC, 77 Summer Street, 10th Floor, Boston, MA 02110-1006; phone: 1-617-523-8089; fax: 1-617-523-7398; online at www.consumerlaw.org.

Mortgages

The Banker's Secret Audiotape: If you aren't prepaying your mortgage, why not? Marc Eisenson shatters the myths that keep Americans in the hole in his thirty-minute audiotape; cost, $12.95. Available through Good Advice Press.

Fannie Mae offers a variety of good resources for prospective homebuyers. Visit www.fanniemae.com.

If you want to buy a home, the Mortgage Bankers Association offers a variety of brochures on mortgage topics in English and Spanish. Visit www.mbaa.org. To request publications or to obtain a list, send a self-addressed, stamped envelope to Mortgage Bankers Association of America, Attn: Consumer Affairs, 1919 Pennsylvania Ave NW, Washington, D.C. 20006.

Privacy

The Privacy Rights Clearinghouse provides fact sheets on a variety of privacy topics, available on its Web site or for a nominal charge by mail. Visit www.privacyrights.org or send a self-addressed, stamped envelope to Privacy Rights Clearinghouse, Order Form, 3100-5th Ave., Ste. B, San Diego, CA 92103; phone: 1-619-298-3396.

Saving Money/Cutting Debt

The Cheapskate Monthly is a newsletter dedicated to helping those who are struggling to live within their means find practical and realistic solutions for their financial problems. An on-line version is available at www.cheapskatemonthly.com, or to order a mailed version call 1-800-550-3502.

The Pocket Change Investor is a quarterly newsletter designed to help you put more money in your pocket. It features painless ways to save on credit cards, taxes, cars, insurance, groceries, and more. A one-year subscription is $12.95, two for $19.95. Available from Good Advice Press.

Traveling

Using Credit and Charge Cards Overseas: A Traveler's Companion is a booklet detailing tips for using plastic overseas. Available on-line at www.pueblo.gsa.gov.

U.S. Public Interest Research Group

This organization works tirelessly on behalf of consumers. PIRG has fact sheets about credit reports, how to contact credit bureaus, identity theft, etc. Visit www.pirg.org; contact U.S. Public Interest Research Group, 218 D Street SE, Washington, D.C. 20003; or call 1-202-546-9707.

Recommended Books

It is difficult to list all the books I recommend to consumers, but here are a few. For a more complete list, visit www.goodadvice press.com. These books should be available at your library or local bookstore, or can be ordered directly through Good Advice Press, Box 78, Elizaville, NY 12523. (Add $3.95 shipping for priority mail, per order—not per book. Credit card orders call 1-800-255-0899.)

The Banker's Secret by Marc Eisenson ($14.95) will show you how to save thousands on your mortgage and other loans by just adding a little extra to your monthly payments. Packed with charts that show you how much you can save.

How to Get Out of Debt, Stay Out of Debt and Live Prosperously by Jerrold Mundis ($6.99). Based on the proven principles of Alcoholics Anonymous, this book lays out a clear, simple way for debtaholics to free themselves from debt. For his free e-mail newsletter, "Solvency/Making Peace With Money," send an e-mail to jmundis@att.net with the words "subscribe solvency" in the subject line.

Invest in Yourself: Six Secrets to a Rich Life by Marc Eisenson, Nancy Castleman, and Gerri Detweiler. This is our comprehensive guide to creating the life you want on any income ($11.95).

Money Is My Friend by Phil Laut offers training to harness the power of your mind to immediate improvement in your finances; 400,000 copies sold in sixteen languages. Order at shopping cart at www.phillaut.com. A free monthly e-mail newsletter is also available with timely financial tips. To subscribe send an e-mail to plaut@mba1970.hbs.edu

The Savage Truth on Money by Terry Savage. Terry is one of the best personal finance writers I know. This comprehensive guide will get you on the right track ($24.95).

Slash Your Debt, Save Money and Secure Your Future by Gerri Detweiler, Marc Eisenson, and Nancy Castleman ($10.95).

We wrote this no-nonsense guide in response to the frequent question, "What's the best way to consolidate my debts?"

Nolo.com offers understandable and easy-to-use books, tapes, and software. Most are written by attorneys and equip you with the information you need to solve your own problems.

Money Troubles: Legal Strategies to Cope with Your Debts by Robin Leonard ($29.95).

How to File for Chapter 7 Bankruptcy by Stephen Elias, Albin Renaur, and Robin Leonard ($34.95).

Chapter 13 Bankruptcy: Repay Your Debts by Robin Leonard ($34.95).

Everybody's Guide to Small Claims Court by Ralph E. Warner ($24.95).

Divorce and Money by Violet Woodhouse ($34.95).

Resources for Financial Educators

Experian offers "Reports on Credit and Other Financial Issues," a series of reproducible fact sheets on various credit topics, direct marketing, real estate credit, and business data. For ordering information, call 1-800-947-7990.

Financial Literacy Center: Publishes humorous, colorful, and easy-to-understand information on personal finance. They are best known for the Loose Change newsletter, which is distributed through the employers. Visit www.flconline.com or contact Financial Literacy Center, 15 Corporate Circle, Albany, NY 12203; phone: 1-866-352-1234.

JumpStart Coalition for Personal Financial Literacy is dedicated to encouraging curriculum enrichment to insure that basic personal financial management skills are attained during the K–12 educational experience. Offers a variety of resources to financial educators. Visit wwwjumpstart.org or call 1-888-45-EDUCATE.

National Coalition for Consumer Education is a nonprofit coalition of consumer educators, businesses, and government agencies dedicated to consumer education. Offers membership and newsletter. Contact NCCE c/o National Consumers League, 1701 K Street NW, Ste. 1200, Washington, D.C. 20006; phone: 1-202-835-3323; on-line at www.lifesmarts.org.

The National Institute for Consumer Education offers a bibliography of credit education materials available through many sources. Contact NICE, G12 Boone Hall, Eastern Michigan University, Ypsilanti, MI 48197; phone: 1-734-487-2292; on-line at www.nice.emich.edu.

Contacting Gerri

You'll get updates on information in this book, as well as have the opportunity to ask me your confidential questions at www.ultimatecredit.com. I look forward to hearing from you!

INDEX

Deficiency judgment, 224, 228
Delinquencies, 14, 17, 22–23,
    38, 86, 89, 120, 136, 161,
    281
    see also late payments
Department-store cards, 57,
    60, 129, 136, 142, 155, 173
    and credit reports, 21
    interest rates, 60, 77
    paying back, 200
Diner's Club, 62
Direct mail lists, 285
Direct Marketing Association,
    285, 286
Discharge, *see* bankruptcy
Discover Card, 135–136
    acceptance, 299
    address, 332
    CDW coverage, 298–299
    described, 59
    personal information, 274
    see also Private Issue
Discrimination, 26, 28,
    125–127
    age, 19, 140
Disputes, credit card, *see*
    billing errors
Disputes, credit reports, *see*
    credit reports
Divorce, 44, 85, 88, 120, 126,
    129–132, 161
    and bankruptcy, 245

E

Electronic Funds Transfer Act,
    269, 271
Employment, 8–10, 24, 25, 26,
    41, 45–46, 51, 54, 115

Enhancements, 78–79, 289,
    299–301, 308–309
Entrepreneurs, 147–148
Equal Credit Opportunity Act,
    116–118
Equifax, 8, 9, 34, 41, 44, 190,
    330
Experian, 8, 9, 13, 32, 41,
    44–45, 330, 339
Extended warranties, 299, 302
Eviction, 145–146, 237

F

Fair Credit Billing Act,
    250–252, 254, 261, 265,
    267, 272, 294, 321
    and fraud, 278
    and overseas purchases, 296
Fair Credit and Charge Card
    Disclosure Act, 61
Fair Credit Reporting Act,
    31–32, 35, 40, 43–44, 46,
    47, 49, 50, 51, 52, 53, 93,
    98, 99, 119
    amendments to, 14, 31, 33,
    35, 40, 44–47, 49, 51, 52,
    55, 90
Fair Debt Collection Practices
    Act, 207, 211–215
Federal Trade Commission,
    45, 209, 218, 278–279,
    334, 336
Federal Reserve Board, 251,
    260, 267
Fees
    cash advance, 64–65, 297
    currency conversion,
    290–291
    debit card, 82